PHOTOSHOP®

CHANNEL

CHOPS

David Biedny

Bert Monroy

Nathan Mood

New Riders Publishing, Indianapolis, Indiana

Photoshop® Channel Chops

By David Biedny
Bert Monroy
Nathan Moody

Published by:
New Riders Publishing
201 West 103rd Street
Indianapolis, IN 46290 USA

Printed in the United States of America 1 2 3 4 5 6 7 8 9 0

Library of Congress Cataloging-in-Publication Data

97-80800

ISBN: 1-56205-723-5

This book was produced digitally by Macmillan Computer Publishing and manufactured using computer-to-plate technology (a film-less process) by GAC/Shepard Poorman, Indianapolis, Indiana.

Warning and Disclaimer

This book is designed to provide information about Photoshop. Every effort has been made to make this book as complete and as accurate as possible, but no warranty or fitness is implied.

The information is provided on an "as is" basis. The authors and New Riders Publishing shall have neither liability nor responsibility to any person or entity with respect to any loss or damages arising from the information contained in this book or from the use of the discs or programs that may accompany it.

Publisher *Jordan Gold*

Executive Editor *Beth Millett*

Managing Editor *Brice P. Gosnell*

Development Editor
John Kane

Project Editor
Howard Jones

Manufacturing Coordinator
Paul Gilchrist

Book Designer
Glenn Larsen

Cover Designers
Nathan Moody
Travis Estrella

Director of Production
Larry Klein

Production Team Manager
Juli Cook

Production Analysts
Dan Harris
Erich J. Richter

Production Team
Linda Knose, Michael Henry,
Mark Walchle

About the Authors

David Biedny is a leading digital effects, graphics, and multimedia expert, and owner of IDIG (Interactive Digital Intelligence Group), Inc., a polymedia design and production firm. Working at Industrial Light and Magic, he produced digital effects for movies such as *Terminator 2, The Rocketeer, Memoirs of an Invisible Man,* and *Hook,* as well serving as a Special Effects Supervisor (for IDIG) on the motion picture *Spawn.* He is currently a Contributing Editor for *MacWorld, New Media,* and the *Macromedia User Journal.* Biedny has been a top-rated teacher, lecturer, and speaker at the Kodak Center for Creative Imaging, Seybold Seminars, Stanford University, San Francisco State University Multimedia Studies Program, The School of Visual Arts, and MacWorld Expo. David and Bert co-authored the very first book ever written about Photoshop.

Bert Monroy is considered one of the pioneers of digital art. Bert's work has been featured in scores of books and can be seen in *MacWorld, MacUser, Byte, Verbum,* and *MacWeek* magazines. Bert has done a considerable amount of film work, including digital matte paintings for *Forrest Gump.* Bert's work appears on the Deluxe CD-ROM versions of both Adobe Illustrator and Adobe Photoshop.

Nathan S. Moody is an artist and production manager at IDIG, Inc. and a freelance illustrator. He has produced graphics for many World Wide Web sites, CD covers, and commercial CD-ROM projects. He has co-authored many software and hardware reviews with David Biedny, and, with Biedny, Monroy, and the rest of the IDIG production team, produced digital effects for the movie *Spawn.*

Trademark Acknowledgments

All terms mentioned in this book that are known to be trademarks or service marks have been appropriately capitalized. New Riders Publishing cannot attest to the accuracy of this information. Use of a term in this book should not be regarded as affecting the validity of any trademark or service mark.

Dedications

dB: To my lovely Hellene, and her parents Selma and Leo Orenstein, for their love and support over the years.

BM: I dedicate my humble contribution to this book to my wife Zosia, with whom I will grow old, for the best is yet to be.

NM: I dedicate my contribution to this book to my parents, Roger and Audrey, without whom I'd never have, well, been born.

Acknowledgments

The authors have some people to thank, collectively and individually.

First and foremost, deepest thanks to David Dwyer and Don Fowley from Macmillan Computer Publishing, the guys who are responsible for making this book happen. After all of our negative experiences with book publishers, these gentlemen have restored our hopes and made us want to write this book. Their patience and support bordered on being downright angelic. David, thanks for taking that e-mail outline seriously; and Don, thanks for being so understanding about our reality during *Spawn*. You guys are champs! We would (and will) work for you again without hesitation.

And then there's our editor, John Kane—the kind of guy that can't be as cool and friendly as he seems, but actually *is*. John's patience and understanding during this project went far above and beyond the norm, and his warm, dynamic personality helped pull us through some tight situations. His editing prowess is unmatched, and helped make this book better than it was when it left our hands. Besides, his taste in music is simply the most refined of any editor we've known. You rock, John. Oh, and now that our book is done, how about sending us some of those books you promised, eh?

Thanks also to Howard Jones for his insightful editing comments, and Jennifer Eberhardt for production smarts. And we'd like to extend thanks to all of the other folks at New Riders who have worked on this book. And, of course, hugs and thanks go to Lynda Weinman (Queen of Web Graphics), for being supportive of us going with NRP (they *are* cool, Lynda!).

From Adobe, we'd like to thank Mark Hamburg for the tech data, and Patricia Pane for being the coolest PR lady we've ever dealt with at Adobe (which is probably why they let her get away—your loss, folks). Special thanks to Sonya Schaefer for her support, as well as Russell Brown, George Jardine, and John Ledd. Other Adobe friends we'd like to acknowledge: Stephen Kilisky, Therese Bruno, Patrice Anderson, The Daves H&S (so what's up with AE 4.0?), Sara Daley (gone but not forgotten), Keith Zentner, Patrick Ames, and Andrei (even though we don't necessarily agree with what he's doing, he's still a nice guy!).

Technological kudos to Chris Athanas at DigiEffects for his friendship and cool After Effects plug-ins, Roger Kasten from Newer Technologies for access to their excellent hardware products, the folks at Umax for use of their superior scanners (the PowerLook II rules!), the fine folks at Photodisc for the use of their great stock image library (the only source of stock images in this, and all, of our books), Karen Raz and Jay Roth at Electric Image, Rob Sonner and Scott Hawthorne at MetaCreations, Steve Guttman at Macromedia, the folks at Terran Interactive, and Lisa Auslen at A&R Partners. And a **very special** thanks to Mark Dippé, Clint Goldman, and Steve "Spaz" Williams (at Pull Down Your Pants Productions), as well as Tom Peitzman, for bringing us along for the ride on *Spawn*, as well as for giving us permission to use some images from that project in our book. On that count, thanks to New Line Cinema as well.

Special thanks to our pal Joe Ranno at Flash Photo, in the lovely Red Hill Shopping Center. Besides the fact that he's full of (mostly) funny jokes, he has been extremely supportive and helpful in all matters photographic. And let's not mention the way cool boat rides. You're a real mensch, Joe. And then there's the Easy Street Cafe next door, home of much of the food that fueled us during the production of the book. Jody, Robin (or is it Barbara, or Diane?...), Robbie, and Robert made sure that we were well fed.

A big breakout thanks to the newest member of our family, Travis "Big Dog" Estrella, who asked good questions and kept us laughing like drunk hyenas during the last few months of the book. Travis, where has that bone been? Mike, you have one hell of a son. Susan, he's eating better now, don't worry.

Finally, we'd like to thank Travis Estrella for designing the snazzy eyeball icon you'll see beside the tips in this book.

Personal Acknowledgments

dB: Warm Thanks to my friends who, in one way or another, helped me while we wrote this book: David Schargel, Frank "Red Sneaks" Colin, Stuart Sharpe, Paul Mavrides (thanks again for the amazing tattoo!), Brooke Wheeler, Scott (& Claire & Taylor!) Myers, Ron and Jackie Meckler, Steve "Wookie" Mitchell, Judy Van Wicklen, Teja Van Wicklen, Cathy Benante, Wendall Harrington, Bo Erickson, Tony Bove and Cheryl Rhoades, Lawrence Kaplan, Chuck Farnham, Dan Gray at Stanford, Karl Marmaduke, Dr. Eric Feintuch, Andy and Elaine from Invision, David Berry, Bruce Walters, RoseAnn Alspektor, Erwin Schalker, Maureen Garrett and H.P. Thanks also to the folks at Seybold—Liz Grady, Arlene Karsh, Craig Cline and Alison (I never *did* find out your last name!). And, AV Rick, you are the best, buddy.

I also want to acknowledge some of the people who were in my thoughts (and life) during this project: Paul & Christine Rosenfeld, Jim "Jimbolaya" Harris and Claire Nilsen at Maximum Music, Joyce, Yale and Mark Gasper at House of Bagels, Erika Penner (Fuzzy Boots!), Sean and Erika Monroy, Suzanne Kramer, Dr. David "Capuchita" Bajayo, Taroo Berry, Roger Dean (I miss those phone calls, Roger!), Noam Chomsky, Isaac Asimov, Willi Penner, Karin Åberg, Miles Perkins (thanks for trying!), Oma, Opa, Cecilia Cohen, Bill Vellekoop, Mary Hoogeveen, Randy Rhodes, Jimi, Stevie Ray Vaughn, Ken Parker (you are the best of the new way), Paul Reed Smith (you are the best of the traditional way), Alan Rosen at Bananas At Large (you'll likely be getting a chunk of my income from this book), Salvadore Dali, Mike Levine, Thea Grigsby, Steven Kellam, Dean-O Fernandez, Spencer Maines and Dean Wilcox (and other friendly forces at Landor Associates), Barry & Amy, those wacky kids in South Park, Tony, and Brandon Lee.

My personal Special Thanks to Nathan and Bert, two of the best friends and collaborators anyone could ever hope for—I hope we remain close forever.

And a final, loving acknowledgment to my parents, Louis and Felicity Biedny, who brought me up the right way and taught me what was *really* important in life. May you both Live and Love in the Light.

BM: Through the years I have come across many who have inspired and directed me to where I am today. A few stand out from the rest, and it is they whom I wish to acknowledge in this book. Sister St. Helen in grammar school and Mr. Richardt in high school, who gave me confidence in my artistic abilities; my mother, Irma Monroy and Sally Schnur (my Jewish mother) for guidance during those tumultuous years of youth; my daughter Erika, son Sean, and extended family member Mark Surawski for adding richness to my life; Sisters Diana and Irene, nephew Joey, and my brother-in-law Richie for the sense of family and all that goes with it; Richard Estes and Maxfield Parrish for my artistic inspiration; M.C. Escher for proving there is always another side to the story; Jimi Hendrix and Jim Morrison for background noise and serenity; last, and mostly, all those whom I have the grandest pleasure of calling my friends—you know who you are, with the other two guys on the cover of this book, at the top of the list.

NM: I'd never have gotten this far without the understanding and assistance of David, Bert, Ralph Vittuccio, Tom Clancey, Fred Carlson, James Pike, and Gudrun Tarr. Deep thanks also go out to everyone else who has been supportive and put up with me during the production of this book, especially John Alldredge, Paul Dickey, Travis Estrella, Luz Longa, and Gunnar and Colleen Proppe. A special tip of the chapeau goes out to those "children of the night," without whom I would be utterly insane: Don Blanchard (and the crew at 21st Circuitry Records), Andrea Bruns, Greg Cardinale, Krista Fechner, Gayle Grimes, Ed Klein, Wayne A. Lee, Steve Watkins and the rest of you crazy rivetheads (you know who you are, just admit it). Inspirational gratitude goes out to Richard Diebenkorn, Albrecht Dürer, Paul Mavrides, Dave McKean, Egon Schiele, Carlos Segura, the Brothers Quay, Joel Peter Witkin, and Andrew Wyeth; I'd have lost the faith without your brilliance.

Contents at a Glance

Table of Contents

Welcome to the Photoshop Channel Chops book. We're glad you could make it to our little show. I'm David Biedny—Bert Monroy, Nathan Moody and I are your hosts for the duration of this program. Please don't change the channel (or, if you do, read this book first so you can get a better idea of which channel you want to see)...

So why did we decide to write another Photoshop book, when the market is inundated with books on just about every Photoshop-related topic imaginable? When it gets to the point where there are books on using Photoshop to design interfaces and create special type effects, we can definitively say that the market is officially saturated. Why risk doing another Photoshop book? Are we crazy? (Our closer friends would probably respond with an enthusiastic "yes!")

The answer was very clear to us: While there are many books about getting up to speed on the basics of using Photoshop (many of these being nothing more than thinly-veiled, rehashed interpretations of the basic Photoshop documentation), and a number of very good books on specific, vertical topics related to using Photoshop, the fact is that no one has really attempted to write a relatively advanced book about working with alpha channels, multi-channel documents, and the Calculations commands.

The last book that Bert & I wrote, *Adobe Photoshop: A Visual Guide* (for another, much less hip publisher than New Riders Publishing) received a number of good reviews. Everyone really seemed to like the section of the book devoted to explaining alpha channels, (even though it was relatively brief and basic). So why not create a book devoted to the topics that we've been teaching people for years, topics that typically get little to no coverage in most other Photoshop instructional products? We decided that

- The idea made good sense.
- People wanted a book covering these somewhat obscure (but *critical*) topics.
- The book didn't already exist.
- The three of us, in our working careers as production-oriented creative multimedia artists, had accumulated valuable techniques that we wanted to share with a larger audience than our regular students.
- If we continued to wait for someone to create such a book, we would wait a *long* time. We're tired of waiting. We decided to write the book so that *you* don't have to wait any longer, either.

So the book that you're now holding in your hands is the result of our wanting to get this information out into the world, along with the cooperation and understanding of New Riders Publishing.

Before we get into the meat of the book, we feel it's necessary to explain some of our own personal history with Photoshop (David and Bert were two of the earliest Photoshop users, working with the program in an early alpha version a full year before Adobe ever *saw* the program). We also provide related background historical information about the image processing world that you'll rarely hear about or ever read about in any book—so many computer books are downright sterile, leaving out the fact that there are *actual people* involved in the process of creating software and deriving creative techniques with those tools. We'll also give you a bit of insight into our particular approach to writing this book.

This isn't going to be like other introduction chapters you're likely to see in other books, and we suspect that our publisher is going to raise eyebrows at some of our caustic comments. Well, that's just too bad—we shoot from the hip and tell it like it is, without worrying about what some of our associates in the industry will think or feel. You, the reader, deserve to know a bit about the reality of this business, and we're happy to let you in on some things that other people *don't want you to know.* Sometimes the truth hurts.

There's an old saying, popular among bodybuilders: **no pain, no gain.** So here we go.

Author's Note

A disclaimer: This entire introduction is being written by me, David Biedny. If anyone wants to dispute any of the revelations in this introduction, I'm the one with the smoking gun. While Bert and Nathan have both seen this chapter, and provided me with their feedback and comments, **I am taking full responsibility for all of its content.** If anyone wants to dispute any of the information presented here, **I'm your target. Let the shooting begin.**

The reason that you're reading this book is that you're interested in learning more about how Photoshop works with the channels that constitute any digital image. These channels can consist of actual color information, which is the foundation of any computer graphic image. Another common usage of extra channels are *alpha channels,* which define the opacity of a graphic element. A primary focus of this book is combining digital images together in convincing ways: this process has historically been referred to as *compositing.* Any time you combine multiple images together to make a new visual, you've created a *composite image.*

As you might expect, we'll be getting into extensive detail on these subjects throughout this book. But before we do, we'd like to briefly touch on the early history of the process of combining visual imagery to create composites. Yes, before computers and digital technology, people were compositing visual elements in a variety of mediums. Perhaps the most visible of these fields is the world of motion picture special effects.

Before Digital There Was Film

To better understand digital compositing, let's take a look into how traditional film compositing, or *optical compositing,* was done.

Long before the digital media revolution began in the late eighties (with the proliferation of desktop computers and capable software applications such as Photoshop), the art of optical special effects and compositing exerted its influence on the minds and imaginations of moviegoers around the world in a more innocent, impressionable time (as far as visual effects are concerned). Starting with the epic blockbuster *King Kong* in 1933, the art of optical compositing was born, and quickly found a place in the palette of tools used to create motion picture magic. (Even though there was some earlier work done in this field, it's generally acknowledged that King Kong was the first commercial success for optical compositing.)

In that classic movie a small-scale gorilla model is combined with other miniature elements and live action to form a seamless (for the time—somewhat crude by today's standards) visual "reality." The process of *Stop Motion* was used to animate King Kong and the other creatures on the island.

Stop Motion is a painstaking technique used to animate—in the case of *King Kong*—a miniature creature based on an articulated armature covered with a variety of materials (clay, metal, fabric) and a fur layer. The figure is moved slightly, and a frame of film is exposed; the figure is moved a little more, another film frame is shot, and so on. Perhaps the best contemporary example of stop motion animation can be found in the amazing Tim Burton movie *The Nightmare Before Christmas.*

You can learn more about the hardware currently used to create stop-motion animation by visiting the following URL:

http://www.didi.com/www/monkey2.shtml

This site contains a description of a popular, commercial armature device called the Monkey. A deep, technical paper on armatures and the Monkey can be found on the same site:

http://www.didi.com/www/m_paper.shtml

What does stop-motion have to do with compositing? Everything, in fact. King Kong was a frightening monster primarily due to his perceived massive size. The fact that he was shown next to realistic elements such as trees, people, and skyscrapers enhanced this perception (though, in fact, many of these elements were also small-scale models). The basic theory and techniques of designing, lighting and directing live-action actors that are then composited together with stop-motion animated characters and scale-model backgrounds are still alive and well today. Except that many of these elements start—and end—in the computer.

In the traditional process of optical compositing, at least three pieces of film are required to create a basic composite:

- The **foreground element**, which holds the object to be composited. This is footage of the spaceship, flying superhero, or gigantic dinosaur that is to be set onto a different background.

- The **matte**, which determines the opacity of the foreground element during the compositing process. The matte outside the foreground element is black, masking out the background in the foreground element. The foreground element itself is left exposed through clear film. This was done on monochrome (black-and-white) film, since actual colors weren't (and still aren't) necessary for determining transparency of the matte.

- The **background plate**, the backdrop onto which the foreground will be composited: a star field for the spaceship, a city skyline for the superhero, or an open field for the dinosaur. This background is usually either a filmed background (such as a real landscape or city skyline), a miniature model, or a matte painting (an ultra-realistic painting of scenery that serves as a faux backdrop for foreground elements).

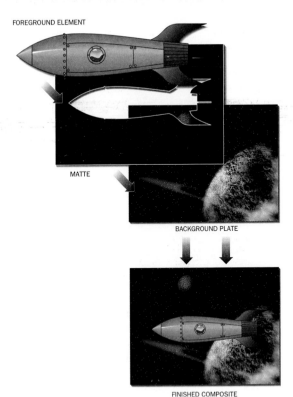

FOREGROUND ELEMENT

MATTE

BACKGROUND PLATE

FINISHED COMPOSITE

The essentials of the compositing process. The foreground element is laid onto the background through a matte, which determines exactly how the foreground element will interact with the new background plate. While the actual implementation of this technique usually involves many more elements (or layers) than this example, the basic concept follows the same logic.

When the compositing process takes place, the foreground element is exposed, through the matte, with the background plate onto a fourth strip of film. Exposure occurs only where the matte is clear, compositing the foreground element image onto the background plate image. In its most simple configuration, that fourth piece of film now holds the *composite*.

In an animated element, the three components usually aren't stationary. For example, a spaceship is typically flying around space so that both the foreground (spaceship) and background (star field) elements are changing from frame to frame. The matte used to track the spaceship and keep its opacity uniform is often referred to as a *traveling matte*.

This basic technique has been employed and refined over practically the entire history of motion picture production, with the accuracy and effectiveness of the process improving over time. Notable examples of cutting-edge compositing work include the vast works of Ray Harryhausen (who learned the special effects craft from Willis O'Brien, the stop-motion animator on *King Kong*) on movies such as *The Seventh Voyage of Sinbad* and *Jason and the Argonauts*, among other classics.

If you go back and look at some of these movies today, the limitations of the compositing process become quite clear. In the case of one of our favorite examples, the infamous skeleton warrior battle at the end of *Jason and the Argonauts*, the stop-motion animated skeletons look quite convincing (especially given that the movie was made in 1963), but the illusion begins to fall apart when you realize that they don't cast shadows on their surroundings. This was a considerably difficult thing to do with the optical compositing techniques of the time, but is a relatively straightforward process with current digital techniques, as you'll see in this book.

Even though various compositing techniques were used through the fifties and sixties (including outstanding examples such as *Forbidden Planet* and *2001: A Space Odyssey*), the field exploded in the mid-seventies with *Star Wars*, which took the art to an entirely new level of visual sophistication and technical complexity. The use of motion-control cameras, the ability to exactly repeat camera moves with computer control (critical for giving multiple elements the exact same motion characteristics), and the refinement of the optical compositing process were combined with the detailed models of space vehicles to produce movie history. The results were astounding at the time, and helped cement the *Star Wars* movies into mass culture in a way that had not been done at any time before.

In recent years, digital compositing tools and techniques have driven the state-of-the-art in motion picture compositing, such as the groundbreaking work done by Industrial Light and Magic for *The Abyss, Terminator 2: Judgment Day,* and *Jurassic Park*. Aside from the advanced 3D modeling, rendering, and animation techniques introduced in these movies, the seamless digital compositing of artificial characters into live action (as well as computer enhanced and generated environments) helped to define the overall realism of the special effects in those motion pictures. Digital compositing has taken its place as one of the central features in special effects production for a diverse range of media, including motion pictures, broadcast television, video post production, and multimedia title development.

The process of compositing allows multiple layers of media (still images, digital video, and animation) to be combined into a single, layered composition. In order to create convincing composites, a multitude of factors must be controlled for each layer, including brightness and density values, transparencies, foreground-background prioritization, shadows, edge characteristics, and more. For example, live actors filmed against a blue screen background and composited with a matte painted background or optical effects (such as a star field) must be made to match the overall color and lighting conditions of the background. In the traditional optical compositing process, many tests had to be done in order to match up all of the desired parameters to attempt to achieve an optimum composite—a time consuming process.

A bigger drawback presented itself in the form of generational loss: typically, only two elements can be composited together at a time with an optical process, with the results of each compositing pass sent along to be processed with the next element in line. The problem with this approach is that each precomposite stage evokes a noticeable quality hit, or *generational loss*, which dramatically reduces the overall quality of the final composite (especially with composites that have a larger number of elements). With the advent of digital tools and digital formats for graphics, the issues of generational loss have quickly faded into the background. Digital technology has brought the field of compositing to a new level of realism and efficiency. Given enough time, resources, and creativity, virtually any visual scene that can be imagined can be created.

A Brief History of Photoshop

Over the many combined years that the authors have been using various genres of creative technology, the realization has set in that in order to best understand any particular piece of technology (or the results of any creative endeavor, for that matter), it's extremely useful to look at the human element behind the technology. In the case of microcomputer software applications, getting to know the folks who actually write the code that makes up a program tells you more about the software than any manual or book.

Back in the days when Photoshop was nary a glimmer in Adobe's eye, we got our first look at what was to become the industry standard in digital image processing. And we got *really* excited, because it was clear to us that Photoshop was an entirely new type of beast. At the time, Bert and I were good friends with Mark Zimmer and Tom Hedges of Fractal Design, the rather remarkable programmers behind such important software as ImageStudio (the first industrial-strength, grayscale image editing program) and ColorStudio (the only competitor that could have given Photoshop a real run for the money had it not been for Letraset).

Bert and I were both under retainer to Letraset, providing a wide variety of technical and marketing advice, which fell on largely deaf ears at the company. Bert created the very first print ad for ImageStudio: a reconstructed Roman Coliseum that was, to the best of our knowledge, the first published image of an image digitally rebuilt on a desktop microcomputer, using an off-the-shelf software package. We have been working with digital imaging tools for longer than we care to remember.

One day, a friend at a then-prominent Silicon Valley software publisher gave us a call. She had been asked to evaluate a program that had been brought to her by a young Industrial Light and Magic artisan. The program was the fruit of efforts by this fellow and his brother, and they were beginning to shop an early version of the software around, looking for a potential publisher. The ILM employee was John Knoll, the brother Tom Knoll, and the program was called Photoshop (yes, that *was* the original name of the software). This friend sent us an early alpha version of the program, looking for our objective opinion (we were also doing some work for that company at the time, as we did not have an exclusive deal with Letraset).

I clearly remember loading Photoshop on my then state-of-the-art Macintosh II, launching the application, opening an image I had just scanned on our $10,000 Howtek scanner/boat anchor, and applying a Gaussian Blur filter to the scan. The resulting euphoric blast that rushed through my brain was something like what I felt the very first time I used a Macintosh (December 1983, right before it was introduced to the public); I thought "game over, this is the way to use a computer."

> ## Author's Note
> Qualifier: My first computer experiences were with the venerable Apple II, and I used to train people in the use of WordStar running on CP/M machines in the early 80's. The Macintosh was my *best*, not first, experience with a microcomputer.

Why did I personally come to that conclusion about Photoshop? A large part of my feelings were based on the first five minutes spent with the then-primitive implementation of the Calculation commands, including some options that never even made it into the first commercially-released version of the program. I spent an entire night and early morning with Photoshop that first time—nine hours straight, though it may actually have been longer—and was simply blown away by what I saw. Within days, Bert spent a similar evening with Photoshop, and was amazed at the promise that the program displayed. It was clear to us that Photoshop was the future. We were won over.

> ## Author's Note
> At the time, Bert was known as the ultimate PixelPaint artist, a program written by our friends Keith McGreggor and Jerry Harris. PixelPaint was the leading color paint program in those early days of the color Macintosh. Bert and I had both contributed a number of ideas and suggestions to the authors, and had become very friendly with them, even visiting them in their Atlanta offices—where we saw the very first pressure-sensitive mouse, a product that never did get to market.

Shortly thereafter, I called our friend at the software company, and told her "grab this thing right now, it's the hottest graphics program I've ever seen." To make a *very* long story short, they passed on it (and I turned down further work from them in protest), I got directly in touch with John Knoll, and over the course of months we spent many hours on the phone, discussing his software, things that he and his brother needed to add to it, and generally forming a somewhat unconventional phone friendship. John wanted to know who had given us the software. I wouldn't tell him, but we became friends regardless, given that he understood that *we* understood what he and Tom were trying to accomplish. We were fans from the word go.

After being rejected by most of the graphics software publishers in Silicon Valley, John Knoll ended up taking Photoshop to Adobe. How many software executives ended up kicking themselves in the pants years later, realizing that they could have had the leading image processing program *in the world*, but were too shortsighted to understand what they were seeing?

We give the Adobe folks credit in that they immediately saw the potential of Photoshop, and snapped it up. The rest is history. As we predicted, Photoshop became synonymous with image processing, and no other program has been able to play the role of competitor—and not due to any lack of effort by companies such as Microsoft, Micrografx, Macromedia, Letraset, Live Picture and others.

Bert and I went on to write the very first book on Photoshop, and over the years our names have been very closely associated with the program. The three of us have done work for Adobe in recent years, and often end up fielding questions about Photoshop as if we were Adobe employees or spokespeople (neither of which is accurate). Our insights into—and our knowledge of—this program goes far beyond the standard editorial interest, or the perspective of the working artist using the tool to create content.

Alright, let's get back to our main point. So what was it about Photoshop that won us over? Was it the filters? The extensive support for a wide range of bitmapped file formats? The cool, original application icon (a miniature one-hour photo shop booth)?

None of the above. It was the interchannel processing, and the robust support for alpha channels, a concept not yet familiar to the masses at the time, but certainly to those of us involved with the more esoteric computer graphics field. Photoshop's color reduction capabilities were also killer, and directly assisted us in some of our early multimedia work—we started working with what was to become Macromedia Director in early 1985, and did some of the first color animation work in VideoWorks II, the first color version of that program. (Video Works was also the first program with color painting tools for our original Macintosh II, the very first one in New York City. Apple was not amused when we showed the color Macintosh before their own official release event—but that's another story.)

Using Photoshop, we were able to make better images for Director than almost anyone else at the time, thanks to the (then) excellent color reduction capabilities present in the very first versions of the program. Bert also fell in love with the Airbrush tool. At the time, he emphatically stated that it was "the best digital equivalent to the analog version I have ever seen."

In 1990, at the invitation of John Knoll, I moved out to California to work with John at Industrial Light and Magic, using Photoshop to create digital composites for motion pictures. The fledgling Digital Effects group was a kind of rebel outfit, not particularly loved by the folks in the ILM optical department (who saw us as a serious threat to their continued viability) or the 3D artists who were beginning to rule the place (who generally looked at 2D compositing as a lowly rung of the lofty digital ladder). While there were people in both departments who understood that the reality was far more subtle and complex than these gross simplifications (in particular, Dennis Muren and John Ellis stand out in my memory as the most enlightened of the "old-school," while John Knoll was a one-man dynamo who convinced ILM management that Photoshop was a completely viable production tool for many aspects of motion picture special effects work), in general, we weren't taken very seriously. All that changed while I was there (less than a year, but with the crazy hours, it felt like much longer), and, to the best of our knowledge,

Photoshop is still used to create *digital matte paintings* (ultra-realistic scenes that are used as backdrops for the placement of live or 3D elements).

> ## Author's Note
> Bert did a stint at ILM as a digital matte painter on movies such as *Forrest Gump*, *Baby's Day Out*, and *Star Trek: Generations*.

Why Are You Reading This?

In a marketplace crowded with over 50 books devoted to Photoshop, it became clear that most authors were simply rewriting large portions of the Adobe documentation. Or there are the books that concentrate on specific applications of Photoshop techniques, some successfully (such as the highly recommendable *Photoshop in Black and White*, by Jim Rich & Sandy Bozek, Peachpit Press), some that we thought were more than slightly gratuitous (do we really need an entire book devoted to cheesy type effects? Perhaps not...), and some that are downright bad (any books with the words "Quick Start" in the title are sure to be less than satisfying). All the while, we waited for someone to write the book we know almost everyone needed and wanted—a serious, practical guide to employing alpha channels, advanced masking techniques, interchannel mathematics, and creative use of layers. And we waited. It's been over six years, and the book never materialized. Until now.

This is **not** a book on making "colored blinking lights" (thanks to Howard Penner for that great phrase). We will *not* mention Kai's Power Tools in this book (oops, well maybe that one time!). The focus is on information that doesn't require the use of any third-party software; if you have a copy of Photoshop, you've got all you need to use this book.

It's always surprising to us that many people look outside of Photoshop to solve problems, when a creative approach and some insight into how channel processing works yields results that rival the potential of many third-party add-ons. Although we appreciate the fact that innovative software developers are constantly writing plug-ins for Photoshop, do we really need more than a single dropshadow or embossing filter? No, especially if you take the time to learn a little about channel operations (which we've handily abbreviated to the word *CHOPS*).

We will offer our opinions on many topics, and you'll quickly find out that we often feel strongly about certain things, and aren't afraid to express ourselves with little to no restraint (the three of us are from the east coast of the U.S., so we're a bit more cynical than the typical west coast multimedia crowd). While we use Photoshop as the basis for our explanations and examples, the general principles and techniques can be applied to any situation where you're making use of alpha channels, such as compositing a 3D rendered element from Infini-D or an Electric Image onto some live video using Adobe After Effects. The Macintosh is our collective platform of choice, but the described techniques work just fine on the PC and UNIX versions of Photoshop. Just substitute the appropriate keyboard equivalents:

Macintosh Command = PC Control

Macintosh Option = PC Alt

What about UNIX? Well, we're not a UNIX house, and we don't have UNIX machines. We're not even sure if Adobe has released version 4.0 for UNIX, and frankly, we don't care. Did we mention we're all from the east coast of the U.S.? What bad attitudes...

Monkeys Push Buttons, Humans Push Their Brains

Before we jump into the thick of this book, we'd like to briefly discuss our philosophy of learning. We adhere to it in our classes and in this book, and we feel you should know something about how we approach the learning process.

There's an ugly trend in digital imaging, a nasty truth that pervades not only the world of computer graphics technology but just about every complex aspect of life in general. People who work with technology (in general) and computers (specifically) tend to want to get their work done and don't really care about the inner workings of the technology. Instead of increasing the potential for creativity, people end up spending most of their time watching screen savers (does anyone realize that screen savers are the best-selling product in the general utility market? Frightening!), trying to get their systems to work (whether you use a Macintosh, Intel-based PC, or UNIX box, system crashes are a part and parcel of daily computer interaction), or just trying to get their designated workload out the door. The concept of "push a button, get something useful" is pervasive, and as more computers get into the hands of more people, this trend shows no sign of decreasing (or even leveling out).

In the case of Photoshop, an entire after-market has sprung up around plug-in products that make it easy to create specific effects (drop shadows and embossing are two obvious examples that come to mind) that can often be easily created using the built-in tools in Photoshop. All it takes is a little understanding and a tiny bit of effort, with the payoff of being able to customize and edit the effect with far greater precision and control than most plug–ins allow. We just have to laugh when we see people spending money on a plug-in to do dropshadows, an effect easily created with channels, and now made positively simplistic with the addition of layers to Photoshop (as of version 3.0).

It boils down to a simple fact: Most people seem not to want to understand how to do things; they just want to press a button, get a result, and move on. Well, this approach might make some sense if you're not interested in being creative or exploring the limits of the technology in your hands, or if you just want to get work out of the way so that you can get going on that golf or skiing trip (endeavors not typically enjoyed by any of the authors of this book). If you're producing the same kind of imagery day in/day out, and your boss and the client is ecstatically happy, then you might think that you don't *need* to understand how things work.

Wrong. The very second that routine changes, the moment that the client wants something out of the ordinary (and we'll stab a guess that has never happened to anyone reading this book, right? Yes, we're just joking!), the standard button-pushing routine is suddenly completely useless. There are times when there's simply no substitute for human creativity.

Author's Note

A Biedny anecdote: To this day, people come up to me (and Bert) and ask how to get a job at ILM. The key to the answer? Learn how to be a creative problem solver. Memorizing sequences of commands in a graphics program isn't the way to such enlightenment. Learning the intricacies of channels and masking is a much better route to honing your creativity and visual problem-solving skills, and is more likely to get you noticed than a good-looking resume or being able to recite the names of all of the third-party plug-in products for Photoshop.

In this book, we'll do our best to instill you with some useful, real-world image, visual problem-solving skills. It's going to require some effort, but the reward is well worth it. And we'll do our best to make the trip comfortable and enjoyable. Buckle up.

Photoshop 4

A question sure to cross the mind of the inquisitive reader:

"Is this a Photoshop 4 book?"

The simple answer is "Yes." If you use Photoshop 4, this book is for you. We use 4.0 as the basis for all of the screenshots and descriptions of the techniques presented in this book.

The longer, more accurate response is that we've approached this book with the philosophy that channel manipulation work has actually not changed much since the very first version of Photoshop. The addition of layers was perhaps the first (and arguably, only) major shift in how channels could be processed, but, in reality, the core theory and functionality of channels didn't change significantly with the arrival of layers.

So if you're still using version 3.05 of Photoshop (as we tend to do in our day-to-day work; we're definitely not happy with many of the changes in version 4.0, and find little reason to switch at this point), absolutely *all* of the information in this book is relevant. And we strongly suspect that all of the techniques presented here will be totally relevant and usable in the next version of Photoshop. Much of the theory discussed here is even useful for those using other imaging programs.

Worry not—your investment in this book is sound, regardless of what version of Photoshop you're running, or whatever hardware platform it's running on. We promise.

General Book Organization

In order to get the most out of Photoshop Channel Chops, there are just a few important pointers to keep in mind:

- This book has been written in linear order. Unlike many other books, we recommend that you try going through the book in a sequential fashion (or simply stated: from beginning to end). After a first read, you'll probably find yourself going directly to different topics. At the least, please read the Channels chapter before diving into the rest of the book.

- This is an advanced Photoshop book. We are assuming a certain level of familiarity with the program (as well as your computer of choice). If you've just purchased Photoshop, and are new to the field of digital imaging, this isn't the best choice for your very first instructional book. There are many other alternatives out there; the Photoshop manual that came in the box, as well as our *Adobe Photoshop: A Visual Guide* book (Addison Wesley) or *Real World Photoshop* (Peachpit Press), are decent places to start your learning experience. When you're finished with those reference sources, come back to *Photoshop Channel Chops*. You'll then get a lot more out of our knowledge.

- If you consider yourself a Photoshop Power User or imaging guru, please turn directly to the bluescreen chapter. If your brain absorbs and comprehends this chapter without too much effort, then you're indeed a Photoshop monster. You have our deepest respect. You have reached Photoshop nirvana. Go take a vacation, and get some fresh air. You probably need it!

- The Internet, and the World Wide Web in particular, are fantastic resources for many different types of information. You'll notice that we will often mention a specific web site while explaining a concept, and give you the URL (Universal Resource Locator). Instead of duplicating the gargantuan effort of people who are generous enough to share their knowledge with anyone who cares, we've decided to send you to your Internet browser for specific information that we feel you might benefit from—but this doesn't mean that you *must* have Internet access to make this most of this book.

Terminology Note

One of the things that's going to drive our publisher crazy (and might make you a little confused at certain points in the book) is our slight tendency to fall back on science fiction and pop terminology. While any self-respecting book editor will go to great lengths and overtime effort to discourage writers from using non-standard language, we've found that there are times when certain words fit *just right*. Have you ever read a review of a software product that was bad, where the review simply stated "don't buy this program, because it's *junk*"? No, we didn't think you had. Have you bought a program, gone home, installed it on your computer, worked with it for a half an hour, and ended up screaming, "What a piece of crap!" at your screen? We bet you have.

In particular, we sometimes mention the word "Grok." This is a weird and wonderful expression from the incredibly important science fiction book *Stranger in a Strange Land* by Robert A. Heinlein (Ace Books). In the book, the principal character, Michael Valentine Smith (an earthling raised on the planet Mars), has the ability to "grok" things. We looked on the Internet, and found the following definition for the word:

> grok: /grok/, var. /grohk/ vt. [from the novel *Stranger in a Strange Land*, by Robert A. Heinlein, where it is a Martian word meaning literally `to drink' and metaphorically `to be one with'] The emphatic form is `grok in fullness'. 1. To understand, usually in a global sense. Connotes intimate and exhaustive knowledge.
>
> The Jargon File 3.2.0
>
> http://t2r.uwasa.fi:80/jargon/grok.html

With that aside, let's get down to business.

First stop, Channels.

One

Channels

While this book covers many specific creative and technical issues relating to digital image processing, channels are at the core of all of these issues.

Channels are at the beginning and end of many important image manipulation tasks, and everywhere in-between. Just about everything discussed in this book relates to channels in one form or another.

Within Photoshop, people often take channels for granted. For example, when you scan an image with a desktop color scanner, you might not pay too much attention to the individual RGB channels of the image once it's been scanned. Crop, adjust brightness and contrast, run that new filter you just got in the mail—but mess with the channels? That's only for advanced geeks! Well, the fact is that you can learn quite a bit from understanding a little bit about *what* the different channels of that RGB scan actually represent. Even though you can adjust brightness and contrast as a global process to the entire image, by addressing specific channels of information you can limit your actions to only occur *when* and *where* necessary, yielding better-looking results. And who doesn't want that?

In order to get over the initial hesitation that many folks share when getting into understanding *why* things work, along with the *how*, it's important to understand some of the theory that supports the actual practice. In the case of Photoshop, or any software you're likely to use in your computing adventures, the fact is that there are always two sides to the coin: the face of the program that you, the user, see and interact with as you do your work, and the stuff under the hood—the guts of the software that do the actual nitty-gritty processing work. While you might be looking at a full-color image, unaware of the utility and power of channels, the graphics program that you're using is acutely aware of channels—in fact, it uses them when processing just about every command or feature you invoke.

Like so much terminology that overlaps the world of digital technology and the world of everyday life, channels have a specific set of meanings when we talk about digital imaging. Alpha channels are one expression of the potential functionality of channels in image processing. But it's critical to remember that, in discussing image processing software, the term *alpha channel* is likely to be virtually interchangeable with *masks*. If you speak to an experienced airbrush artist about masks, you're likely to hear a diatribe about *friskets*—a mask by any other name. And none of this addresses the fact that channels are the basic building blocks of any image, regardless of color space or graphics program or whether or not you use or care about alpha channels or masks. (After reading this book, you *will* care about these things. We promise.)

This book is about channels. Learn them. Love them. They will serve you well.

The 8-Bit Imaging Universe

In order to start to wrap your arms around the intricacies of channels and inter-channel processing, it's important to clear up some basic core concepts relating to how microcomputers (in general) and Photoshop (specifically) work with images and visual data. The concepts that we'll cover in this section are primarily based on the Macintosh and Intel PC platforms. (The Silicon Graphics platform handles graphics differently due to SGI core graphics formats being based on more than 8 bits per channel.)

Fear not: This isn't an engineering manual. We're not going to revisit the nightmares of many college math classes. We reluctantly admit that none of us were *exactly enamored* of math during our school years—we all passed our math classes, but we definitely preferred pictures over numbers. A little theory, though, never hurt anyone, and is necessary in order to get the most from this book, as well as from Photoshop.

Perhaps the most essential atom of information in Photoshop (or any professional imaging application, for that matter)—besides pixels—are the individual channels that make up *any* image, color, or otherwise.

Everything in Photoshop is measured based on the reference of 8 bits of information. No, not the 8-bit graphics produced by converting images to indexed color mode. We're talking about the 8 bits of visual information that make up each channel of an image.

When working with images destined to be used for CD-ROM or Web applications, the file formats that tend to be used (such as PICT on the Macintosh, BMP on the PC, and GIF for Web) are usually 8-bit indexed color. Instead of the 8 bits of grayscale information we find in Photoshop channels, these indexed 8-bit (or lower) images have restrained color sets, expressed as groups of colors called palettes. While an indexed color image can have up to 256 colors, it also can have lesser bit depths (a 6-bit GIF image can have up to 64 distinct colors); discrete channels on microcomputer platforms (specifically, Photoshop image channels on the Macintosh and PC versions of the software) tend to always be expressed in 8 bits of grayscale data, or 256 levels of gray.

An RGB image consists of three channels, or components, of information.

In order to clarify the meaning of an 8-bit channel, let's take a look at the relationship of bit–depth and color (or the mechanics of how a bucket of bits actually translates into useful information).

Every pixel (short for **Picture Element**—hey, don't ask us where the X comes from, we didn't invent the term!) on a computer screen is associated with some physical memory (that's the job of the VRAM in your computer, if you've ever wondered). On a black-and-white screen, each pixel has a single bit of memory. A bit can possess one of two states—on or off, black or white. This concept is the most basic core of binary arithmetic and, while relevant to many aspects of how computers work, is made very clear by placing it in the context of how a pixel is displayed on a screen.

As we devote more memory to each pixel, the number of colors that a specific pixel can choose from to display on the screen increases accordingly. If we increase the number of bits for a pixel to eight, the number of possible pixel values increases to 256. Why? Because each bit can have one of two states (on or off)—and there are 8 bits—this results in 256 combinations (or *permutations*) of possible arrangements of those eight bits. This mathematically translates to 2 raised to the 8th power, which totals 256.

8-bit color depth can be used in two ways:

1. To designate a set of 256 color (different hues, as well as brightness and saturation) values to represent an image.
2. To represent 256 shades of gray, with no hue (color tonality) information.

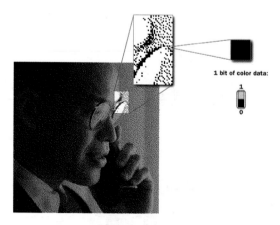

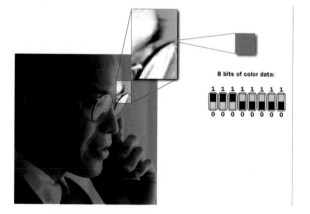

A black-and-white pixel with its one bit of associated memory. The bit can be either on or off; as a result, the pixel can be either black or white.

An 8-bit pixel with associated memory. There are 256 possible configurations of the eight bits of memory, yielding 256 distinct shades, colors, or values.

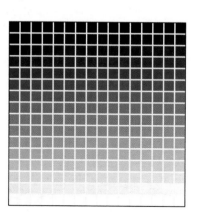

The 256 possible gray values found in an 8-bits-per-channel world. They are the foundation of all image processing in Photoshop.

The second case is the one we're interested in at the moment. In an 8-bit grayscale image, the 256 permutations are used to represent the complete brightness range, from pure black to pure white, with 254 shades of gray in between. Solid black is given a value of zero, and the value of pure white is expressed as 255 (zero to 255 still expresses a total of 256 permutations).

This range of gray values is critical to the purpose and mission of this book. These 256 gray values constitute the entire foundation of channel processing in Photoshop, as well as any other imaging program you're likely to use on the Macintosh or PC.

Photoshop Channel Fundamentals: Understanding Multi-Channel Documents

Since its inception, one of the most distinctive traits of Photoshop was that it understood and dealt with the concept of multiple-channel documents, additionally providing the digital artisan with direct editing access to the channels. Most other graphics software at the time, which allowed you to work with 8- or 24-bit RGB images (such as PixelPaint or ColorStudio), only let you go so far as seeing and adjusting all of the channels simultaneously. (While early versions of ColorStudio enabled a restrained level of access to individual color channels, it was greatly over-shadowed by Photoshop's channel access from the moment the latter program was released.)

Almost every document in Photoshop consists of at least a single 8-bit channel of information—the specific exceptions are "bitmap" images, which contain only pure black-and-white pixels, containing no intermediate gray values whatsoever. While the color component channels of an image are directly used to represent the actual image data (such as the RGB channels in a standard 24-bit color image), channels also are used for information other than the actual image data; alpha channels are perhaps the best example. Alpha channels are used for masking and compositing (which is discussed in more detail later in this book). These masks might have the task of isolating a specific element or portion of an image from the rest of the background, or might be used to create special effects for image blending and compositing.

Besides serving as the foundation for representing color images, different color spaces, and masks, other uses for extra channels include

- **Annotation layers**, for adding comments to an image that can be non-destructively overlaid on top of an image document, such as notes for informing a production artist where to work on an image needing retouching.

- **Positioning guides**, which were often needed for aligning multiple elements in Photoshop. The addition of guides to Photoshop 4 has reduced the necessity of creating guides in alpha channels, with the added benefit that the integrated Photoshop 4 guides can be snapped-to, much like the guides familiar to Illustrator and PageMaker users (and, of course, the built-in guides in Photoshop 4 take up less memory than an alpha channel). Guides and grids, however, don't supplant the technique of making vanishing point and perspective guides using alpha channels. The two techniques are complementary.

- **Text.** Very often, instead of creating color text directly onto a layer in Photoshop, you'll want to create text in an alpha channel and load that channel onto the color image as a selection; this enables you to fill the selection with different colors (for solid colored type), apply advanced color fills such as the multicolor gradients, and create filter effects between the text alpha and the background image. These general techniques enable you to create special effects that cannot be created any other way, outside of buying third-party filters, many of which don't deliver the degree of control attainable through less-automatic alpha channel techniques.

Alpha channels can be used to create overlays of comments for production situations without affecting the actual image data. This technique is incredibly obvious, useful, and often overlooked.

Two examples of using alpha channels for type effects. Notice how they interact with their backgrounds, something that's often hard to achieve by just using layers.

Photoshop Image Modes

The Image>Mode submenu choices determine a variety of factors, the most important of which is the overall bit depth and number of channels of an image. Generally speaking, the number of channels and the bit depth increase as you move down the available mode choices, detailed in the following sections.

Bitmap

A bitmap has 1 bit per pixel, with pure black (0) and white (255) values. No grayscale values are allowed here. While it might seem that the Bitmap mode has very limited appeal, the fact is that it delivers unique opportunities for both special effects and output applications.

The Bitmap mode has a variety of useful (and some rather esoteric) applications in everyday work. As far as special effects are concerned, you can create custom patterns as halftoning screens for achieving attractive (or distinctly ugly, based on the specified textures) mezzotint effects. Bitmap mode also is very handy for printing images with custom halftone screens on non-PostScript printers (such as many models of the popular Hewlett-Packard LaserJet line), which typically lack advanced halftoning handling in their imaging engines.

> Images meant to be reproduced in print are always prepared by creating halftone screens. Without spending thousands of words on the subject (which is covered in extreme depth in many other Photoshop books, especially those oriented towards printing images from Photoshop), we can describe the halftoning process as breaking an image down into clusters of different shaped and spaced dots. In the case of black-and-white printing—with newspaper and laser printing as prime examples—there is no such thing as gray ink values; instead, black ink is laid onto white paper, and the illusion of intermediate shades of gray is achieved by creating clusters of black dots that exploit various deficiencies in the way that the human eye resolves detail in a visual image.
>
> In the traditional methodology of preparing continuous tone images for black-and-white printing, a fine mesh screen was literally placed over the image and a special type of photographic exposure of the image-screen sandwich was produced, resulting in a version of the image that was broken down into the dots made by the holes in the screen. Even in the digital version of this method, the term *screening* has been retained.

Perhaps the most basic example of custom halftone screens is easily achieved by using the standard Photoshop Noise filter to create noise to be used as a halftone pattern.

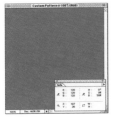

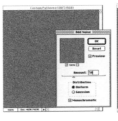

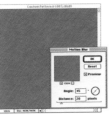

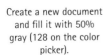

Create a new document and fill it with 50% gray (128 on the color picker).

Using the Add Noise filter, create some monochromatic noise, with a setting of 50. Either Photoshop Uniform or Gaussian are fine; the differences are minimal for this exercise.

Now we'll apply the Motion Blur filter (Filter>Blur>Motion Blur) to the noise pattern to create a streaked-looking metal texture. We'll use an angle of 45 degrees and a 20-pixel distance for the Motion Blur filter.

Apply the Equalize command (Image>Adjust>Equalize), which will expand the dynamic range of the motion-blurred noise.

Choose Select>All and define the document as a pattern by selecting Define Pattern from the Edit menu.

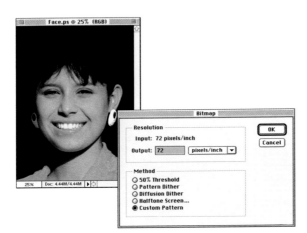

It's time to apply the custom-defined pattern as a halftone. Choose an image to process, and start the process of converting it down to Bitmap mode. You'll probably have to convert to grayscale as an intermediate step (using the Image>Mode>Grayscale command), and once you choose Bitmap mode, you'll be presented with an options dialog box. Make sure to choose Custom Pattern as the method. (If this option is dimmed out in the Bitmap dialog box, you probably forgot the previous step of creating the custom pattern.)

Using this technique, any image or texture can be used to create a custom screen effect. Why is this cool? Simple: Printers that lack PostScript are typically challenged in the custom screening department. With this custom screening technique, you can squeeze custom halftones from any printer, or take advantage of the obvious special effects potential of creating endless varieties of custom screening effects. All built into Photoshop with no third-party filters required!

Grayscale

With 8 bits per channel and 256 fixed shades of gray, Grayscale is most useful for printing images to black-and-white output devices (such as black-and-white laser printers) and processing grayscale scans. Grayscale is also the standard mode for single-channel mask documents. Of course, you'll need to switch to a color mode (such as RGB) in order to tint grayscale images with color/hue variations.

 Tip: In previous versions of Photoshop, adding an alpha channel to a grayscale image would turn the image into multichannel mode. This is no longer true in Photoshop 4.0; adding alpha channels to images in grayscale mode simply creates grayscale-mode documents with multiple channels.

Duotone

Duotone has 8 bits per channel, with up to 4 channels. Each channel represents a solid ink. This mode is only partially properly named, due to the fact that it represents one-channel (monotone), two-channel (duotone), three-channel (tritone) and four-channel (quadtone) documents. Each channel holds a representation of a standard process or spot ink type. Once converted to any of the duotone formats, the separate channels of the duo/tri/quadtone can be individually viewed or edited within Photoshop by converting the document to Multichannel mode, which places each ink plate into a separate channel.

Indexed Color

Indexed Color has 8 bits per pixel, one channel. An 8-bit image in Indexed mode, unlike Grayscale mode, can be in color; a specific 8-bit color palette (sometimes referred to as a color lookup table, or *CLUT*) attached to the file determines what colors are represented. Colors that aren't part of that palette are either dithered or discarded. You can directly access, view, and edit the derived color palette (Image>Mode>Color Table).

RGB

RGB is the native working mode in Photoshop, and has up to 24 channels of 8-bit information. Three of the channels are always dedicated to the RGB components, while the rest are alpha channels. Many file formats, however, store only one alpha channel with an RGB image; Photoshop's native format stores all 24 channels, if necessary.

 Tip: If you delete an individual RGB component layer from an RGB document, the image is automatically converted to Multichannel mode.

CMYK

CMYK is the native color space of four-color process color reproduction. CMYK files contain four color channels, with 8 bits each; only the Photoshop and TIFF file formats support more than four channels per document. The primary channels are cyan, magenta, yellow, and black, representing the four colors of ink used on a printing press. This is based on the subtractive color model. We don't spend too much time with this color space in this book, for two reasons.

Reason A: If you primarily work with CMYK scans, for output to CMYK separations, the only real importance of RGB color is to create masks—for use in the CMYK base images. Remember, it's entirely feasible to

- Duplicate your CMYK scan document (using the Duplicate command in the Image menu).
- Convert the duplicate from CMYK to RGB color.
- Use the RGB-based techniques described in this book to generate masks.
- Copy the RGB-derived masks back over to the CMYK, as additional channels. Use these new masks as desired.

This approach gives you the best of both worlds of CMYK and RGB. We have no problem confessing that the majority of our work is done for multimedia, video, and Internet applications, so we don't spend as much time in CMYK mode as we do in other color modes. Of course, like many other Photoshop artists, we often have to print our images on processed dead tree pulp, but we usually start with RGB data and leave the CMYK conversion process as one of the final steps in preparing images for print reproduction.

Reason B: If you want the deepest knowledge available on the theory and practice of doing deep, channels-related work with CMYK files, run right out and buy the amazing *Professional Photoshop*, by Dan Margulis (John Wiley & Sons). This book is the last word on CMYK color in Photoshop, and we felt that it would be silly to try and duplicate Dan's excellent efforts and skills. While we don't necessarily agree with absolutely everything Dan says in his book (he seems to have little interest in RGB color, and proclaims that CMYK is a better color space for many image processing tasks), we recognize genius when we see it. This guy is a bona fide CMYK genius. 'Nuff said.

Lab Color

This is Photoshop's very own color mode: one channel of luminance (lightness) and two channels of chrominance (color), labeled A (the green-red axis) and B (the blue-yellow axis), hence the acronym *Lab*. In truth, Lab was originally developed back in the earlier part of this century. It was proposed as a color space standard by the Commission Internationale d'Eclairage (CIE) in 1931, and updated in 1976, at which time it was officially dubbed CIE L*a*b*. The idea was to create a truly device-independent color modeling scheme that would preserve color values (hue, saturation, and lightness) across a variety of mechanical and digital hardware platforms (printers, displays, software, and so on).

> For an excellent (and deep) technical discussion of the Lab color model, power up your Web browser and go to
>
> http://www.ls.com:80/cielab.html
>
> Ed Granger, a senior scientist at LightSource (makers of the excellent Colortron color measuring and calibration system), has posted an exceptionally relevant paper on the history—and inherent problems—of the Lab color space. Highly recommended reading from one of the great minds of the field.

While Lab looks like an arcane color space on the surface, it turns out that it's actually something of interest to any Photoshop user. Why?

- It's the native color space of PostScript Level 2. If you have a color printer with this version of PostScript, be aware that image files sent to it are converted to Lab space as part of the raster image processing (RIP) stage. Many people have reported great results converting images from RGB to Lab before printing directly from Photoshop to a PostScript Level 2 color output device.

- Lab is the closest thing left to the HSB (hue, saturation, and brightness) color mode in earlier versions of Photoshop. This mode was incredibly useful for processing the detail of an image (the brightness channel) while leaving the actual color information of the image intact.

- When you convert images between different color spaces (such as RGB to CMYK), Photoshop uses the Lab mode as an invisible, intermediary part of the color space conversion process.

Tip: Here's a time-saving Lab tip: If you spend significant amounts of time applying Unsharp Masking to large (20+ megabyte) scans, you can save some time required to apply the Unsharp Masking filter (not one of the fastest filters in the Photoshop toolbox) by converting your image to Lab and running the Unsharp Masking on the L (lightness or luminosity) channel exclusively. This also creates the desired sharpening effect on the detail areas of the image while leaving the color components intact, reducing the possibility of *halation* around strong color boundaries. The word halation is derived from halo: a particular problem with high frequency edges of an image, when being processed through contrast enhancement processes such as Unsharp Masking. Halation also can be seen with images taken with digital camera technology, especially if you do further Unsharp Masking to the digital camera image before converting it to CMYK for color output.

An image with the Unsharp Mask filter applied equally to all color channels. Note the visible halo effect around the edges of the foreground object.

An image converted to Lab color space, with Unsharp Mask filter applied only to the Luminosity channel. Note that the halation effect seen around the edges of the foreground image isn't as obtrusive as the results of the previous figure.

Multichannel

Multichannel is the Swiss Army Knife of Photoshop's Mode menu. It's primarily used for the following reasons:

- Directly view and edit the results of a Duotone conversion. (Normal Duotone mode doesn't allow the separate plates to be viewed or edited discretely.)

- Prepare spot-color composites. For example, a grayscale image in one channel might accompany a type knock-out area designated in a second grayscale channel; the contents of the knock-out are assigned to a specific Pantone color, which prints on top of the grayscale image in the first channel. While Multichannel mode can be used to emulate spot color plates, it isn't a technique we recommend for a serious production environment, and certainly isn't a replacement for a real spot color capability in Photoshop (perhaps the most overdue feature still not found in the current release of the program).

Viewing multichannel documents in Photoshop results in only viewing one separate grayscale channel at a time. Multichannel format is often a decent choice for storing alpha channels outside of your main working document (the one that the alpha channels would actually be used on). Because Photoshop allows the saving of selections to external documents, all the masks for an image can be stored in a different document, if needed.

Bit Depth and Color

Most people involved in imaging know that the lower the bit depth, the fewer colors you can fit into your image. We've all seen it: beautiful 24-bit images that show up on the World Wide Web looking pretty lousy in 8-bit color. Some artists wonder why their final CMYK print has weird moiré patterns and other artifacts when their scan was done in 8-bit color mode, converted to RGB, and printed in CMYK.

An indexed color image has a relatively limited number of colors. If we look at the Indexed Color dialog box in Photoshop, it's obvious that an image can have fewer than 8 bits of memory for each pixel, resulting in fewer colors (which translates into smaller overall file sizes). The relationship between the value of the pixel depth (for example, 5 bits per pixel) and the number of colors in a particular image is relatively straightforward: raise 2 (the possible state of a bit: on or off, 0 or 1) to the power of the image's pixel depth (how many bits of color data each pixel contains) to find out exactly how many colors are in it (the maximum number of possible color permutations available for a single pixel). For example, an 8-bit color image can have a maximum of 256 colors in it; raise two to the eighth power and the result is 256.

Given this exponential relationship, the difference in size and range of possible color variations between two images of different color depths is more significant than you might expect. An 8-bit color image, with 256 colors, is much more than twice as big as an image with 4-bit color, which only has 16 colors in it!

The following series of figures is an example of an image indexed down to different color depths and converted with different tools. These tools include Digital Frontiers' excellent HVS Color plug-ins for Photoshop, as well as Debabelizer.

A 24-bit original RGB color image.

An 8-bit adaptive palette, dithered in Photoshop.

A 4-bit adaptive palette, dithered in Photoshop.

An 8-bit adaptive palette, dithered using HVS Color.

A 4-bit adaptive palette, dithered using HVS Color.

An 8-bit Macintosh system palette, dithered in Photoshop.

An 8-bit adaptive palette, dithered in Debabelizer.

A 4-bit adaptive palette, dithered in Debabelizer.

An 8-bit Macintosh system palette, dithered in Debabelizer.

Let's say that you scan an image in grayscale mode with a typical desktop scanner. Even though the original image might be color, and your scanner is a color model, you can scan a single channel of information. This yields a single channel, 8-bit grayscale image in Photoshop.

If the same image is scanned in RGB format, a 3-channel, 24-bit image is the result.

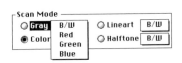

A scanner plug-in module in Photoshop.

The Channels palette, displaying the channels of a 24-bit RGB image.

Tip: We consider the HVS color reduction technology to be one of the better investments that you can make for your Web-related imaging work. You can find the publisher, Digital Frontiers, on the Web at

http://www.digfrontiers.com/

Digital Frontiers HVS ColorGIF 2.0 and HVS JPEG 2.0 are excellent—the HVS (Human Visual Systems) color reduction algorithm goes far beyond the standard color-polling techniques used by programs like Photoshop and results in far more accurate color representation using far fewer colors than anything produced by any other program we've seen (not even DeBabelizer can touch it!). And, yes, they make the plug-ins for both the Macintosh and PC hardware platforms.

Color Depth and Channels

So how do full-color, 24-bit images fit into this 8-bits-per-channel paradigm? Quite easily, in fact. Without going too deep into color and visual theory, the short answer goes something like this...

Unlike a grayscale image, which has a *single* channel (which therefore grants it 256 levels of brightness), an RGB image has *three* component color channels: one Red, one Green, and one Blue. This is called *transmissive*, or *additive*, color, wherein red, green, and blue light are displayed simultaneously on a cathode ray tube. This is how images are shown on computer monitors, television screens, and video displays of all kinds. Each of these color channels, like a single-channel grayscale image, contains 8 bits of data, or 256 different tones. Three of these 8-bit channels in a single image (eight bits per channel, multiplied by three channels) yields a single image with *24 bits of color*. When all three RGB components are displayed at full strength (a full 255 brightness readout for each), the resulting color is white. An absence of all three RGB components (0 readout for each component) results in pure black.

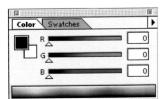

Photoshop's Color palette is a tiny, self-contained education in basic color theory. As you can see, when all three RGB values are set to 0, the result is black.

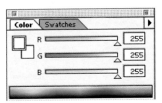

Pump all three RGB sliders up to their full possible value (255), and the result is pure white. And look at the actual color readouts within the slider bars themselves, which shows you how color components interact. Isn't it interesting to see that when you have all three RGB sliders set to full value, the Color palette is trying to tell us something about the relationship between RGB and CMYK.

As you'll see, it's the interaction of these three color channels that produces the ultimate full-color image. In a single color channel, black indicates the absence of that particular color, while white represents full-color presence. Let's assume a particular pixel in a 24-bit RGB image is black in the red channel, 50% gray in the green channel and white in the blue channel. This pixel's RGB color is 0% red, 50% green, and 100% blue, resulting in a light blue hue. The total possible permutations of hue in a 24-bit color image is upwards of 16 million different colors (16,777,216 colors to be exact, the result of 2 to the 24th power).

Specifically, when discussing the actual color channels of an image, the presence of brightness in a component color channel (as expressed in values getting close to pure white) indicates the presence of that component color in the overall image. Let's look at the example of a typical color photograph.

If we take a look at the blue channel of this image—by selecting it from the channels palette, or pressing Command-3 (Control-3 for Windows users) from the keyboard—it's clear that the area of the blue sky contains predominantly brighter pixels, especially when compared to the same area of the image in either the red or green channels. (In the case of a blue sky, the red channel is relatively dark, while the contents of the green channel in the sky area fall somewhere in between the brightness values of the red and blue channels.)

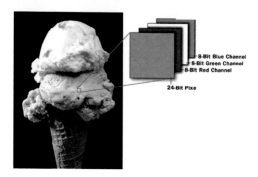

RGB images have three 8-bit channels, one for each color. The interactions of these channels create full-color, 24-bit images.

A typical 24-bit RGB image from our stock photo library.

The red, green, and blue channels of our sky image. In Photoshop, the name of the channel appears in the title bar of the document window. Note that the pixels in the sky area in the blue channel are significantly lighter than the same areas of the red and green channels.

The only times that RGB images have more than 24 bits of data per pixel are

- If they have embedded *alpha channels*, 8-bit channels used for masking and compositing, effectively making them 32-bit image files (with no increase in potential colors).

- If they have been scanned on high-resolution scanners. Drum scanners, and even some flatbed models, can scan images with up to 16 bits of data per color channel. This extended bit depth primarily asserts itself in the image as extended detail in darker (shadow) regions of the image, as well as in smoother color gradations, which involve subtle variations of a base color (such as gradients between pure black and white). Images originating on SGI systems also often have more than 24 bits of data.

Photoshop has some limited support for handling 16-bits-per-channel images. The toggle for 8- or 16-bit modes can be seen in the Image>Mode submenu. Normally, the default setting is 8 bits per channel (in all color modes, with the exception of Bitmap, in which neither 8 nor 16 bits are active), with the 16-bit option appearing in both Grayscale and RGB modes.

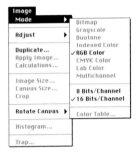

If you have a Grayscale or RGB scan created with a typical desktop scanner, it's most likely that they will default to the 8-bit setting. Some higher-end flatbeds, as well as a number of slide and film scanners, have the ability to generate 16-bits-per-pixel scans, which significantly extends response in shadow areas (yielding greater detail in predominantly dark portions of a scan). Photoshop can actually import and display a 16-bits-per-pixel file.

In Grayscale and RGB modes, you can choose from either 8 or 16 bits per channel.

What's the use of 16 bits of color data per channel? Four words: *greater dynamic color range*. If you get a 24-bit color scan (8 bits per channel) that's both dark and lacking in contrast, using Levels or Curves actually discards some image data in favor of some level of aesthetic improvement. You can visually see this by opening up the Levels dialog box, where you'll see empty bands in the image's histogram, indicating missing colors or tones.

With a 48-bit scan (16 bits per channel), doing drastic color or brightness correction still leaves a good deal of data intact. Looking at the Levels dialog box of a 48-bit scan after significant color correction still shows a histogram with a full dynamic range of tones. Of course, after initial scan tweaking you'll have to convert your images into 24-bit mode for filtering or other significant editing.

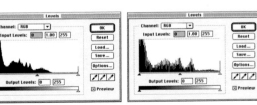
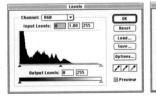
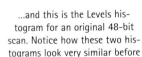
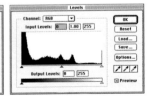

This is the Levels histogram display for an original 24-bit scan...

...and this is the Levels histogram for an original 48-bit scan. Notice how these two histograms look very similar before any image editing is done.

This is the same 24-bit scan *after* Levels has been used for contrast enhancement. You can start to see the empty vertical bands where color data has been lost.

When the 48-bit scan has the same Levels command applied to it, however, the histogram looks entirely intact; when converted to 24-bit mode, it has a greater range of color data than the 24-bit scan.

Color Spaces and Channels

Color space, in the context of this book, is an abstracted method of color representation on the computer. RGB, CMYK, CIE, Lab, Indexed–the color modes in the Image>Mode menu of Photoshop–are all individual color spaces. Despite many experts, many opinions, and untold numbers of international standards organizations, there is no single universal method of constructing a color space that can display color on all devices for all occasions. That's why there are several different standard color spaces in Photoshop and other applications. Each color space has its own intended use.

Color images usually have a dedicated channel for each component color in the image's designated color space: one channel each for red, green, and blue for an RGB image (three channels total); one channel each for cyan, magenta, yellow, and black in a CMYK image (four channels total); and so on. One exception to this rule is the Indexed Color mode, which uses only a single channel to represent a specific set of colors; this set of colors is called a *look-up table* (LUT for short, sometimes called a *CLUT* for color look-up table).

Channels Reveal Their Secrets

The different color space options offered by Photoshop each have their appropriate use, depending on the context of the acquisition and final application of an image. For example, images scanned on professional laser drum scanners are typically delivered as CMYK files right from the scanner, while images scanned on most desktop scanners are typically in RGB format (with the exception of a newer generation of desktop laser drum scanners, which have begun to appear on the market in the last couple of years).

The Importance of RGB

Much of this book deals primarily with the RGB color mode in Photoshop, often at the expense of coverage of the other useful color models (such as CMYK) found in Photoshop. Why did we decide to do this?

The Electromagnetic Spectrum

Color, brightness, and saturation–terms you're likely familiar with from working with Photoshop, as well as other imaging software–are ways to describe particular characteristics of the portion of light that human beings can see. The visible spectrum of light is part of a larger construct of physical reality (no, we didn't just go New Age on you, we're talking about actual empirical physics here), a world that's called the *electromagnetic spectrum*. Did you ever wonder how broadcast television and radio work? Or how it is that a sound of a frying hamburger reaches your ears?

Authors' Note

At this point, you're probably wondering why we're taking this little detour into physics... "Hey, this is supposed to be a Photoshop book!" Well, the fact of the matter is image processing is largely based on the concepts of signal processing, which are more generalized that visual imagery, but can help you understand the more complex topics encountered in learning advanced image processing.

The truth is that much of David Biedny's knowledge of image processing is derived from his intense interest at an early age in audio processing, which shares many base concepts with image processing. (Ever notice the High Pass filter in Photoshop? Wonder what it does? The concept has an extremely important and useful counterpart in audio signal processing, and is an important link in the audio equalization chain.) But let's get back to channels!

Most of the devices used by human beings to perceive and interpret color are inherently based on the RGB color model. The light gathering mechanisms of the human eye are based on RGB color, as are the computer and display monitors used by anyone reading this book.

Well, as discussed in the preceding paragraphs, it's the native color space for most input devices that you're likely to use in daily work (with the notable exception of high-end pre-press drum scanners, which typically create scans in CMYK color space). RGB also is the native color space for your computer, the monitor on your desk, and your own internal optical input devices (*eyes*, by any other name). Most important to the mission of this book, though, is the fact that RGB is perhaps the most revealing of the color spaces, in terms of how light works and the characteristic behavior of light when described in RGB.

Although Photoshop can display images in other color spaces, the actual colors on your screen are still physically created by the RGB guns in the Cathode Ray Tube (CRT). In the day–to–day world of image creation and reproduction, just about the only time you'll likely deal without another color model is in the four-color printing process—combinations of cyan, magenta, yellow, and black inks. Hey, face it: It's an RGB world, after all.

 Tip: One of the options in the Display & Cursors screen of Photoshop's Preferences dialog box is the capability to display color component channels in either grayscale or the actual component color. You'll always want to make sure that you're looking at channels in Grayscale mode, given that the actual brightness values of the pixels in each component channel are of any actual value; looking at the blue channel in shades of blue can be quite distracting, making it harder to actually evaluate the real information present in the channel.

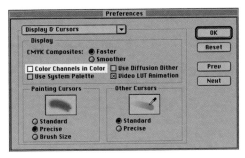

Make sure that you've unchecked the Color Channels in Color option in the Display & Cursors Preferences dialog box (screen three) as the method for displaying individual channels.

The Red Channel

The red channel is the ultimate proof of life on Mars. Okay, maybe not. Like the other channels, the red channel displays the amount of red component in an image. Perhaps the most noticeable example of this is seen when looking at a shot of a typically lit human head. Human flesh tones have a significant amount of red component, represented by brightness in the red channel.

In a general sense, the red channel tends to contain the greatest range, or *spread*, of contrast values in an image. If you want to know a bit about the brightest and darkest values in a photographic image, you'll usually start by taking a look at the red component channel (which can be directly accessed by pressing Command-1).

The red channel is always active where human flesh is involved.

The Green Channel

Of all of the RGB channels, green is extremely useful in general image processing work. While the red channel tends to hold the contrast spread, the green channel is the place where all high-level or high-frequency detail in a photographic image can be found.

What is high-frequency detail? Does it have something to do with your stereo system? Is there a treble control involved? Well, not quite, but the ideas are actually related.

In discussing image processing, the concept of high frequency is placed into a specific context. Let's take the example of the most extreme case of a high-frequency edge.

The area where the two regions meet is considered a very high-frequency edge. If you sample the black-and-white areas with the eyedropper tool, it's clear that the difference between the two values is as extreme as it gets.

In the case of CMYK, for example, the distinctive, recognizable details of an image are primarily contained in the black channel (often called the black plate by those in the printing and pre-press world). This is the primary reason that Photoshop enables you to get very specific about how you want the black channel derived from the mixture of red, green, and blue when doing color space conversions from RGB to CMYK.

Any edge that displays a significant differential in brightness values is where the actual defining detail of an image can be found, and as it turns out, the green channel of an RGB document tends to contain the best representation of high-frequency edges in a color composite image. The green channel can be accessed by pressing Command-2.

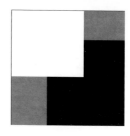

This represents the most high-frequency edge you can find in image processing: a border between two regions of absolute black and white.

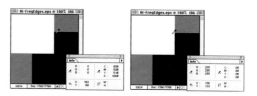

It's obvious that there's a 255 value spread between white (255) and black (0).

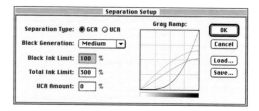

The density of the black plate of a CMYK document (converted from an RGB source image) is determined by specifying the Black Generation tonality curve and the Total Ink Limits (Total Ink Limit describes the relationship between the amount of mixture of CMYK inks and the derivation of black values from that mixture).

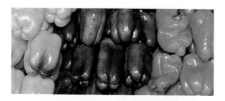

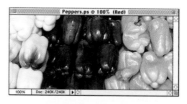

If you look closely, it becomes obvious that the best representation of the fine detail in an image can be found in the green channel.

The Blue Channel

In the food chain of RGB channels, blue is at the bottom of the heap. No, that doesn't mean that the blue channel is bad—but very often the bad things about a color image try to hide themselves in the blue channel of a color image. Of course, if you're scanning lots of images of blue skies, blank blue screens, blue-colored construction paper, or a new fashion line of pure blue clothing, you would expect significant activity in the blue channel (remember, the presence of a color component in an image is represented by brightness values in that component channel). But for most natural images, the blue channel is the place where you can find

- Noise artifacts
- Film emulsion grain characteristics
- Scanner noise and undesirable artifacts
- Video jitter (in the case of images grabbed or digitized from video sources)

One way to tell how well any scanner performs (in terms of overall image quality) is to take a look at the blue channel by itself (press Command-3 to display just the blue channel in the active RGB document window).

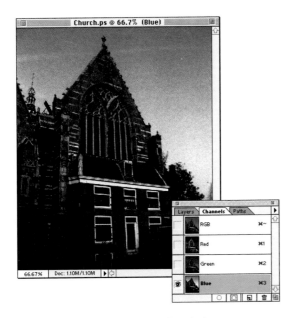

A typical blue channel of a color image.

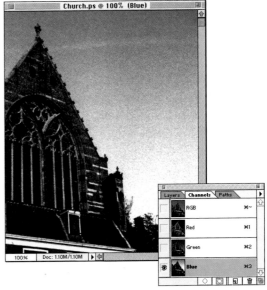

The emulsion characteristics of a specific type of film are always visible in the blue channel of a scan of the slide.

If you're evaluating the blue channel of an image scanned from film (such as a 35 mm slide), you'll notice a distinctive grain pattern underlying the overall image.

Different types of film display distinctive film grain emulsion characteristics. If you take a look at the ASA rating of a roll of film, the film rated with lower ASA numbers (such as 100 ASA slide film) has a finer (smaller) grain size than film with higher ASA ratings (such as a 400 ASA print film). The higher the ASA value, the larger the grain. A smaller grain results in greater detail (and requires more light when actually taking a picture; this is one reason that higher ASA rated film is used for lower-light situations, as well as for fast action).

Very often, by applying small amounts of specific filter effects to the blue channel of an image scanned from film, you can reduce the overall film grain noise in the overall color image. This technique also can be used to minimize the jitter often seen when images are grabbed from video sources such as VHS decks and low-end camcorders.

Deriving Grayscale from RGB

When you use the grayscale mode command in Photoshop, an image in a color space (such as RGB, CMYK, or just about any other deeper color space) is converted to a single channel image devoid of color tonality (or hue) information. For the purposes of this discussion, we're going to concentrate on the mechanism used to convert RGB to grayscale and explore a better methodology for accomplishing this process.

When you choose the Image>Mode>Grayscale image mode, a three-channel document is converted into a single channel of 256 gray levels. How does Photoshop determine how to reduce the information and create the single channel from three? What does it mean when Photoshop tells you that it's going to Discard Color Information?

The Grayscale conversion dialog box. Not exactly the whole truth of the matter.

When you choose the Image>Mode>Grayscale image mode, a three-channel document is reduced to a single channel. Color information is lost as a result of the process, but it's not like Photoshop is extracting just the straight brightness information of the image, leaving the hue information behind.

The process takes a majority percentage of green (for detail), a minority percentage of red (for contrast), and a smaller percentage of blue. In fact, we asked Mark Hamburg, one of the lead Photoshop engineers at Adobe, exactly how grayscale information is derived from a color image. His response is directly quoted in the following note.

> RGB to grayscale conversion via the mode menu (or when converting in the info palette) is based on converting from RGB to XYZ using the information in Monitor Setup and then converting Y to gray based either on the information in Monitor Setup or the information in Printing Inks Setup, depending on whether the use dot gain for grayscale option is enabled. When we need a fast approximation to luminance, we use 30% red, 59% green, and 11% blue. This gets used in things like Luminosity mode and is the gray channel option supplied in the Calculations and Apply Image dialog boxes.

But what if the results of the pre-defined methodology don't give you what you want? The answer lies in using the red and green channels of an image to derive your own grayscale document, with full control over the blend of the green and red channels. (Under most conditions, you'll rarely want to incorporate any percentage of the blue channel into the conversion process.)

This technique can be applied to image acquisition and scanning as well: simply scan your grayscale image in RGB mode. You'll get, of course, an RGB color image, but it's the individual color channels that you're after. If you scan in or reduce RGB to Grayscale mode, you're getting what Photoshop and your scanner think is an optimal gray image, as described in the preceding paragraphs. If you have an RGB image, you can choose what channel (or combination of channels) will get you your *own* balance of contrast, detail, and film grain.

Using inter-channel calculations, you can make your own custom grayscale recipe, spiking more with different channels to enhance overall contrast, brightness, or inherent grain or texture, depending on the look you're going for.

So let's try the technique. It involves that most daunting of Photoshop commands... the Calculations command.

We devote an entire chapter (Chapter 4, aptly titled "Calculations") to the intricacies of the Calculations command. But, in brief, Calculations enables you to compare and process the pixels in different channels of a document, or between channels of different documents—with the one caveat that all documents and channels that you wish to process are the exact same physical size, in pixels and overall resolution. Why, you ask? Read the Calculations chapter and find out!

Make sure that the RGB image you want to convert to grayscale is the currently active document. The document should consist of a single background layer with the actual image data and no other layers of any type.

Select the Calculations command (Image> Calculations).

While many Calculation commands are sensitive to the order of the channels specified as the Sources, we're not going to worry about it just yet.

Let's make the example image active by making sure it's checked in the Windows menu.

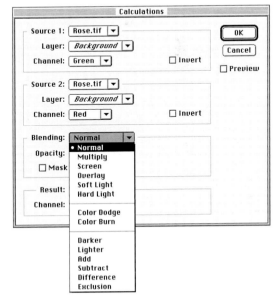

In the Calculations dialog box, Source 1 and Source 2 are the two channels that we wish to process. Select the green channel of the active document for Source 1, and the red channel for Source 2.

Make sure that the Blending mode is set to Normal.

The Normal mode gives you the ability to create straight cross-faded blends between the two channels, without any extra mathematical processing typically incurred by most of the other Blend modes.

It's time to set the blending value between the green and red channels. The Opacity value in the Calculations dialog box is referring to the percentage of Source 1 factored into the calculation. Yes, we know that this is somewhat less than obvious, and if it were up to us, we would redesign the entire Calculations interface. We'll share more of our complaints with you in the Chapter 4.

As we discovered from Mark Hamburg, the relationship of green to red in the standard Photoshop grayscale conversion process is roughly 2:1. We'll use Calculations to experiment with changing this ratio.

So let's say that you want to increase the overall detail of the image while losing some of the contrast value. The trick is to increase the percentage of the green channel considered processed in the Calculation.

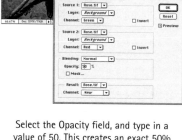

| Turning on the Preview checkbox in the Calculations dialog box enables you to see the results of your settings in real-time, in the active document window. | Select the Opacity field, and type in a value of 50. This creates an exact 50% split between the green and red channels of the image. The result is slightly more contrast in the overall grayscale image as compared to Photoshop's standard conversion results. | Select the Opacity field and type in a value of 75. This results in 75% of the green channel being combined with 25% (the remainder of the total 100%) of the red channel. The result is an image with more detail and slightly less contrast. |

Once you have a combination that seems pleasing, the next step is to save the results as a separate channel/image. The options at the bottom of the Calculations dialog box enable you to specify where to place the results of the Calculation process. While you can send the results into an existing channel, or even create a new layer, for this exercise specify a new document for the resulting grayscale image.

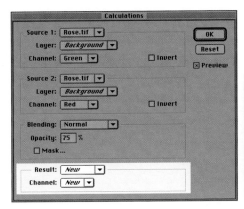

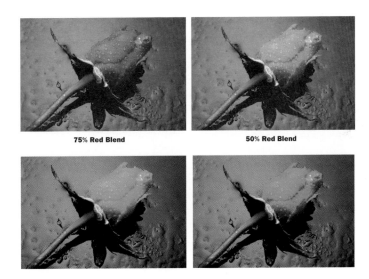

Specify a new document as the target for the results of the calculation. Click the OK button.

A great thing about Calculations is that you can continue processing the results with the channels of the original image as long as you haven't resized the original or new documents. Let's say that you want to add a little of the original red component back to the newly derived green-heavy grayscale image resulting from the last step. Make the single-channel grayscale result of the previous Calculation active, choose the Calculation, and blend it back with the red component of the original image.

75% Red Blend   **50% Red Blend**

We can blend the newly derived grayscale image back with the red channel of the original document to bring out more contrast in the final grayscale image.

So why use Calculations instead of copying the green and red channels to separate layers in a file and using the opacity controls to control their relative interaction? For starters, if the image you're working on is a large, high-resolution scan, making new layers and manipulating those layers can be a time–consuming (as well as scratch–disk intensive) chore. Using the direct memory pipeline inherent in the Calculations command dramatically streamlines memory overhead and usage, and doesn't actually create new image data until you press the OK button in the Calculations dialog box. There also are other reasons, which we'll explore more in-depth in Chapter 4.

When we set out to create this book, we were originally going to make alpha channels—the primary mechanism for masking and compositing in the digital realm—the main focus of the text; in fact, the publisher specifically wanted the words "alpha channel" in the title of the book. As you can see, good sense prevailed. We expanded the focus of the book by folding alpha channels into the overall concept of thinking of an image as discrete channels of information. But the fact of the matter is that alpha channels are perhaps the most pragmatic expression of the usefulness of image channels, and are the most important application of channels for the day-to-day work of any imaging artist.

In this chapter, we're going to take a brief historical look at how the concept of the alpha channel was devised. This information should help you understand the usefulness and versatility presented by the creative and judicious use of these helpful entities. We also will explore specific examples of how alpha channels are used to combine separate visual elements into complex, multi-layered composites. You'll find a reasonable mixture of theory and practice, both necessary for understanding the inner workings of the dark art of *masking*.

The Zen of Alpha Channels

Before getting into the meaty details of masking and alpha channels operations, we'd like to take a step back, out of Photoshop, computer graphics, and imaging. In order to set the stage for full comprehension of the concept (and reality) of the alpha channel, we have to get a bit philosophical. Yes, philosophy is a somewhat strange thing to find in a technique-oriented computer graphics book, but you've probably figured out that this is *not* your standard kind of computer book.

In order to deeply *grok* the functionality of alpha channels, it's critical to cover some basic concepts that are often taken for granted by advanced computer users, but aren't usually considered by the casual computer artist.

Summed up in a single sentence:

Take **this**, and do **that** to it.

Seems simple, right? Let's talk more about this elementary concept for just a moment.

Computers are useful devices, but generally speaking, they aren't too smart about knowing what we want to do with them. In order to get any work done on a computer, we find that it's necessary to be quite specific about our intentions. Computers aren't too good at figuring out *purpose*, though they are excellent at actual *processing*. Whenever you sit down with a computer, you'll find that much of the work involved in *producing results* is wrapped up in prompting the computer to follow your exact commands—selecting menu items, typing in a word to find something in a text document, highlighting some text (with a mouse or a keyboard sequence), choosing a color to use with the paint bucket tool, or just about *any* operation where you explicitly instruct the computer to accomplish a specific task.

Computers aren't very good at anticipating human intention. And even when software can look ahead and try to guess what you want, the results are often incorrect (at best) or infuriating (at worst). For example, there have been attempts to add a level of automation to the process of writing words on a computer. A number of utility software developers, along with some of the bigger word processing application players, have released software that looks at what you type into the computer at any given moment and automatically expands upon what you've typed in; this is done by recognizing what you're starting to type and using a reference dictionary to instantly finish typing a word. For example, you might set the software up to recognize the characters "brook" and instantly replace them with the full text string "Brooklyn, New York" as you were typing. While this might seem useful, upon close inspection, the concept rapidly loses practical merit, for computers are really bad at figuring out the context of word usage (one of the biggest barriers to the continued advancement of the field of Artificial Intelligence). If you were writing a report on the water flow patterns of brooks and streams, this feature would instantly make your work nightmarish.

So how does any of this discussion relate to the feeding and care of alpha channels, you ask? Simple: When you work with visual images, there are certain things that are reasonable to expect that you'll want to do with the image. Such predictable image processing behavior includes, but is not limited to, the following:

The quick brown fox jumped over the lazy dog.

In order to change or alter text, you need to select it first. The word processor has no idea that you want to do this—selecting the text is part of a *selective filtration process* you must do in order for the computer to do its part. The selection is an alpha channel for text.

- Cropping
- Scaling
- Brightness and contrast enhancement
- Tinting/colorization
- Filtering
- Combining an image with other images

At the most elemental level, these phases of image processing functionality come into play more often than not. Of course, there are many other things that you can do with an image, but the basic idea is clear: Images are brought into the computer, where they are manipulated using whatever tools are available.

And this is where your intentions and desires usually get a bit more specific and defined. We might know that we want to manipulate an image, but commonly it's only a portion of the picture that needs to be worked on, and not the entire image. It's clear that many types of editing functions are often applied to an entire image (scaling is a good example), but in the real world, it's likely that you'll only want to do things to specific parts, or regions, of a complete picture.

The issue of *selective processing* or *selective filtration* has always been present in image processing and computer graphics. It's critical to understand that these fields of study have actually been around for significantly longer than graphical-interface computers such as the Macintosh. Research work on visual interaction with computation devices can be traced back to the early sixties. Some of the most important pioneering work was accomplished by Doug Engelbart, the inventor of the mouse, the first windowing systems for computer screens, and a host of other important technological innovations. The mouse was the first significant and universal step beyond the QWERTY keyboard that enabled users to communicate intent and desire to a computer, and has lasted with us until current times. But the alpha channel has its own history and players.

Why discuss the historical origins of the alpha channel? For no other reason, we feel compelled to set the record straight on this somewhat obscure subject (at least for people not normally informed about the historical development of this industry). At a major Photoshop conference we attended a couple of years ago, a well-known Photoshop book author was teaching (in our opinion) a rather sloppy advanced masking session. Someone in the audience asked him where the term alpha channel originated, and instead of admitting that he didn't have a clue, he claimed that "Apple Computer invented the alpha channel, and it was labeled 'alpha' because the word started with the letter 'A,' just like Apple." When we hear this kind of nonsense, we feel compelled to act and uncover the *reality* of the situation. Read on.

Historical Overview—Traditional Masking

Before we even get down to the specifics of the origin of alpha channels, it's critical to understand that the process of masking in the creation of artwork has been around for a long time. If you visit various types of graphics artists, you'll find that they use masks that have specific types of names, but that all work in similar ways.

Just about everyone has their first experience with masks in grade school–using paper stencils and crayons to create specific letter forms on paper. The holes in the stencil allow the crayon to be applied to the underlying paper in

This was probably the very first time you used masks in your creative work-stencils and crayons (or Magic Markers, or even colored pencils). The process is fairly obvious. The holes in the stencil allow the medium to be applied to the underlying paper in order to create specific shapes in a controlled, relatively predictable manner. The stencil is effectively an alpha channel, but lacks the variable transparency and flexibility of digital alpha channels. Of course, this technique works on a desert island, while you'll need electricity and computers for the digital method.

a specific fashion, or shape, while the rest of the paper is protected from the crayon by the solid parts of the stencil.

Speak to an airbrush artist and you'll find that they refer to masks as *friskets*, which are really almost exactly like a paper stencil-the only real difference is that the airbrush artists charges much more to make the frisket than a student would charge to cut a stencil! A production artist working in a print production environment often has to cut *Rubylith* in order to designate parts of a page or image as protected, or to specify that specific areas of a page (designated by falling inside the Rubylith-masked region) are to be printed in a specific spot color, metallic ink, or with a certain type of finish (such as a glossy varnish).

Rubylith: A sheet of clear acetate or plastic with a thin coating of red plastic bonded to the top of the material. A shape for a mask or overlay can be cut with an X-Acto knife, with the unwanted areas peeled away to leave a solid region. The red areas look black to an optical plate-making camera, and are opaque to the light used for making contact exposures from negatives. *Amberlith* is a similar material with an orange rather than red coating, and is used for identical purposes.

As an example, a gradient of blue color will be applied to the sky in the following image, using this traditional method of masking.

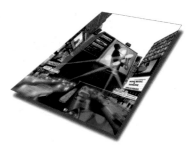

The original image with the unpainted sky.

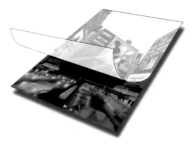

A sheet of frisket material or vellum is placed over the art.

 Tip: One of the big issues in traditional masking is the process of deciding which type of material to use to make the mask. In the case of grade school stencils, the masking material is opaque, making it more difficult to actually cut the hole for the revealed area in the exact position with respect to the actual image. Semi-transparent materials such as Rubylith enable the artist to actually see the underlying image as he or she cuts the desired areas away from the overlay. The equivalent in Photoshop is to display the channel in QuickMask mode, or to turn on the display for an alpha channel by clicking the Eye icon for the desired alpha channel in the channels palette. Each mode displays the mask overlaid onto the underlying image with a degree of transparency, and with a specific color. The controls for these parameters can be accessed by double-clicking the desired channel in the Channels palette.

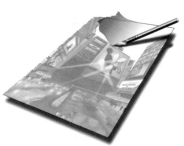  

The area to be modified is cut out from the frisket with a knife. The cut-out area exposes the underlying artwork while the remaining frisket protects the artwork from any modification.

Paint is applied to the exposed area of the art.

The completed art with the sky colorized.

Once the modification is complete, the mask is removed and the modified art can be viewed without the mask.

If you want to think about this process in a completely non-computer context, take a look at house painters getting ready to paint a wall with windows. Usually, they'll place masking tape over the glass surfaces of the window pane, as well as any other parts of the molding that are supposed to remain unpainted. The exposed areas (walls) receive the full load of paint, while the taped areas are left untouched.

This process is essential to understanding how digital masks work. While the range of types of processes that can be masked through an alpha channel is much greater than any analog equivalent, the core concept of functionality is exactly the same. The alpha channel is a kind of digital frisket, but (as you'll soon find out) is much more versatile and, unlike the analog version, won't give you headaches from the paint fumes.

Photoshop Alpha Channels

An alpha channel has the same utility as a frisket, or stencil. 100 percent black in an alpha channel represents the frisket and 100 percent white equals the cutout. When an alpha channel is applied to an image, wherever the alpha channel is black, the image is protected from modification (the mask is opaque). Where an alpha channel is white, the image will be modified (the mask is transparent). Any modification that can be applied to an image in Photoshop can be applied through an alpha channel. This includes all the Adjust controls, filters, painting tools, and Paste Into commands.

Unlike a frisket, which totally exposes or covers an area, the alpha channel grants varying levels of masking. An alpha channel is an 8-bit channel, containing black, white, and up to 254 different levels of gray; given that black masks the image and white exposes the image to manipulation, grays determine the opacity of the effect applied to the image. The level of gray determines the opacity level of the effect applied to the image. For example, a 50 percent gray exposes the image to a 50 percent modification. Using the Rubylith comparison, imagine being able to paint away varying thickness of the Rubylith to allow varying amounts of ink though to the image. Instead of an X-Acto knife, we can use a brush dipped in virtual HCL (hydrochloric acid, nasty stuff that burns plastic to a crisp) to eat away at the frisket's thickness and opacity.

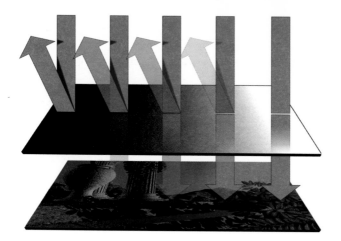

Photoshop's alpha channels can be thought of as advanced friskets. Instead of only having masked (black) and unmasked (white) areas, alpha channels can have varying levels of mask opacity based on grayscale brightness.

Like any grayscale channel or file, any tool or filter can be used on an alpha channel. In fact, both blurring and filtering alpha channels are essential elements of creative and professional image compositing (see the following section on making masks).

Alpha channels, then, are channels that determine transparency. An RGB image has three channels for its actual colors (red, green, and blue), as well as a fourth channel for determining opacity. Like the color channels, the alpha channel has 8 bits of information with which it can determine varying levels of opacity. An RGB image with an alpha channel has 32 bits of information per pixel: 24 bits of color data and 8 bits of opacity data.

Historical Overview—The Alpha Channel

In the realm of computer graphics, the concept of the alpha channel has its origins in pioneering work done at the New York Institute of Technology (NYIT) by Alvy Ray Smith and Ed Catmull (two of the original founding members of the seminal computer graphics company Pixar), who date their invention of the integrated alpha channel to the year 1977. The graphics work that they were doing at the time involved having to re-render a foreground image element every time it was moved onto a different background element (or even moved into a new position over the background image), eating up large amounts of time and money.

> The framebuffers (an exotic term for dedicated graphics memory) that Smith and Catmull were using at the time were more expensive than many SGI machines today!

Catmull realized that rendering times could be drastically decreased if the foreground graphic could have its own opacity information embedded into its file structure, preventing the need to fully re-render the image every time it was introduced onto a different background. Each pixel would have its own opacity setting, allowing for variable, non-linear transparency of the image over the background (in the most practical application of this technique, the edges of the foreground element could have variable transparency with respect to the background; today, we call this *anti-aliasing*). In one day, Smith formulated a new image file architecture: RGBA, or RGB+Alpha.

Tip: The term *alpha*, used to designate a channel that determines opacity, was chosen by Alvy Ray Smith when he originally designed the format. Its name comes from part of an equation, where alpha controls the amount of linear interpolation, or blending, between two composited images.

With RGB+Alpha, the need for a separate digital file to act as the equivalent of the third piece of monochrome film (from the original optical process) that holds the matte is eliminated. The foreground element has its own color and opacity data, stored in a single file. Another traditional compositing dilemma is also solved by the integrated, or embedded, alpha channel: the traveling matte. Traveling mattes were masks tied to the motion of a foreground object. A traveling matte wasn't only a *spatial* matte, which masked out the background of the composited element, but a *temporal* matte as well, a matte whose position (and perhaps shape) could be changed over time. If an image could have its own opacity data, moving the image across the background plate would still result in a perfect composite. Its opacity is integral with its color, and moves with it. (Traveling mattes are still a necessary evil, especially when digital elements lack embedded alpha channels or when alpha channels need to be significantly changed over time.)

With the advent of 3D software, the concept of the embedded alpha channel became even more crucial. 3D renderings usually generate an alpha channel for each frame at render time, streamlining the compositing process.

Alpha Channels and Digital Compositing

An easy way to understand digital compositing is by visualizing a 1-bit mask possessing only black or white pixels. This is exactly how real-world masking works, like Rubyliths and friskets. Such a mask is sometimes referred to as a *threshold mask* or *bitmask*, just like an image in *bitmap* mode has a color depth of one bit. Where this 1-bit mask is white, there is 100 percent transparency, and the foreground element shows through the mask. Where the mask is black, however, the image is masked, having 0 percent transparency. Note that bitmasks aren't just theory: transparent GIF files for World Wide Web pages only have 1 bit of transparency information (such as one background color).

The drawback of a 1-bit mask, however, is that with only black/white, transparent/opaque, on/off masking capability, the composited image has harsh edges, which manifest in the stair-stepping jaggies we've all come to know and hate. That's why most masks have 8 bits of transparency data, just like a color channel holds 8 bits of color data; with 256 levels of opacity, this allows for anti-aliased and feathered edges, greatly enhancing the realism of a composite.

Why use a 1-bit mask? In the development of arcade video games, 1-bit masks were easy to calculate for every frame of animation of a character in the game. The prevailing (and largely correct) theory was that while the object was moving and the game play was occurring, the user wouldn't notice the rough edges of the animated element. In today's world, dedicated video game platforms (and many games that run on PC-compatibles and Macintoshes), there is finally enough computing power to

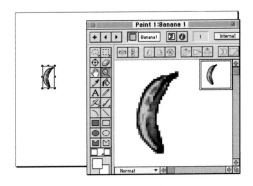

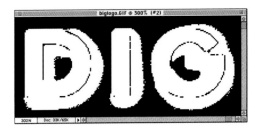

With a 1-bit mask, a foreground element can be combined with a new background, but with a relatively rough edge where the two meet. This example is the alpha channel of a Web-ready GIF file.

In the case of Macromedia Director, castmembers (Director terminology for an individually animated element) can only have one transparent color, which is exactly the same as having a 1-bit mask. Commercial add-ons have appeared that allow Director to handle images with 8-bit alpha channels, but this has the effect of slowing down overall animation playback speeds.

deal with more than one level of transparency. This is also the reason why the currently popular GIF file format may be supplanted by the PNG format on the World Wide Web: GIF files have only 1-bit masks, while PNG file can have 8-bit masks, allowing for significantly smoother edges and varying levels of transparency against custom backgrounds (this will be especially useful for Web designers who insist on creating backgrounds out of tiled images, a practice we generally frown upon).

Photoshop and Alpha Channels

Now that we've established a bit of background on the origin of alpha channels, let's get back to Photoshop and how alpha channels work and play.

Selections—A Mask in the Rough

The natural way to get our brains around alpha channels is to discuss one of the primary results of using alpha channels: selections. If we take a look at the Photoshop tool palette, the top of the palette holds some of the handiest tools that you're likely to encounter in your imaging adventures, all designed to select portions of an image.

The Marquee, Lasso, and Magic Wand tools are all designed to select portions of an image. The Move Tool is used to, you guessed it, move the contents of a selection. This also can be done with the other selection tools by holding down the Command key.

Of course, let's not forget the Path tool, located in its own floating palette. Used to create vector-based masks, Paths can be converted to selections with the click of a mouse. Paths have their own chapter in this book, so we'll get back to them later.

As we touched upon earlier in this chapter, in order to *do something* to an image, it's critical to guide the computer to the exact source of your desired manipulation. Selecting something tells the computer "whatever I'm about to ask you to do, I want you to do to *this* stuff." In Photoshop, using any of the selection tools to isolate portions of an image is critical to most processing tasks. When a selection is active, anything that you do is restrained to the exact area of the selection. This includes the following:

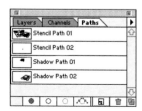

The Paths palette enables you to use vector-based tools to isolate portions of an image.

- Filters
- Painting tools
- Adjustment controls (levels, curves, and so on)
- Copy/Paste commands

... and just about anything else that you can do in Photoshop.

Once a selection is made and active (displayed by the marching ants effects around the border of the selection), any action is constrained to the inside of the selection.

To show where the mask is acting as an active selection, Photoshop creates a visual selection marquee around the areas where over 50 percent of an effect will be applied. Following this metaphor, alpha channels are almost always useful specifically when used to produce selections, and this is where the Load Selection and Save Selection commands come in.

Although selections normally made with the various Selection tools are basically masks, they are only temporary in nature. If you deselect those pixels (for any reason, or at any time), the selection is dropped and your temporary mask has vanished. Selections made with any of the many selection tools can be saved into a Photoshop file as alpha channels, and recalled at any time. This permanent nature is what makes alpha channels an essential extension of the selection process.

The Select Menu

Select	
All	⌘A
None	⌘D
Inverse	⇧⌘I
Color Range...	
Feather...	⇧⌘D
Modify	▶
Grow	
Similar	
Load Selection...	
Save Selection...	

Any time a selection is active, the Select menu items become activated, allowing you to modify and enhance the selection in a variety of ways.

The Select menu in Photoshop contains commands that are directly linked to the functionality and modification of selections.

● All. The All command simply selects every pixel in a document's visible area (or canvas). Note that the All command doesn't always select every pixel in your document, per se. The All command won't select image data beyond the visible portion of your image (for example, data left over from pasting in an element larger than your image's canvas size). Photoshop 4.0's ability to retain image data beyond the boundaries of the canvas is called *big data* (a term reportedly coined by Jeff Schewe, digital artist extraordinaire and a key alpha and beta tester of Photoshop 4.0), and the only way to delete that excess data is to invoke the Select>All command, and then the Image>Crop command, cropping your document at the edges of your canvas.

● **None.** This de-selects every pixel in your image, dropping any active selections.

● **Inverse.** Inverse reverses the selection region, selecting everything *outside* your original selection. It's the equivalent of applying an Invert command to an alpha channel before loading it. In technical terms, this process is called "inverting the *polarity* of the alpha channel."

The rest of the commands within the Select menu—Color Range, Feather, Modify, Grow, Similar, Load Selection, and Save Selection—are more involved and are covered in the following sections.

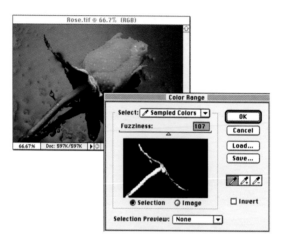

Color Range

The incredibly useful Color Range command (Select>Color Range) gives you a way to make masks and selections based on color and brightness values. The Color Range tool generates a selection over the active document, which is then made into a selection on the active document when you press OK in the Color Range dialog box. (The resulting selection can be saved into an alpha channel, if you desire, using the Select>Save Selection command.) While this capability has always existed in Photoshop (by direct channel manipulation), Color Range adds interactivity and a slick interface, making the process a lot less painful. Color Range is a great way to further familiarize yourself with masking, because its interface uses the same metaphors as alpha channels.

Color Range is extremely useful for selecting specific ranges of color, with interactive selection parameters and real-time previewing. Note how the preview looks awfully similar to an alpha channel—because it *is*! Or, at least, could be.

The current document (or contents of current selection) appears in the center preview area of the Color Range dialog box. Colors can be selected in the dialog box preview (by pressing the Control key); the actual color data is shown in a reduced view in the preview area, or you can place your cursor in the active document window and select colors from the active image view.

 Tip: As with any other instance in which a dialog box is open in Photoshop, you can pan around the image in the document window with the Hand tool by pressing the Spacebar while dragging the cursor in the active document.

The Magnifying Glass tool also can be invoked by pressing the Command and Spacebar keys while positioning the cursor in the image window, to more accurately select specific colors from magnified views of the image. Add the Option key to the mix, and you can zoom out from the current magnification.

When you first open Color Range, the foreground color is the default basis for the potential mask. The leftmost eyedropper tool selects the baseline color for your mask; your initial color range starts with a single color value. Using the Shift key, or using the middle *additive* eyedropper tool, adds more colors to the selected color range. The Option key with the main eyedropper, or selecting the right *subtractive* eyedropper tool, subtracts selected colors from your color range. With judicious use of these tools, you can gradually build up a rather decent mask without any direct channel manipulation.

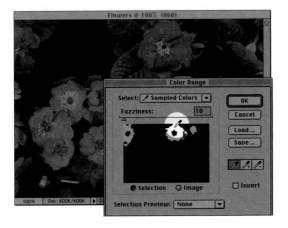

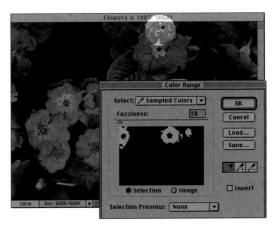

These cursors allow you to select colors either in the dialog box's preview...

... or in the active image window.

 Tip: In other sections of this book, we discuss using individual color channels as the basis for creating masks. If you activate a single color channel of an RGB image (by clicking its name in the Channels palette) before invoking the Color Range tool, you'll be able to use Color Range to select specific brightness ranges of *only* the active color channel.

The *Fuzziness* parameter is a slider-based equivalent of the Grow command (described in a later section of this chapter) or the Magic Wand tool's Tolerance parameter (which controls the normal Grow command value as well). Raising the Fuzziness setting increases the number of contiguous colors that are selected; its default setting is 40. One of the great benefits to using Color Range is being able to interactively alter the Fuzziness and see the potential selection update in real time.

There are other methods for selecting colors besides using the eyedropper tools. The Select pop-up menu offers a number of options for the basis of a selection. Some of these options for deriving color ranges can't easily be duplicated by other selection methods, making them very appealing for specific types of selection tasks.

- Color Sets: Color Range can use a standard range of certain colors (reds, yellows, and so on) as the basis of defining

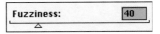

The Fuzziness control, which controls the range of contiguous colors to be selected. A question we've often wondered about: Why can't Adobe just call this parameter Tolerance or Grow?

These color selection methods are alternatives to defining a color range by hand.

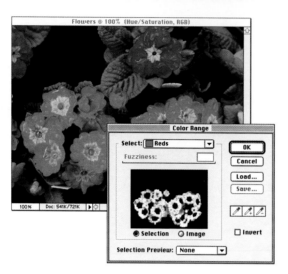

With red selected, Color Range automatically derives a mask
for all the red flower petals in the image.

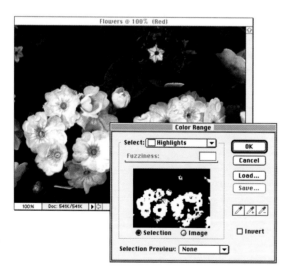

Another way to select the reds in this RGB image is to use
Color Range to select the highlights in the red channel.

the selection. Note that these color sets are derived from RGB and CMY, an interesting correlation to the RGB and CMYK color modes. This suggests that certain color sets are best used on either RGB or CMYK color space images. For example, the red, green, and blue color sets, when used to define color in an RGB image, are basing their selections directly on the contents of specific color channels. The same is true of using the cyan, magenta, and yellow color sets on a CMYK image.

The main drawback to using these selection parameters is that the color range is automatically defined: You have no control over the spread of colors selected (for example, the Fuzziness control). It's a good idea to try these methods if your image has a lot of sharply defined, saturated colors, but it's rarely a one-stop solution (requiring further tweaking to the resulting selection or mask).

● **Tonal Ranges:** These are simply broad categories of brightness. Like the specific color sets, you don't have access to the Fuzziness control to expand or contract the selection ranges. These methods are typically useful if you want to select the shadows, midtones, or highlights of a single color channel (which, of course, is grayscale); this often winds up being more accurate than using Color Range's built-in color sets in an image's composite color channels.

● **Out-of-Gamut Colors:** Color Range is a perfect place to start for creating desaturation masks for CMYK pre-press images. Using the Out-of-Gamut option in Color Range automatically selects over-saturated values (determined by the color separation tables being used by Photoshop, set in the File>Color Preferences> Separation Tables); you then simply use Hue/Saturation or an adjustment layer to reign in the offending hues.

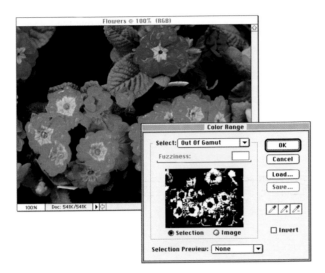

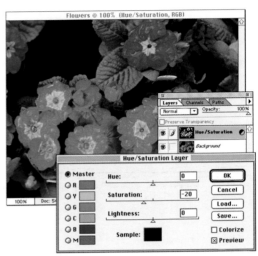

This image has some very clear out-of-gamut colors. Color Range is used to select these unprintable colors.

With the selection made, a Hue/Saturation adjustment layer is made. Because the selection was active when the adjustment layer was created, the colors within the gamut of printable colors are masked from the effect. The colors are now safely within the printable CMYK color gamut.

 Tip: If you're trying out the previous technique, there are two important little tricks to keep in mind:

1. Use the Color Range tool to select the out-of-gamut regions of the image, create the selection, then save the selection as an alpha channel. Apply small amounts of Gaussian Blur to the entire resulting channel to soften the often hard edges of the mask created by Color Range. This helps reduce hard edge artifacts often found in selections created using the Out-of-Gamut mode in Color Range.

2. Try turning on the Gamut Warning command in the View menu as you use the Hue/Saturation reduction techniques described in step 1; as you gradually turn down saturation values, the visible Gamut warning gradually disappears when you bump down the saturation of the selection. This technique enables you to interactively determine the appropriate amounts of desaturation. The Sponge tool (set to Desaturate mode) also can be used to paint away color saturation, with the Gamut warning gradually fading away under your Sponge brush strokes. Try adjusting the Pressure control to fine-tune the overall build of the desaturation effect. We like to combine the two methods: using the Hue/Saturation tool to get into the general ball-park, then using the Sponge tool to touch up specific problem areas of the image.

The image preview in the Color Range dialog box defaults to showing you the selected colors in white, and the uns-elected colors in black—just like an alpha channel!

 Tip: To even further grok the relationship between selections and channels, make the Channels palette visible before you invoke the Color Range command. You'll see that a temporary alpha channel is added while the Color Range dialog box is open; it disappears, however, once the OK button is hit and this temporary mask is activated as a selection.

Selections also can be inverted from within the dialog box by clicking on the Invert checkbox. The image preview swaps the white (affected) areas with the black (masked) areas to select everything *but* the specified colors.

Inverse vs. Invert Tip: Notice what the Invert button is doing in the Color Range dialog box, and the resulting selection. The Select>Inverse command is exactly the same as using Image>Adjust>Invert command on an alpha channel. This is another crucial key in understanding alpha channels.

The Selection and Image radio buttons underneath the image preview toggle between displaying Color Range's mask and the actual image. In either mode, the eyedropper tools can still be used to alter the currently selected color range.

Tip: Pressing the Control or Command keys while in the Color Range dialog box toggles between the Selection and Image previews in the dialog box; if you're often moving between the Selection and Image previews, this is much more convenient than using the two radio buttons.

To help visualize your potential selection, these Selection Preview modes display Color Range's mask on your image itself.

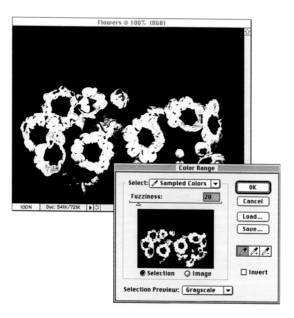

If you're used to working with alpha channels, the Grayscale Selection Preview is an easy preview method to follow. It's also perfect for understanding the relationship between selections and alpha channels.

The final Color Range variable is the Selection Preview pop-up menu, which determines how the Color Range mask is displayed in the actual document window.

- None: The image shows no indication of Color Range's mask.

- Grayscale: The image window is filled with a grayscale mask as it appears in the Selection preview in the Color Range dialog box. If the resulting selection is saved as an alpha channel, this is what that channel will look like. It's also the most useful mode for being able to zoom into the mask and evaluate exactly what's going on with the actual high-resolution data of the image, critical for analyzing fine edge details.

- Black/White Matte: These modes are very similar, but each is appropriate for different kinds of images. The selected areas of the image show through, but the masked regions are obscured with black or white (these overlays are called *mattes*). One way to think of this is that you'll see what the selected regions look like if they were composited with a light or dark background. This preview mode works well if you're selecting highlights, bright colors, or out-of-gamut colors. If you're selecting shadows, dark tones, or muted colors, you'll

In trying to create a mask for the dog and the balloons, this user decided to start by making a Color Range mask by selecting those similar tones in the background and then inverting the mask. That's an okay start, but this is hardly a good time to use...

...Black Matte. If parts of the dog are being accidentally masked, it's very hard to tell.

find that White Matte is visually easier to interpret. Try each one and it will immediately become visually obvious which is more appropriate for any given combination of values in the selected pixels.

● **Quick Mask:** This displays the resulting selection in Quick Mask mode. A color tint (red is the default) is displayed where the image is masked (outside the selection), and the original image is shown untinted, within the areas that will be selected. (See the following in-depth description of Quick Mask for more information.)

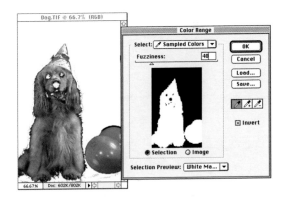

White Matte is a much better method of seeing the same selection on the same image.

It's important to remember, though, that Color Range isn't isolated from other selection tools and mask-making techniques. Color Range often gets you close to your goal, yielding a decent, workable mask, but perfecting that mask takes some more work. Levels and Curves, for example, can be used to isolate and clamp specific brightness ranges once your selection is saved as a selection. Before we get to that, however, let's keep looking at the different selection tools and methods you can use.

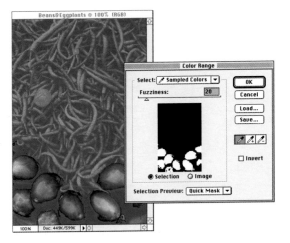

Quick Mask mode overlays the masked areas of an image with a red tint, like a piece of virtual Rubylith.

Feather

While many selections are automatically anti-aliased, you'll often find situations where the border of your selection needs to be much softer. This is where Feather comes in. The Feather value is the number of pixels by which your selection is softened, or blurred; this softening occurs equally on both sides of the original selection. This means that a Feather of 4 softens your selection by two pixels outward and two pixels inward. In masking parlance, Feather is the equivalent of blurring an alpha channel.

Applying Feathering to a selection is the same as creating a non-feathered alpha channel and applying amounts of blurring to the entire channel. If you look at Gaussian Blur and Feather, both are specific in image pixels. In fact, typing the same value in either command yields the same final results. A 5-pixel feather looks exactly the same as a 5-pixel Gaussian Blur on a clean, unfeathered version of the primary selection. We like to recommend to our students that they get into the habit of creating clean, crisp masks and feather only as a post-process, by blurring the alpha channel version of a selection. This gives you three benefits:

- You always have a clean version of the mask, which will probably come in handy at some point. If you define a Feather value for your selection tool (such as the lasso) ahead of time, you'll have to do more work to get a clean, unblurred version of the selection mask.

- You can use Levels/Curves to slide the antialiasing in or out of the central mask boundary, by using the interactive choking and spreading techniques described elsewhere in this chapter. This delivers a significantly greater level of control over the quality and accuracy of the resulting mask.

- If you want to apply different amounts of softening to separate areas of the selection, you can use the Blur tool to manually soften up desired portions of the selection edge, leaving other parts of the edge crisp and intact.

Modify

The Modify submenu, which focuses on modifying the edges of selections.

The Modify submenu and its commands offer ways to affect the edges of your selections. An active selection must be present, of course, in order to use these commands. The numeric limits, in pixels, of these commands are the same. The minimum value is one, and the maximum value is sixteen.

Tip: Remember, these parameters are specified in relation to the resolution of the document you're currently working on; high resolution images have smaller pixels, low resolution images have larger pixels. A 5-pixel value for Smooth, for example, is going to be a lot less obvious on a high resolution (300 DPI) image, when in fact it will probably have a significant effect on a low resolution (75 DPI) image.

- **Border.** The edge of the active selection is outlined to create a new selection. This border has a width, in pixels, based on the Amount entered in the Border dialog box. The border is created on either side of the selection: A 4-pixel border selects 2 pixels on either side of the current selection border. Once you invoke and use the Border command, the previously selected interior of the selection is no longer selected—just a band around the selection.

So what can you use this command for? One of the primary applications is to re-introduce antialiasing into the edges of a defringed layer (the technique is covered in detail in Chapter 3, "Layers") by using the Blur filter with Bordered selections.

Another cheesy special effect made possible with the Border command is quick and simple glows around selected objects. With an alpha channel for a foreground object loaded as a selection.

1. Copy the selected object.

2. Apply a large border (try 30).

3. Feather the bordered selection (around half of the specified border—in this case, 15).

4. Fill with desired glow color.

5. Paste selected object back into image (or stop at step 4, if you want the glow to spill over the edges of the object).

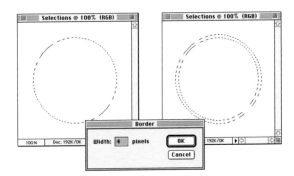

The Border command outlines a pre-existing selection by an absolute number of pixels.

Why didn't we break this out into an illustrated, step-by-step example? Because we covered this technique in our first book (the *first* book ever on Photoshop), so we assume that this is a tired lick by now. But feel free to use it for some cheap glowing thrills.

- **Smooth.** Smooth softens angular edges of a selection region. The amount of Smoothing is based on a pixel radius around the harsh edges in question: the wider the radius, the greater the smoothing.

- **Expand.** Expand extends the edge of a selection region outward, effectively spreading the selection.

- **Contract.** Expand brings the edge of a selection region inward, choking the selection.

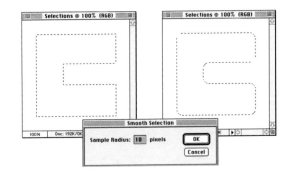

Smooth rounds off sharp edges, based on a smoothing radius.

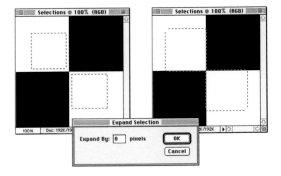

Notice that Expand doesn't preserve hard angles or edges if its setting is high (or even moderate); if that's a problem, you should re-examine your selection before significantly expanding it.

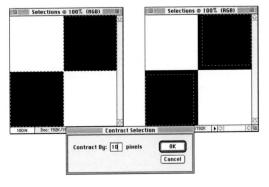

It's important to remember that Contract won't affect edges of a selection that meet the edge of the canvas; here you see the inner edges have receded while the outer edges haven't moved.

Later in this chapter we'll look at some more extensive techniques for choking and spreading masks with a bit more control and flexibility than the Expand and Contract commands. That doesn't mean that the Expand and Contract commands become irrelevant as you learn more about masking—in fact, they'll do for more than half of the mask fine-tuning you're likely to do during your working day.

Grow and Similar

These two commands, while having no dialog box controls, operate according to the Tolerance setting in the Magic Wand tool.

Grow spreads your selection area to similar adjacent tones based on the Wand's Tolerance. For example, most photographs of blue skies aren't the same tone of blue throughout; clicking on a mid-range blue tone with the magic wand often gets you going, and using the Grow command (barring any clouds) expands your selection to the next-most-similar blue tones.

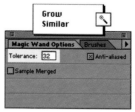

Grow, Similar, and the Magic Wand tool: Separated at birth? All three features operate based on one shared parameter: the Magic Wand's Tolerance setting.

Similar selects all of the currently-selected hue and brightness ranges in your image. In our hypothetical photograph of a blue sky, if there's a tree in the scene, there are probably little islands of blue color between its branches and leaves. Rather than using the Magic Wand tool hundreds of times to select each little blue chunk of sky, selecting a reasonable spread of blue sky colors enables you to use Similar and select every pixel that has the same colors as the currently selected pixels.

 Tip: The Grow and Similar commands can be used with any existing selection, regardless of the methodology used to create the selection. For example, you can use the Rectangular Marquee tool in conjunction with the Shift key to select multiple areas of an image, each with a different color. When you use the Similar command, it will find and select *all* colors similar to the colors contained in the multiple selections.

An important note: Because selection modifiers (such as those found in the Select menu) are expressed in pixels (*absolute* values), the values used in defining such modifiers are *relative* in effect, based on the resolution of your image. For example, if you make a selection in both a 72-pixel-per-inch document (such as Web graphics or multimedia screens) and a 300-pixel-per-inch (ppi) document (like a CD cover or magazine illustration) and feather both selections by 30 pixels, the feathering in the 300-ppi image looks less extreme than in the 72-ppi image: The feathering amount, in pixels, is the same, but there are more pixels to be affected in the larger image. This 30-pixel feathering appears less than half of an inch thick in the 72-ppi image, but will be less than one-eighth of an inch thick in the 300-ppi image.

This is true about all of the selection tools and modifiers that request pixel values: Feather, Modify (Expand, Contract, Border and Smooth), Defringing, Grow, and Similar all demand *absolute* pixel values, but are *relative* in effect, based on the resolution of your image.

Load Selection

The Load Selection command can create a selection based on a channel's grayscale contents (brightness). While selections can certainly be made using any of an image's color channels, this feature is intended to be used in conjunction with pre-existing alpha channels.

Tip: In fact, the Load Selection dialog box doesn't allow you to select a color component channel to be loaded as a selection. If you want to do this, you would have to copy the color channel into a new alpha channel before using the Load Selection command. At that point, it's easier to simply Command–click on the desired color channel in the Channel palette, or drag the color channel to the Make Selection icon at the bottom of the Channel palette.

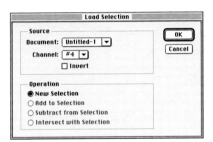

The Load Selection dialog box, which uses an image's channels to create selections.

The white portions of a channel are selected; black areas are command totally unselected. Gray areas essentially represent feathered selection regions, based on their brightness value.

- **Source.** Load Selection can use any channel, in any open document that has the *exact same physical size, resolution, and dimensions* as the source document, as a selection.

- **Invert.** This automatically inverts the selection when it's activated. The same as selecting Inverse from the Select menu immediately after loading the selection.

- **Operation.** This parameter determines the interaction between the new selection (created with Load Selection) and previously existing selections. New Selection discards the previous selection in favor of the new one, Add to Selection adds the new selection area to the existing one, Subtract from Channel subtracts the new selection area from the existing one, and Intersect with Channel creates a new selection based on the overlap between the new selection and the existing one.

The Add, Subtract, and Intersect options are dimmed out if there is no selection activated immediately before invoking the Load Selection command.

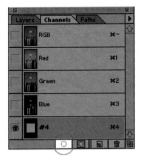

The selection icon, in the Channels palette. It loads a selected channel by simply clicking on the selection icon itself or by dragging a channel onto it.

Loading a selection from a channel also can be done from within the Channels palette. Holding down the Command key while clicking on a channel and dragging that channel onto the command selection icon loads that channel as a selection.

These actions can be modified with the Shift key (which acts as the Add to Channel option), the Option key (which acts as the Subtract from Channel option), or the Shift and Option keys simultaneously (which act as the Intersect with Channel option). Note that these key modifiers are identical to those used with the selection tools.

The Command key can also be used to activate and make a selection out of a layer's transparency in the Layers palette. By holding down the Command key while clicking on a layer, the transparency mask for that layer is loaded as a selection. The same modifier keys that affect the loading of a channel as a selection—Shift, Option, and Shift + Option—have the same effect in the Layers palette. If you have multiple layers in a document, try loading the transparency mask for a layer by option clicking it. Then try using the Shift key in conjunction with the Command key, and click another layer. The transparency masks for both layers command are combined into a single selection.

Tip: You can combine layer transparency masks and channels into complex composite selections by clicking between the Layers and Channels palettes and using the various modifier keys described in the preceding sections.

Save Selection

Save Selection command stores an active selection as an 8-bit alpha channel. Just as the Load Selection command uses the brightness of a channel to determine a selection region, a selection region can be saved as an 8-bit grayscale alpha channel. It's different from using the Create Channel from Selection icon from the bottom of the Channels palette in that you can specifically designate an exact destination instead of always creating a new channel (the default behavior of the Create Channel icon).

Where the selection is 100 percent active, the alpha channel appears white, and unselected pixels appear black. Feathered and anti-aliased selection areas appear as varying levels of gray.

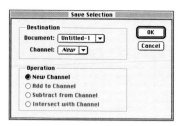

● Destination. Not only can you save selections as alpha channels in the current document, you can save them into another file entirely or, in some cases, into layer masks. This is particularly useful if you're trying to avoid immense file sizes in your primary image document. You can store a selection into new or existing channels.

The Save Selection command enables selections to be saved as alpha channels for later use.

Tip: If you try to save your selection into another currently open document, you'll notice the same limitation imposed by the Load Selection command. The target document must have the same size and resolution as the source document.

This Save Selection command is often used to shunt all of the masks for a particular image into a different image file entirely, loading them as selections as needed. This keeps the file size of your main image to a minimum, and is a RAM-friendly technique if your image is very large or has lots of layers.

Tip: Beware of saving selections over existing channels: Photoshop assumes that you know what you're doing, and doesn't warn you that you're about to save a selection over the intricate alpha channel you just spent four hours creating.

● Operation. When saving a selection into a previously existing alpha channel, there are several options you can choose to control the interaction between the new and old selection areas. New Channel creates a new alpha channel, Add to Channel performs the functional equivalent of a Screen calculation to add the new selection area to the older alpha channel, Subtract from Channel fills the older alpha channel with black where the new selection is active, and Intersect with Channel fills the older alpha channel with black outside the current selection.

Tip: The extremely useful Hide/Show Edges command, which hides the marching ants marquee that visually defines an active selection, has been moved from the Select menu to the View menu in Photoshop 4.0. The key command, however, is the same (Command-H).

Quick Mask Mode

Quick Mask Mode allows you to cut masks quickly; it is a middle-ground of complexity between straight selection methods (using the selection tools) and creating alpha channels. The Quick Mask controls are near the bottom of the Toolbox, and consist of two buttons: the Standard Mode button on the left and the Quick Mask Mode button on the right.

InstaPaintaMask: the Quick Mask buttons.

Quick Mask Mode allows you to cut masks quickly.

Standard Mode shows channel; a color tint is displayed where the image is masked, so you can see the original image underneath your Quick Mask. If selections are active before turning on Quick Mask Mode, the areas outside the selection are tinted to indicate that they're masked. Quick Masks are temporary alpha channels, because like selections, they disappear unless saved.

While in Quick Mask Mode, you can use any painting tools; the only difference is that they only affect the Quick Mask itself. You can blur, paint, erase, and smudge the edges of your Quick Mask. The process consists of essentially painting a selection around objects, which is particularly useful for masking/selecting hair, lace, and other high-detail images. Our previous frisket metaphor of a Rubylith mask is especially helpful in understanding Quick Mask, because it displays masked areas under a red overlay (of course, you can change the display color and transparency). Remember, just like masks, the clear areas are exposed to modification and the colored areas are protected.

To turn your Quick Mask into a selection you can use, click the Standard Mode icon. The Quick Mask disappears, and the unmasked areas turn into a selection. If you've made a selection already, click the Quick Mask icon and the selection turns into a Quick Mask; this is a good method for fixing selections that are close but not perfect.

Double-clicking the Quick Mask Mode buttons enables you to specify a number of other Quick Mask parameters as well.

- **Color Indicates:** This parameter determines whether or not the color tint in Quick Mask Mode shows masked areas or selected areas. The default setting is to tint the masked areas, and we find this to be the most intuitive mode of working: clear areas are going to be affected, and colored areas are masked, just as white areas of masks reveal while black areas obscure.

The Quick Mask Options dialog box lets you customize how this feature works.

This representation of masking is also known as a *white core mask*.

Many Photoshoppers find that switching this default (having the tinted regions represent revealed areas and the clear regions represent masked areas) is a rather counter-intuitive way to display a Quick Mask.

- **Color and Opacity:** The user can specify the Quick Mask color as well as its opacity in relationship to the image itself; try to keep the opacity low so that the Quick Mask doesn't obscure what you want to mask out underneath. This becomes important, for example, when the colors in an image are primarily red—imagine trying to mask red peppers or tomatoes! Being able to change the color and opacity of the Quick Mask helps keep it visible, and, as we all know, seeing an accurate representation of your working mask data is essential.

In a similar vein, alpha channels have their own controls over how they may be overlaid onto an image's other channels. By making an alpha channel visible while another channel is visible (by clicking on the layer's visibility icon), a Quick Mask–like overlay appears. Double-clicking an alpha channel invokes the Channel Options dialog box, which differs from the Quick Mask Options dialog box only in the capability to re-name the selected alpha channel. Using a different overlay color for each alpha channel is very convenient for visualizing the interactions of multiple alpha channels.

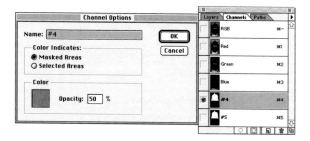

Double-clicking an alpha channel opens the Channel Options dialog box. This option isn't available for color channels (red, green, or blue, in this case), and differs from the Quick Mask Options dialog box only in the capability to re-name the selected alpha channel.

We generally find ourselves using alpha channels more than Quick Mask. Why? For starters, alpha channels are *permanent*. Every operation you do to an alpha channel is saved when the image file is saved. This isn't the case with Quick Mask; like selections, Quick Mask is temporary, intended to create a mask either for one-time use or to be stored later as an alpha channel. Secondly, an alpha channel can be viewed as a Quick Mask by making it visible on top of other channels. Painting directly into an alpha channel in this mode is exactly like painting into a Quick Mask. Our advice: Get into the habit of making explicit alpha channels. You'll thank us.

The Compositing Process

There are two basic distinctions within the greater subject of alpha channels and the compositing process: *creation* and *usage*. Creating alpha channels (also known as *making masks* or *pulling mattes*) is the process of actually making a mask for a given element, making the mask opaque over the background and transparent over the foreground element itself. Alpha channel usage, of course, is the next natural step: using the alpha channel, already having been created, to composite elements together.

While mask creation and mask usage are separate disciplines and require different methods, it's important to keep in mind the *usage* (how it will be used) during the *creation* process (how it's made). The mask usage can directly impact your approach to mask creation. This depends on a wide variety of factors, but it starts with knowing whether the background element is moving or static; whether it has generally dark, light, or widely varying tones; and what its predominant colors are.

To illustrate this relationship, let's look at two images we'd like to composite together.

This image is the foreground element in our composite; we need to mask out the blue sky and isolate the mountain, tree-line, and two large palm trees.

This sunset is our background, onto which the palms and mountain will be composited.

On one hand, the job of masking the sky should be relatively easy; because there are no clouds, we can use the blue color channel as the basis for our mask. (We'll deal with the specifics of how to do this in a moment.)

On the other hand, there are some obvious issues to deal with. First is the new background; its color is not only different from the sky in the foreground image, its orange color is a direct complement (or inverse) of the foreground's blue sky. This will probably result in some undesirable (such as, light blue) colors in the edges of the leaves once the trees are composited onto the background. This alerts us to pay extra attention to the edges of the palm tree foliage.

Our preliminary alpha channel, derived from the blue color channel.

Here's the initial composite, and a close-up of the tops of the palms. The blue edges of the individual leaves really stand out against this darker orange background.

Just because a composite isn't perfect the first time around doesn't mean it should be abandoned: If at first you don't succeed, try thinking and clicking. If we look closely and experiment a bit, we quickly find that all that's needed to make this composite work is

● Some darkening: Levels or Curves for brightness-matching the two elements.

● Hue shifting: Hue/Saturation or Color Balance for matching the colors of the foreground to the background.

● Edge enhancement: Using layer masks to eliminate the lighter edges—see the "Layers" chapter for more details.

Once again, it's all about developing *visual problem-solving* skills: being able to look at an image and determine the best method of mask creation, based on how the mask will be put to use. Solutions are rarely arrived at in one single step, no matter how skillful the artist; the key is finding the path with the fewest steps to derive the best results. Compositing, per se, is nothing more than mask usage: using a mask to isolate one element from another and putting it on a new background.

Making Masks— Alternate Methods

There are a lots of ways to make masks and selections, and just about every minute of every day Photoshoppers are figuring out how to make a better mask than they could make a week ago. A virtual plethora of masking techniques are floating around the Photoshop world.

A few of these methods have stayed with us, through photography and digital imaging, to become standards (of a sort) in

This is the same composite after a few minutes of work.

the imaging professional's toolbox. Are techniques available in Photoshop filters? No. Are they stand-alone programs? No. Sometimes you need to rely on your own chops, and not just the tools you have at hand.

Recently, a few third-party masking plug-ins have appeared on the market, including offerings from Extensis (Mask Pro) and ChromaGraphics (Magic Mask). They weren't available in time for us to review for this book, but from a quick look at them at Seybold New York 1997, they are both worth a closer look. Do they negate the techniques described in the rest of this chapter? Not a chance. You may want to experiment with them, though; you can find information about them at the following sites:

www.extensis.com

www.chromagraphics.com

These mask-masking methods aren't even explicit, step-by-step recipes. They are time-tested approaches to problem solving. The individual permutations on each technique are unlimited, because every image and compositing task is different. What we'll endeavor to do is show you how to use these concepts, to analyze your image, and how to become skilled in developing a case-by-case *masking strategy*.

Masks Derived from Color Channels

In an RGB image, the presence of white in a color channel represents the presence of that color in the image, and that black in a color channel represents that color's absence in the image.

If we wanted to make a mask for a certain color, we could use Color Range to select that color and then save the selection as an alpha channel. It would probably look okay, but there's going to be at least some editing necessary to make a professional-level mask for that color. The Replace Color command might be able to swap one color with another, but what if we wanted to composite something into that color field?

Take a look at the color channels in the image; you just might find some surprising contrast between the element you want to isolate and the rest of the image.

In this image, the red channel is mostly white in the inner (red) portion of the stop sign, as well as in the light gray and white areas (the sign's trim and the signpost). Notice that the sky appears quite dark in the red channel, indicating the presence of very little red in the sky.

This hints at a certain course of action: duplicating the color channel that holds the best contrast between the color you want isolated and the rest of the image, and using that as the basis for an alpha channel.

Take another look at the red channel. Doesn't its range of whites and blacks almost look like... an alpha channel?

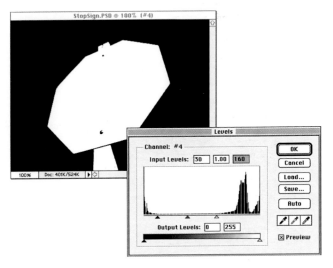

This duplicated red channel becomes the basis for a mask to isolate the stop sign. Notice that the Levels command has yielded a close, albeit unfinished, first-pass mask.

Luminance Masking

Luminance masking, as its name implies, is the process of deriving a mask using the brightness information (and corresponding dynamic range characteristics) that *already exists* in an image, either from a single channel or combinations of channels. Anyone who's used the Magic Wand tool to select a light object on a dark background has done rudimentary luminance masking. What we're going to describe here is more involved, but much more elegant and efficient, and builds upon the concept of using color channels as the basis for masks.

This figure is a good candidate for luminance masking: it's significantly darker than its background, despite many similar hues in each.

Luminance masking is easy if you already have an image with a foreground element that is significantly lighter or darker than its background.

Luminance masking can be done with either the component RGB channel or with individual color channels; the decision of which channel to use is based on determining where the greatest contrast lies. If that contrast isn't quite enough, use Photoshop's image adjustment capabilities to accentuate contrast or brightness.

For deriving our luminance mask, the green channel in this image should be sufficient.

The green channel is duplicated into a new channel, in the same image. The Levels command can be used to increase the contrast enough to create a rough mask.

The white holes are fixed by some minimal touch-up by hand, and the mask is inverted. The mask for the figure is now complete.

Tip: There's nothing that says you can't use tools like the Paintbrush to help you make masks. It's important to realize that minimizing the use of such tools maximizes overall mask creation efforts and greatly increases the speed at which you work. Painting masks by hand, while often useful, is usually best left to fine-tuning a mask defined by channel operations (CHOPS).

There is a more common luminance masking scenario, however: an image that has a few areas of good contrast between the foreground element and the background, but that isn't significant enough to yield a good mask. Images like this often contain fine detail that is insidiously difficult to mask, such as hair.

This image needs a mask for the woman and her hair, but the contrast between the edges of the woman's face and hair against the background isn't drastic enough to jump right into creating a luminance mask. What's an artist to do?

An amazing, *truly* empowering aspect of digital imaging is that you can make exact duplicates of images and process them in any way desired, without having any effect on the original information. Copies can be created, processed beyond obvious use, and then the results can be used with the original, pristine image.

1. Take an image.
2. Duplicate it.
3. Push the contrast of the duplicate to an extreme level.
4. Copy a channel of the processed image back into the original, unprocessed file.
5. Use the processed channel as a mask.

That's exactly what we'll do here: Duplicate the basic image and then alter the duplicate to ease our mask-making woes. The alpha channel can be duplicated back into the original image or simply loaded into the original image as a selection.

Now that the contrast between foreground and background has been enhanced (regardless of what the RGB image looks like), let's dive into the individual color channels of this image.

This image poses a few challenges for the mask-making artist, not the least of which is the fine hair detail.

Using Levels, the image's contrast has been enhanced to assist our mask creation efforts. Notice that this is done to a duplicate of the image, not the original.

How we progress from here is less important than how we got here; the key to this example is the *method*: luminance masking, finding masks based on brightness values contained in an image. Let's take a quick look at how the final mask will be derived.

The red channel of this image, as we'd expect, holds the majority of the image's contrast, good for the hair detail. The green channel has less edge contrast, but the background has more consistent dark tones, good for the mask.

Using Curves in the red channel, the contrast between lights and darks is enhanced.

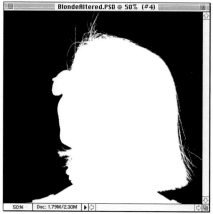

With a little more image adjustment and some minimal hand painting, here we are: an alpha channel ready to be used with the original, unaltered image.

Difference Matting

Difference matting is a more complex method of mask creation that relies on Photoshop's ability to compare the contents of color channels of different images.

The Difference application/transfer mode, found in both Layers and the Calculations command, is the key to this technique. The difference in pixel values between two images is calculated and displayed as a grayscale image; brightness represents the spread between the two compared pixel values. The greater the difference, the lighter the resulting pixels; pixels with no difference whatsoever result in black.

The process of difference matting is a closely guarded secret in special effects circles, and it's based on a deceptively simple concept.

1. Lock a camera down (with a tripod and some tape) so that it's not likely to move around.

2. Assemble some objects or people in a room.

3. Take a photo.

4. Remove the objects and people from the room.

5. Take a photo of the empty room.

Now, think about the two photographs that were just produced. What's the *difference* between them? Easy—the objects and people, and the shadows they were casting on other objects in the room. By using difference matting techniques, you can create a mask for the things that have changed between the two photos. This is the core concept behind difference matting. Now let's take a look at the principle in practice.

The seagull in this composite needs some more work, but the alpha channel has been lost and the image has been flattened. Using the original cloud background (sans seagull) and difference masking, we can derive a new mask for the seagull. As you'll see, difference masking (like most other masking techniques) is used along with other techniques to create a usable mask.

Even without the original seagull image or an alpha channel, the final composite and the cloud background can be used to create a difference mask.

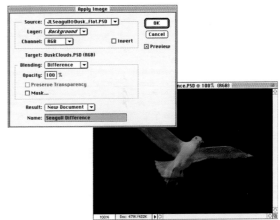

Using the Apply Image command, the difference between the composite and the background is placed into a new document.

The background of the resulting difference is black, perfect for masking out the background. Unfortunately, the area inside the seagull has some errant colors and tones. Looking at the component color channels may uncover a channel with less tonal variation inside the seagull, and clamping this area to white will complete our mask.

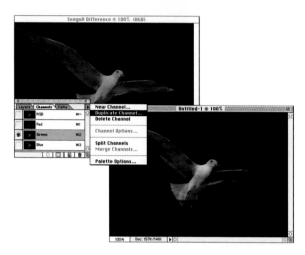

A combination of Levels and Curves is used to clamp the tones inside the seagull to pure white. This results in a usable mask, which can be loaded as a selection into the original composite file.

This image needs to be enhanced to be used as a real mask. The green channel has the overall lightest tones within the seagull; this channel is duplicated as a new grayscale document.

Making Masks—Mask Enhancement

Even the most creative, meticulous channel tricks don't always yield the desired effect. Many of the masks that you create with channel procedures end up needing that extra nudge, the fine tuning that shows that you want the best possible results. Your black mask areas are merely dark, not pure black, and they have little white holes in them. Your white mask areas have a fine haze of light gray sprinkled here and there. Your mask's edges are too tight, too loose, too sharp, too soft... the list of potential pitfalls is endless.

The answer is to manipulate the alpha channel directly. Because alpha channels are really nothing more than grayscale images, any image editing capability offered by Photoshop can be applied to help perfect your masks.

> Remember this mantra: Anything you can do with an image, you can do with an alpha channel. It's the basis for most mask-making and mask-massaging techniques.

We've already established a correlation between alpha channels, opacity, and selections. Let's take a moment and review this.

This chart represents the relationships between grayscale values in alpha channels, mask opacity, and selections.

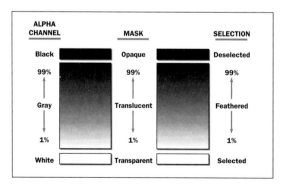

This would suggest, then, some very direct comparisons to be made between selections and alpha channels. Once a given alpha channel is loaded as a selection, are you going to need to invert that selection to isolate what you want? Then you can invert the alpha channel; white becomes black, black becomes white, and the selection is changed appropriately (meaning, it is inverted). Does that selection need to be feathered? Use a Gaussian Blur filter on the alpha channel, creating an increase in grays along harsh edges that results in gently-decreasing mask opacity.

The following sections detail some more finessed ways of massaging unruly masks.

Important technical issue regarding precise mask edge enhancement: All of the techniques that we're about to discuss are going to be influenced by the resolution of the image that you're working with at any given moment. High-resolution images with deep pixel densities simply have more base information, allowing finer degrees of edge play with alpha channels. If you're primarily working with images for web sites, many of these techniques are quite possibly overkill (but knowing how to accomplish them will definitely improve your low-res masking techniques).

Edge Softening/Hardening

Masks and alpha channels are ultimately going to result in selections, in order to process the actual image pixels in a document. We gave a previous example of blurring the contents of an alpha channel for a soft-edged (such as, feathered) selection. This process can be reversed with Levels.

Because the Levels command's input sliders compress the tonal dynamic range of the image, the spread of intermediate grays between black and white are similarly compressed. Let's look at an example.

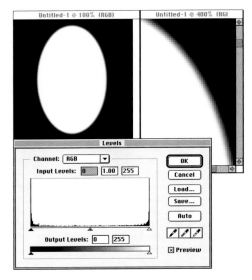

There are usually 256 possible tones in a grayscale image, including black and white (leaving 254 grays in between). We're seeing many of those intermediate pixels in this blurred, white oval on a black background.

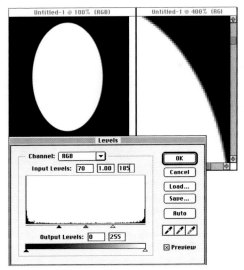

If you alter the input levels of the Levels command to be 70 for white and 185 for black, there are now going to be only 115 levels of gray in between black and white. Notice how the edge has become much harsher.

You can see that blurred edges become sharper as the possible levels of intermediate grays decrease. An increase in contrast results in an increase in edge definition, or sharpness. Another way to look at this is that the change in contrast directly affects the antialiasing values of the edge.

Higher contrast = less dynamic range = harder edge = less antialiasing

Lower contrast = more dynamic range = softer edge = more antialiasing

There are a couple of specific issues regarding the use of Levels for matte edge enhancement:

● The amount of spacing between the shadow, midpoint, and highlights sliders is directly related to the amount of antialiasing along the edges of a matte. When the sliders are close together, there is less dynamic range in the matte edge.

When the sliders have more separation, there are more gray values along the edges of the matte, resulting in a software antialiasing value.

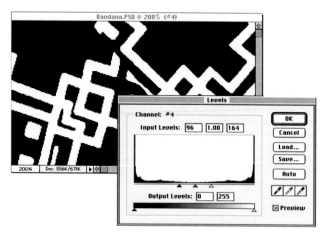

When the input sliders are clustered close together, there are fewer gray values in the edges of the mask, resulting in a harder edge.

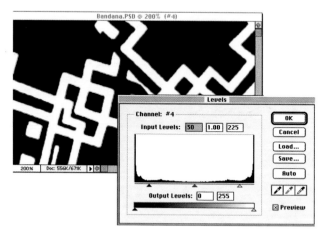

When the input sliders are spaced out, there are more gray values in the edges of the mask, resulting in a softer edge.

● By moving the three sliders together towards the darker or lighter areas of the Input range, you can slide the matte edge in and out of the edge center, delivering an interactive choking and spreading capability that Photoshoppers have been wanting for years. This technique delivers a far finer degree of control than the comparable Expand and Contract commands in the Select menu.

Keep this fact in mind when you're looking at an alpha channel that's too soft along the edges. You can globally adjust the softness, and even use the Blur and Sharpen tools to manually fine-tune regions of mask edges.

Clamping

As mentioned earlier, one of the most common masking challenges is being confronted with a mask that has a common, specific set of problems:

● Dark areas, which should be opaque, aren't consistently black (they are something other than 0 when sampled with the eyedropper).

● Light areas, which should be transparent, aren't consistently white (they are lower than 255).

Yes, you might turn to Levels to make the whites white and the blacks black, but what if you had a spread of intermediate grays that you didn't want to alter? Enter the Curves command and one of its more obscure uses, *clamping.*

Before getting into the specifics of clamping, however, let's take a deeper look at the often-misunderstood Curves command. Perhaps the biggest hurdle in conquering Curves is understanding the graph that maps the relationship between brightness input and output.

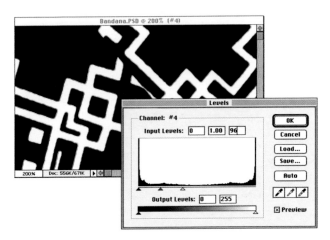

When the three sliders are slid to the left (darker range), the result is that the matte expands outwards.

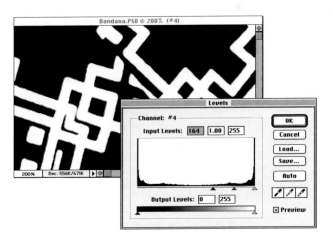

When the three sliders are slid to the right (lighter range), the result is that the matte contracts inwards.

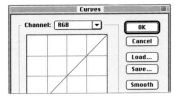

The Curves dialog box is powerful, but often misunderstood.

Users with a pre-press or printing background will find Curves familiar (essentially, the four zones of the curve divide the curve into shadows, quarter tones, halftones, three quarter tones and highlights), but those without such experience might find Curves a bit confusing. This brief detour will demystify the inner workings of the Curves command.

The basic design of the Curves dialog box itself is partly to blame for the confusion many users' have. The graph at the center is just like any other graph, but it charts the brightness input of an image (along the bottom axis, representing the current state of the image) against the brightness output (along the bottom axis, showing the result of the Curves' brightness adjustment).

The only problem with this is that only the bottom axis has an indication of its values: a gray scale, going from black on the left to white on the right (this is switched to white on the left and black on the right in CMYK color mode). So what's the top-to-bottom axis represent? Actually, the same thing: brightness, from white at the bottom to black at the bottom.

The unaltered brightness curve is a straight line, going from the lower-left corner to the upper-right corner. This represents a direct, linear relationship between the input and output values. This means that black is still black, white is still white, and every gray value in between remains the same.

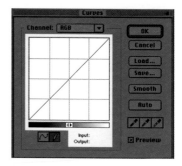

These are the areas of the Curves dialog box that confound users the most: the brightness input/output values and the graph that charts their relationship.

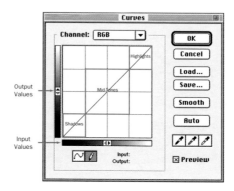

This is the Curves dialog box as it should appear (as far as *we're* concerned). A brightness ramp is on each axis to better convey the relationship of the graph to the corresponding input and output brightness values. General areas of shadows, mid-tones, and highlights follow along the curve, left to right; notice the relationship between these areas and the brightness ramps on each axis.

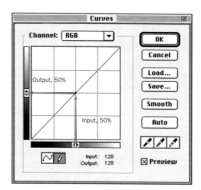

This unchanged Curves dialog box shows the direct relationship between brightness input and output. For example, values at 50 percent gray in the unaltered image (the brightness *input*) will still be 50 percent gray if the current Curves dialog box is used (the brightness *output*). A control point is placed at 50 percent gray on the curve (without changing the curve), so that the input and output readouts both show a value of 128.

The numerical input and output indicators under the graph display resulting input and output values when a control point is added (by simply clicking on the curve and dragging), and update interactively as the control point is moved. These displays also update if you sample colors in the image window.

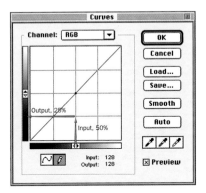

In this curve, a control point has been added and dragged downward. Notice how it's placed: tones in the image that start at 50 percent gray (value 128) are changed to 75 percent gray (value 64).

If the brightness curve is altered, this relationship is altered. Brightness values of the original image (again, the brightness input) are remapped to new values (the brightness output). The manner in which this change occurs depends on how the curve is affected. Pulling the curve up generally lightens the input values, and lowering them darkens them.

Intermediate values around control points (or, if there's only one control point, between it and the corners of the curve) are remapped as well. Finer degrees of control are derived by adding more control points onto a curve, or by using the Arbitrary mode (using the Pencil tool in the Curves dialog box). This latter approach is the key to clamping.

Clamping involves using the Curves' Arbitrary mode to drive light and dark areas to pure white and black respectively, while leaving the mid-tones unaffected.

Let's look at a typical example of clamping involving a product shot, as one might see in a catalog: a white slip on a red background. We need a mask not only for the slip, but for the necklaces as well.

While the red channel may seem like a good place to start the mask—the satin background is almost entirely red—first glances can be deceiving. Unfortunately, in RGB color space, white is represented by the presence of red, green, and blue. This means that the red channel will be predominantly light, and probably won't provide the contrast necessary to derive a decent mask.

Masking the slip in this product shot starts with analyzing the image: the background is red, indicating that we might be able to start by processing the red channel.

In the red channel, the slip is only slightly lighter than the red background, hardly ideal for mask creation.

We're looking for contrast between the slip and the background. Looking again at this image, we can guess that there's little green in the background; green is the complement of red, and isn't likely to be present where there are saturated red hues.

The green channel, duplicated and processed, will become our alpha channel.

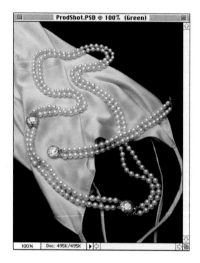

The green channel is our best candidate; there's very little green in the red satin background.

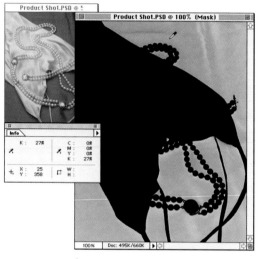

The green channel is duplicated, inverted, and re-named "Mask." Levels have been used to darken the image, making the darkest values (those found in the object we wish to mask) 100 percent black.

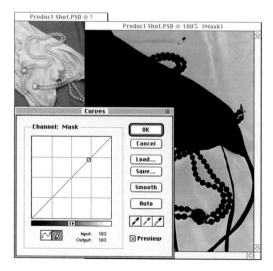

Sampling the background with the Curves dialog box, we find that most of the background tones are lighter than about 70 percent gray. Look for the little bouncing ball in the Curves dialog box, which interactively displays the brightness position of the currently sampled pixel.

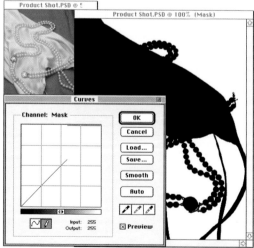

Using Curves' Arbitrary mode, a horizontal line is drawn across the upper right, changing all tones of 60 percent and lighter to pure white.

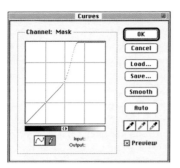

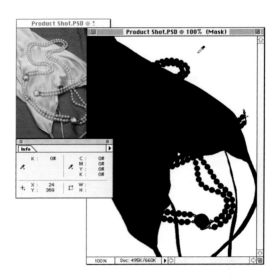

The Smooth button is used twice; the extra 10 percent margin (between 60 percent and 70 percent gray) contributes to the smoothing process, providing a more dynamic edge along the boundary between light and dark values. The result? A smoother, anti-aliased edge.

Looking back at our mask, the background is now entirely white. By inverting the entire channel, we've created a good mask for the foreground element.

Choking

Good, accurate masking is often largely influenced (and judged) by the quality and accuracy of an object's edges against a background. Those familiar with pre-digital compositing work have all seen *matte lines*, those telltale light or dark halos around composited creatures, spaceships, or any number of unlikely things in unlikely places. These lines are typically the result of having a mask that wasn't sharp enough or tight enough around the foreground element; the matte line is a remnant of the original background against which the foreground element was photographed.

Choking a mask causes darker areas of the alpha channel to encroach inward on areas of white. If the matte line is very soft or subtle, it can often be enhanced and tightened by manipulating the relatively small number of intermediate grays normally found in a reasonably sharp anti-aliased edge. Choking by large amounts often involves blurring the alpha channel first, to increase the spread and range of intermediate gray values. The Levels command is usually the best way to accomplish choking; in fact, the process is similar to using Levels for edge sharpening, but involves more fine-tuned control over the placement of midpoint gray values.

A mask has been created for the foreground element in this image. The background layer was duplicated and given a layer mask based on the first mask. The background was then filled with a black-to-white gradient.

This example illustrates choking with a layer mask, but this same technique fully applies to alpha channels as well. (Much more about layer masks is coming up in Chapter 3. Hang tight.)

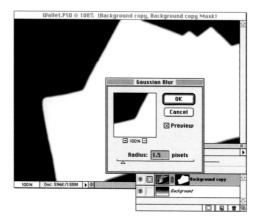

The layer mask is made visible, and a slight blur is added to the layer mask.

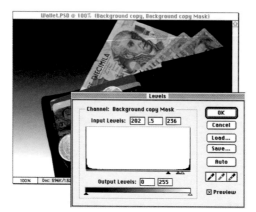

The Levels command is invoked while the RGB portion of the layer is visible (you can see that we're affecting the layer mask in the Levels dialog box channel indicator). This allows us to choke the mask and automatically see the results on the actual color portion of the image.

Notice the blue halo around the foreground element against the gradient background: Those are matte lines, created because the foreground object mask isn't tight enough to fully mask out the previous background (which was, obviously, blue). We need to make sure that, as we choke our mask, the edge of the mask remains anti-aliased. A slight blur assures that we have some grayscale headroom to slide around the edge of the mask.

Choking is perhaps most easily done using the Levels command, altering the Input levels of the alpha channel. To choke the layer mask, we need to push the mid-tone grays toward black, away from white (which results in a tighter edge, closer to the foreground element).

When working with alpha channels (as opposed to the layer masks we altered in the previous example), Photoshop's Quick Mask mode makes it easy to tell if you're going to have matte line problems before you activate the selection.

This is the original image from which the previous foreground element was taken. Making the alpha channel visible in the RGB channel enables you to view the edge of your mask in Quick Mask mode. See that blue edge around the wallet? It's a sure sign that there are going to be potential matte line problems.

Spreading

Clipped edges are the evil cousin of matte lines. Sometimes a mask is so tight around a foreground element that its outer edges are masked, resulting in an unnatural-looking composite.

Spreading is essentially the opposite of choking. It involves pushing white areas of the mask outward towards the dark areas, spreading the mask outwards. Like choking, the process is best approached with Levels.

Like choking, spreading masks involves pushing mid-tone grays around—in this case, away from black and towards white.

In an effort to smooth uneven edges along its mask, this arm suffers from clipped edges. The outer edges of the arm end before they should, which is especially noticeable on the top of the forearm, inside the elbow, and around the fingers.

The extent of this problem becomes visible when we view the mask in Quick Mask mode. The clipped edges are where the red overlay covers portions of the arm.

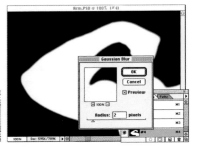

The mask for the arm is blurred to create more intermediate grays to manipulate.

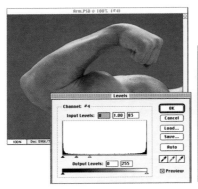
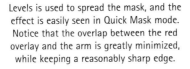

Levels is used to spread the mask, and the effect is easily seen in Quick Mask mode. Notice that the overlap between the red overlay and the arm is greatly minimized, while keeping a reasonably sharp edge.

This is the re-composited arm, after spreading the alpha channel.

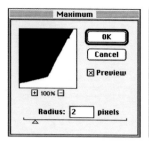 

Maximum and Minimum, Photoshop's filter-based edge enhancement tools.

Minimum and Maximum

Many Photoshop users aren't aware of the true purpose of the Minimum and Maximum filters. When used on grayscale images or channels, they are filter-based methods of choking and spreading masks, respectively. Unlike choking and spreading, they don't require some blurring before their use in order to have some dynamic range to manipulate, but quite often some slight pre-blurring helps.

Now, you might be thinking, "Hold on a minute... this whole choking, spreading, Maximum and Minimum deal sounds similar to yet another method of mask enhancement—the Expand and Contract commands from the Select>Modify submenu."

That's because these three basic methods of mask edge enhancement accomplish basically the same thing, through different methods (grayscale image adjustment, filters, and selections). Which method you use, once again, depends on the nature of your task. Tweaking the edge of a mask with great accuracy is often best accomplished by choking and spreading using various Levels-based techniques. Nudging a high-resolution mask in or out uniformly by a certain number of pixels is certainly an appropriate job for Maximum and Minimum. Choking or spreading an active selection, as opposed to an actual grayscale layer mask or alpha channel, can only be done with Expand and Contract.

To illustrate this relationship, let's compare a mask being choked by the same amount by two different processes: the Minimum filter and the Contract command.

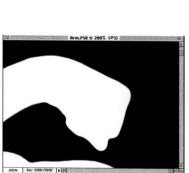

Here's our previous choking and spreading example, magnified to display only the hand.

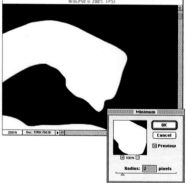

The mask has been choked using the Minimum command at a setting of two pixels.

This is the same mask that has been loaded as a selection and then saved after having been contracted by two pixels.

Admittedly, these two methods of choking seemingly yield very similar results. Upon careful inspection, however, the Contract command tends to gather anti-aliased edges just a bit tighter and more accurately than Minimum does. Because this only affects anti-aliased pixels, not the white core of the mask, this shouldn't have a significant impact on any print-resolution image.

This is the difference between the two masks, created using the Calculations command.

To visualize this difference, we'll create an image that represents the difference between these two images by using the Calculations command and its Difference mode (for more information on Calculations and application modes, see Chapter 4, "Calculations").

The white edges are a result of the difference between how Minimum and Contract deal with mask edges. The black on either side of this border indicates that there's no difference between the mask's white core and solid black background.

One of the biggest problems with using Minimum and Maximum, however, is that they only have one parameter: an amount, in pixels. On the other hand, choking and spreading can be controlled with almost any image adjustment feature in Photoshop: Levels, Curves, the Sharpen/Blur tool, the Dodge/Burn tool, and so on. Minimum and Maximum are best used on high-resolution images, due to the rather heavy effects they create on small files.

Compositing 3D Objects in Photoshop

There's no way around it: 3D graphics are tough. After you finish modeling your objects, arranging them in a scene, and possibly even animating them, the (often dreaded) rendering process arrives. Rendering convincing shadows, reflections, and transparency—the hallmarks of high-quality raytracing—is often extremely time-consuming, and not altogether accurate (from the standpoint of realism) when your 3D images are meant to be composited over 2D elements.

A time-tested approach to compositing 3D objects, either with other 3D objects or 2D image elements, is to render each object *separately*, with no shadows or reflections on/from other objects. This, of course, speeds up the rendering process (especially raytracing) tremendously. This process involves the use of the object's alpha channel to create shadows and reflections as a post-rendering process.

The following example uses a collection of 3D objects and a flat, 2D background. While the objects were all arranged and placed in the same scene, each object was rendered separately, with its own alpha channel (a parameter specified at render time). But it's the process *after* everything has been rendered that we're interested in. That's where that alpha channel magic comes in. (There will be just a bit of non-mask-related work involved, but by using alpha channels we're able to keep it to a minimum, which speeds up our work significantly. And isn't that always a good thing?)

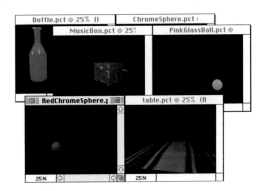

From the same 3D scene, each object is rendered separately. Don't let the solid backgrounds fool you; there's an embedded alpha channel for each object.

After all rendering is complete—one pass for each object, with all other objects hidden—the files are opened in Photoshop. They're all the same size and have straight embedded alpha channels, based on the object's transparency.

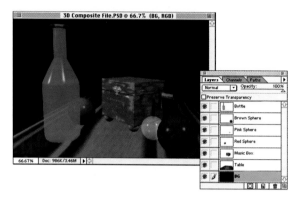

This document is compiled from each separate rendering pass; there is a layer for each object, and a specific background layer, filled with black.

Integrating the Elements

A background document is created, the same size as the rendered frames. Each object is moved onto the new document and given its own layer, in order of depth, so the tabletop is the bottom-most layer and the bottle is the topmost layer. The result is a multi-layer RGB document, each object having its own layer and alpha channel. By loading each object's alpha channel as a selection and inversing the selection, the black background of each object is deleted.

Looking at our preliminary result, there are two things missing: reflections and shadows. To complete this composite, the 3D objects' shadows and reflections need to interact to look realistic.

Creating Reflections

Our first step is to make each object reflect in the table, as if the tabletop had a glossy varnish. This is relatively easy for most of the objects in the scene. The layers containing the spheres and the bottle are duplicated (Layer>Duplicate Layer), flipped vertically (Layer>Transform>Flip Vertical), placed below the original object layers, re-positioned by hand, and dropped to 30 percent Opacity. This yields a satisfactory result; however, the music box will be more problematic.

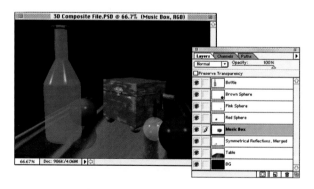

The result of simply flipping some objects around and reducing their opacity. Such Photoshop tricks are so easily done that it may be more productive, and provide greater control, to produce these results *after* render time.

Because it isn't symmetrical, the music box simply can't be duplicated, flipped over, and moved: its feet won't be aligned properly, nor will the reflection of the closer edge of the box. An easy solution for this, however, is to duplicate and align each visible side of the box by hand.

Using the lasso to select the front face of the box, a new layer is made by selecting Layer>New>Layer via Copy (Command-J on the keyboard). Like the other reflections, it is flipped vertically and re-positioned underneath the original music box. The Skew command (Layer>Transform>Skew) helps align the top edge of the reflection layer with the bottom edge of the music box's front face.

A similar approach can be taken with the side face of the music box. Making a selection that encompasses it and the crank, it is also copied into its own layer, flipped vertically, moved, and skewed to be in proportion.

Now for the underside of the music box. Because it simply wasn't visible and didn't get rendered, we'll have to improvise. Drawing a rhombus with the lasso that follows the footprint of the music box should suffice. It's filled with black on its own layer, and aligned with the reflections that are already made.

A similar trick is done to each of the music box's bronze feet. They are copied into their own layers, flipped vertically, and repositioned. Their harsh lower edges are softened using the Blur tool.

The front, side, and underside reflections are merged with the bronze foot reflections to create a single layer for the music box's reflection. Shift its opacity down to 30 percent, to match the other reflections in the image.

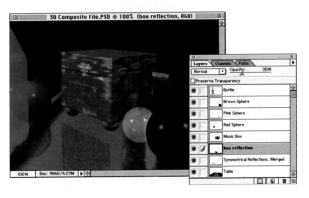

This portion of the music box is in perspective, thanks.

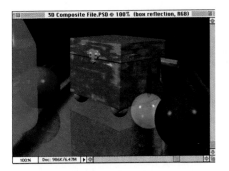

The reflection of the music box starts to take shape.

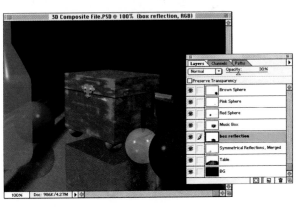

A rhombus-shaped selection is drawn and filled with black to simulate the dark reflection of the music box's underside.

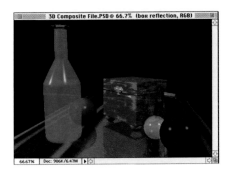

...and the reflections are complete.

Creating Shadows

Many 3D applications produce shadows that aren't very useful in compositing. They're static, often with hard edges (real shadows fall off as they move away from illumination and the object casting them), and won't fall realistically against elements that weren't in the original render. By doing them by hand, we have exact control over all of these parameters. Best of all, the basis for these shadows is already in our layered document: alpha channels.

The lighting on the objects in this still life suggests a light source that's to the left and above the surface of the table, perhaps over the near-left corner. We'll skew the alpha channels for each object up and to the right and use them to create shadow layers. (Notice that the alpha channels bear descriptive names, just like the layers in the image. For complex scenes like this one, descriptively naming your channels and layers will make you happier when you open the file after a couple of weeks of not touching it.)

The red sphere between the bottle and the music box is the first candidate for a shadow. Free Transform (Layer>Free Transform) is used to distort the object mask into a shadow mask. A 2-pixel Gaussian blur is also applied to the mask to give the shadow a soft edge.

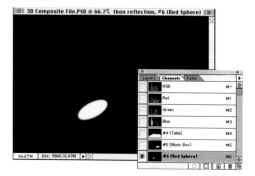

The mask for the red sphere's shadow.

The shadow overlaps the lower-left edge of the music box. In order to look more realistic, the shadow's angle should change inflection when it hits the box. We'll tackle this in the next step, but for now we'll limit this portion of the drop shadow to the tabletop.

When the RGB channel is made active (Command-~), channel #6 is loaded as a selection. Using the Load Selection command, we then load channel #5 (Music Box) and set it to subtract from the current selection; our potential shadow stops at the edge of the music box.

A new layer is created underneath the Red Sphere layer and filled with black, giving us our shadow. A 2-pixel Gaussian blur is applied, and the layer Opacity is set to 50 percent.

Using the alpha channels for both the red sphere and the music box, a selection is created for the potential shadow.

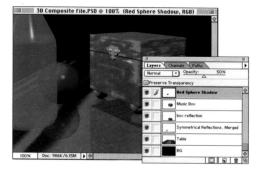

The red sphere's shadow on the tabletop.

Now for the shadow that appears on the music box. The first step is similar to the method used to create the last shadow. Load channel #6 as a selection, then load channel #5 as a selection. This time, channel #5 is intersected with the current selection.

Making sure the Red Sphere Layer is still active, we fill this area with black, then use Free Transform to make it taller and thinner. Dropping the selection, the shadow plays realistically up the front face of the music box. (Note that if we merely blurred the shadow after it had been laid down, the blurring would cause the shadow to bleed onto the music box.)

Now that the first challenge has been met, the shadows for the music box, pink sphere, and brown sphere are very simple, because their shadows don't intersect any other object. Like the original red sphere shadow, Free Transform is used to distort the object masks into shadow masks, and a 2-pixel Gaussian blur is applied. Remember, each shadow goes on its own layer, and is dropped in Opacity (50 percent does the trick in this example).

The selections based on the red sphere shadow and the music box are intersected.

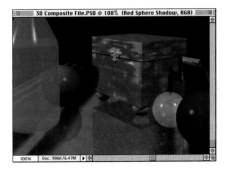

The red sphere's shadow, playing off the front surface of the music box.

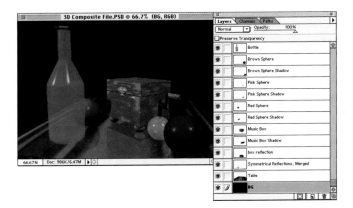

The majority of shadows for the objects are now in place.

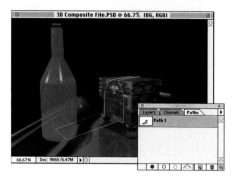

A single path wraps up our shadow-making troubles.

Wrapping up this composite involves one final shadow: the bottle. Looking carefully at the image, we guess that the shadow of the bottle will fall across the table, as well as the front face and the top of the music box. Because we want this to look as realistic as possible, given the potential complexity of the bottle's shadow and its positioning (smack-dab in the center of the image), we decide to do just a bit of hand work. A path is created for the bottle's shadow.

The path is loaded as a selection, feathered, and filled with black on its own layer. Voilà.

The finished composite; a bit involved, but this approach can be a good deal faster than letting reflections and shadows be rendered by 3D software. This is also important because many 3D rendering programs don't support soft-edged shadows.

Text Effects Using Alpha Channels

If you're using Photoshop, chances are you're using layers for a lot of special effects, especially for elements that require depth prioritization, such as drop shadows and highlights to make text look more volumetric. Although that may be the most efficient way of doing such an effect, the fact is that these tricks were first done using alpha channels in one layer only, and can still be done this way. Practically speaking, using alpha channels to do this kind of work is actually beneficial if your project file is very large; adding more memory-devouring layers would bog down Photoshop's speed.

The following example is very easy to duplicate on your own computer; we encourage you to rev up Photoshop, choose a nice hefty typeface, and follow along.

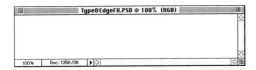

This single-layer document serves as the basis for our type effects.

First, a new RGB document is created (about 500 pixels wide and 100 pixels tall); it should be filled with nothing but white pixels (assuming that this image will be placed in a layout with a white background).

The first step will be to create an alpha channel for the type. In order for the inline type effects to be visible, a heavy sans-serif typeface is ideal.

The first effect we'll apply is a simple color gradient, using the alpha channel to limit it to just the area of the text.

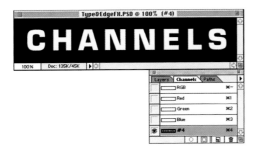

A new layer is created and text is placed in that new channel (using white as the foreground color).

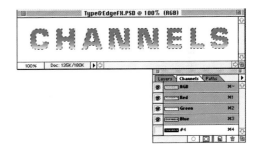

Using the Load Selection command, channel #4 is loaded as a selection. The gradient tool is then used to drop a color gradient through the type.

The text now needs some volume; the easiest way to accomplish that is to add some in-line shadows and highlights. It's crucial that effects like these are consistent, and that you visualize where your hypothetical light source is located. In this example, we'll assume that the light source is in the upper left. We'll start by adding the shadows.

The active selection from our previous step is moved up and to the left by two pixels, using the keyboard arrow keys (a selection tool must be chosen to move only the selection, not its contents).

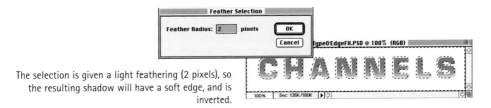

The selection is given a light feathering (2 pixels), so the resulting shadow will have a soft edge, and is inverted.

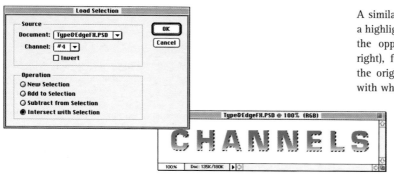

A similar procedure is followed for creating a highlight: the selection is simply nudged in the opposite direction (down and to the right), feathered, inverted, intersected with the original alpha channel, and then filled with white instead of black.

Another common text effect is the drop shadow. In keeping with our current lighting conditions, our drop shadow should fall to the lower-right of the text.

To make sure that our shadow doesn't reach beyond the edge of the text, the Load Selection command is used to intersect our current offset, feathered selection, and the original text alpha channel.

Filling this new selection with black gives us our in-line text shadow.

Our finished in-line highlight and shadow effect.

Channel #4 is once again loaded as a selection, given a moderate feather, and offset down and to the right.

The Load Selection dialog box is invoked to load #4 as a selection and to subtract it from the current selection; this makes the drop shadow appear to be behind the text.

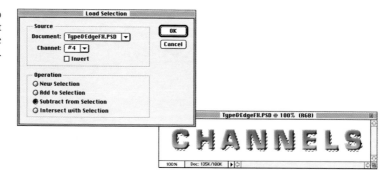

The new selection is filled with black, creating our drop shadow effect.

While our text is looking pretty snazzy, the edge is starting to lose definition now that we have all sorts of lighting effects. Outlining the text will bring it right back into focus.

Of course, this kind of effect—rounded-edge type hovering above a background, casting a drop shadow—is quite common. But what about making text that seems to be *below* the background, recessed into the page (web page, printed page, or any other type of page we haven't heard about)? This is a less-common effect that's just as easily created using alpha channels or layers. Let's take a gander at the alpha-channel approach.

Channel #4 is loaded as a selection, and given a Stroke of one pixel (using Black as the foreground color) at 75 percent Opacity. The result is an outline that isn't too obtrusive.

This image starts just as our previous example did; with an RGB image with text in the alpha channel, used to create a selection through which a color gradient was made.

Our effect hinges on making the white background appear as if it has text-shaped holes in it, casting a drop shadow on what seems to be a color gradient behind the white background. We'll assume, as we did in our previous example, that our light source is coming from the upper left-hand corner.

Channel #4 is loaded as a selection, feathered with a radius of 3, offset by three pixels down and three pixels to the right, and inverted.

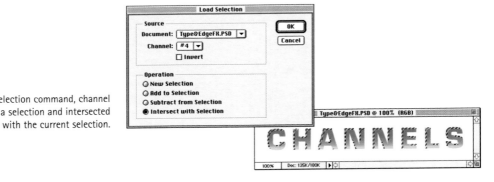

Using the Load Selection command, channel #4 is loaded as a selection and intersected with the current selection.

This new selection is filled with black, creating a drop shadow on the colored text.

To make this cut-out a little more complex, let's add a ridge to make it appear as if the white background was buckling slightly around the cut-out area.

Channel #4 is loaded as a selection, expanded by four pixels (Select>Expand), and feathered with a radius of two.

Using the Stroke command, the selection is outlined by a one-pixel, 30 percent–Opacity black line. Note that it looks fuzzy; that's because our selection is feathered.

Because our theoretical light source is coming from the upper left, it doesn't make sense to have a uniform shadow around the entire ridge. With a little more alpha channel acrobatics, we'll get rid of the upper-left ridge shadows.

The selection region is then offset up and to the left by four pixels each.

Channel #4, loaded as a selection, is subtracted from our current selection to avoid affecting the existing text.

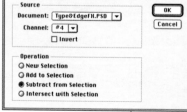

The resulting selection is filled with white.

If there's a ridge around the cut-out area, however, the upper-left edges would still have a slight shadow as they curve inward.

Yet again, Channel #4 is loaded as a selection. It's feathered by one pixel and offset up and to the left by one pixel.

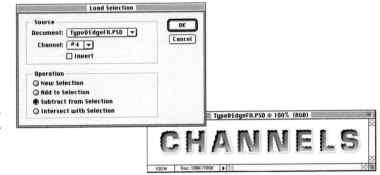

Channel #4, loaded as a selection, is subtracted from the current selection.

Filled with black at 50 percent Opacity, the image is finished.

Don't Change the Channel Yet

You are now a channel warrior. You have more masking knowledge than the majority of Photoshop users on the planet (at least, that's what our students might tell you). We hope that as you approach the process of masking objects in scenes, some of the techniques we've covered in this chapter will help you look at problems in a new light (if not directly deliver the answers).

Next, chocolate layered cake. Well, alright, just Photoshop layers. Get your own chocolate!

Three

Layers

Layers are one of the newest "hot" features in 2D imaging applications. Simply stated, in the case of Photoshop, layers enable images (or color correction adjustments, in the case of Photoshop 4.0) to exist on discrete planes, each separately editable at any time. Each layer can be edited and adjusted separately from everything else in the document. Some people (and software) call them image *objects* or *floaters*, but they are all referring to essentially the same thing: layers.

If you think about it, objects are the foundation of many different kinds of software. The entire desktop publishing model is based on page layout applications, which combine layers of text and graphics as discrete, separate objects. Authoring systems serve up layers of static and dynamic media, the layers linked together for navigation. The concept of database programming is that each information field is arranged and manipulated like, well, an object. Object–oriented programming environments, which makes much more efficient use of programmers' efforts and system resources, are becoming increasingly popular. From this standpoint, layers/objects seem to clearly be the wave of the future.

It's our feeling that, generally speaking, Adobe Photoshop has one of the better implementations of layers on the imaging market today. While we like how layers work in Photoshop, the fact is that Photoshop's layer implementation is far from perfect. Our main goal for this chapter is to bring layers into the light with examples and descriptions of overall functionality, and to introduce some obscure details we've discovered. We also point out ways in which we feel Photoshop layers are lacking, in the hopes that someone at Adobe might take our comments as constructive criticism.

Layer Fundamentals

Variations of the 2D bitmap layer/object concept have appeared in consumer graphics software for almost 10 years, and much longer in experimental situations (like Alvy Ray Smith's pioneering work at the NYIT in the 1970s).

Looking at the history of this software genre on the Macintosh takes us back to the dynamic duo known as ComicWorks and GraphicWorks. Developed by Macromind in 1985-86 (years before the company was renamed Macromedia) for Mindscape, these programs embodied the concept of bitmaps inside of separate frames called *easels*. Each easel could be set to a different resolution, could also have a QuickDraw transfer mode (AND, XOR and many others—remember, this was before the age of Photoshop), and could be moved from level to level in the foreground/background scheme, much like moving cast members from channel to channel in Director, which changes the cast members' 2–dimensional depth prioritization.

Macromedia Director (even in its earlier version, called "VideoWorks") has always had the ability to handle each individual castmember, or bitmap graphic, as a discrete object, with full layering and ink mode functionality, an integrated image "database" arrangement system (the Cast window), precision placement tools (the "Tweak" window), and more.

And then there was Shapes for ColorStudio, the program created by two of the most talented programmers in the Macintosh universe, Mark Zimmer and Tom Hedges (with a little help from their friends, of course). ColorStudio had a feature called Shapes, which allowed PostScript vector art to float in a separate layer above the bitmap background. You could selectively rasterize portions of the vector layer into the bitmap background, a capability that has yet to be reproduced in any contemporary imaging programs. While the current version of Painter has a decent object/layer implementation (called "Floaters"), it still doesn't have the equivalent of Shapes.

Much of the buzz around the most recent versions of Adobe Photoshop, Live Picture, Fractal Design Painter, Macromedia xRes, Micrografx Picture Publisher, and other imaging applications is centered on layers/objects and their specific relationship to memory. Some programs (including Photoshop and Painter) load all the actual pixels into active RAM memory. Photoshop is the better-behaved of the bunch, in that it only loads the pixels of the currently active quadrant, instead of absolutely all of the pixels in the open document.

This ability to only load pixels into RAM as they are needed, combined with various scratch disk techniques, allows manipulation of documents that are larger than the available amount of RAM.

Others programs (including Live Picture and xRes) only load the data that corresponds to the current magnification level displayed on the screen. These "proxy-based" programs apply all editing and manipulation in a final rendering process, much like most 3D programs.

For compositing tasks, the advent of layers means that foreground elements can be imported or placed into an image as separate objects, and maintained as such at all times (unless the artist decides to flatten the image or subsets of layers). Imperfect edges around an object can be manipulated and fixed while previewing the object against the background. The foreground element can remain independent of the background until you are satisfied with the interaction of the various layered elements.

Photoshop Layers

Photoshop Layers are manipulated by controls in the Layers palette. There are two basic types of layers: *image layers*, which contain pixel data (mages), and *adjustment layers*, which hold both color manipulation data (almost anything from the Image>Adjust menu) and pixel data (for masking the color adjustment effect).

While adding layers to a document increases the overall size of the document, only the active pixels in a layer are taken into account—the surrounding transparent areas around the active pixels don't take up any memory. Channels, on the other hand, increase overall document size and RAM requirement, even if the channel consists of a single white area on a large black field.

In working with Photoshop, something that the authors of this book have noticed is that the current release of Photoshop (4.01) has some memory flakiness when adding lots of layers to documents that are already large (100 megabytes or more). If you don't have enough RAM to hold the active contents of all of the layers of your current document, you're likely to run into memory problems. Stability also can take a significant hit if you have a large number of smaller files open in Photoshop simultaneously, each with a relatively large number of layers.

 Tip: It's a good idea to keep a view of your active scratch disk window open in a corner of your screen so you can interactively watch how the space is being used, and whether or not you're running out of disk space. This is most reliably seen under the MacOS; when using Windows 95 or NT, the hard disk information found in the file manager (or Explorer) might need to be refreshed (using the Refresh command, found in the View menu) to show the current disk status.

The older version of Photoshop, 3.0, enables you to have up to 100 layers in a single document (99 individual layers, and the single background layer). Photoshop's layer implementation has become even more robust in its newest version, 4.0. If you make a selection region and use the Float command, a new layer is created instead of a temporary floating selection. Using the Paste command creates a new layer automatically, eliminating the need for the Paste layer command, found in previous versions of the software. Unfortunately, there's no way to turn this new feature off; Paste operations *always* create new layers.

Tip: We cover this point elsewhere in this chapter, but take note now: **Command-E** merges the currently active layer with the underlying layer, which is a pseudo—fix to the new layer "feature."

There are, however, some problems. For example, in previous versions of Photoshop, holding down the Option key while selecting Merge Layers retained the visible layers while creating a new layer that held the merged layers. Pretty useful, right? Well, the new equivalent in Photoshop 4.0—holding down Option while selecting Merge Visible—puts the merged layers into the *currently selected layer*, effectively negating the purpose of leaving the original visible layers intact. You'd have to create a new layer, make it visible with the other layers you want to merge, and then use Option-Merge Visible.

There has been a new technological addition to enhance the way layers work in Photoshop 4.0: *Big Data*. Big Data means that Photoshop retains image data that lies beyond the edges of the canvas. Layers that have been partially moved or scaled out of the image, or that have been placed or pasted from large documents into smaller ones, won't be cropped off. The key to Big Data really being useful is that it keeps this excess, off-canvas data in the image file, keeping all image data (visible or not) between Photoshop sessions.

Tip: The trick to getting rid of excess Big Data you don't need is using the Select All command (Select>Select All) and the Crop command (Image>Crop).

Basic Layer Operations

To manipulate a particular layer, simply click on it in the Layers window to make it the active layer; this is indicated by the layer name being highlighted. The eye icon next to each layer name indicates what layers are visible, so note that an active layer may not be visible! You can only write to one layer at a time. If you need to make an adjustment to all layers in an image, you have to *flatten* the image, thereby cementing the layers together into one background layer. This is covered in more detail later in this chapter, in the section "Merging Layers."

Layers can be re-prioritized in foreground/background space by dragging them in the Layers palette. The hierarchy is top-down: the background layer is at the bottom of the layer list, and is also the furthest object in the background. Layers on top of the background layer are in front of the background layer in the actual document.

The uppermost layer in an image covers the layers beneath it, based on the opacity and applications mode used. The hierarchy of layers can be changed by simply grabbing a layer in the Layers window and dragging it to the position desired.

The contents of the clipboard are automatically placed into a new layer when a Paste operation occurs. If the image is smaller than the layer into which it was pasted, the remaining area of the new layer is transparent (layer transparency is covered in detail later in this chapter).

Layers can be temporarily grouped to be moved together by activating the Link/Unlink anchor for the desired layers. In Photoshop 3.0X, the Link/Unlink option is only good for moving layers together; with Photoshop 4.X, this functionality has been upgraded to work with both moving and dynamic transformations (rotations, skewing, and scaling).

Besides the aforementioned Transformation operations, you can't affect multiple layers simultaneously with Photoshop's filters or painting tools. The new Adjustment Layers found in Photoshop 4.X enable you to create color corrections that process more than one layer at a time.

Adjustment Layers

Adjustment layers are certainly one of the most important new additions to Photoshop 4.0. Compared with a single layer type in Photoshop 3—layers with pixels—there are now two types of layers: normal layers, which contain image data, and adjustment layers, which hold color correction data.

Adjustment layers were created to facilitate making multi-layer tonal adjustment and color corrections. Any number of adjustment layers can be stacked in the Layers palette, each adjustment layer modifying the layers below it. Like an image layer, an adjustment layer doesn't make permanent changes to the underlying image pixels (a behavior termed *non-destructive*). Values can be adjusted at any point in time—as long as you don't merge the adjustment layer with any selected sub-layers.

The following are the specific commands that Adjustment layers can perform:

- Levels
- Curves
- Color Balance
- Brightness & Contrast
- Hue/Saturation
- Selective Color
- Invert
- Threshold
- Posterize

The default method of using adjustment layers is that the adjustments happen globally, to all layers, in all regions of the image.

> **Authors' Note**
>
> While we devote some coverage to our own specific use of some of these image adjustment controls elsewhere in this book, we won't get into extreme detail on the overall functionality of each of these commands. Their usefulness is well documented in many other Photoshop books, as well as in the Photoshop documentation.

While it's not immediately obvious, adjustment layers have actual pixels associated with them: these grayscale pixels are its *layer mask,* and are what you see in the Layers palette preview (unlike normal color image layers, which have a separate layer mask, adjustment layers display their layer mask in the single layer preview in the Layers palette). This layer mask limits the effect of the adjustment layer: White areas let the effect fully show through, while black pixels fully obscure the effect, and varying levels of gray pixels yield transparency based on their brightness. Because adjustment layer masks start as all white, the effects they produce are global. Sound like an alpha channel? You bet. We get deeper into layer masks and how they work later in this chapter.

Masks and Layers

When most people start using Photoshop, one of the first conceptual problems they run into is learning to understand the relationship between layers and masks. The two are linked together in obvious and not-so-obvious ways; both work together to maximize overall *compositing* (blending) options.

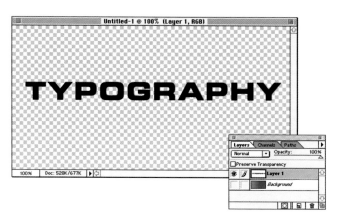

We've created a new layer on top of the default background layer, and turned the background off. Note how the absolute background of the document is displayed as a checkerboard pattern.

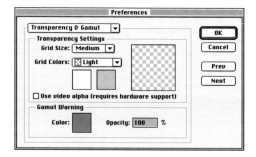

You can choose how Photoshop display's the absolute background in a document, which is useful for analyzing a layer's transparency. The visual appearance of the absolute background in no way affects the functionality of the program; these options are for display purposes only.

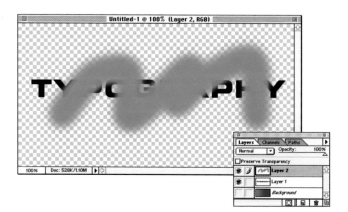

The paint stroke blocks out the contents of layers beneath it; in this example, we've still kept the background layer hidden.

Layer Transparency

When you create a new layer from scratch, with no actual live pixels in the layer, the layer is fully transparent, allowing any underlying layers to show through in their entirety.

 Tip: You can change the way the absolute background is displayed by going to Photoshop's Preferences menu item and choosing Transparency & Gamut.

If you use the paintbrush tool and start painting onto the new layer, the brush stroke will build on top of underlying layers, obscuring them from view.

The pixels laid down by the paintbrush tool are opaque, with soft edges that enable varying amounts of the background to show through.

Seems obvious, doesn't it? Well, there are some hidden mechanisms that are at work when doing this seemingly simplistic operation. How does Photoshop know that the brush stroke covers underlying layers, while still allowing them to show through the parts of the layer that haven't been painted?

In essence, Photoshop is building a mask, on the fly, for the layer; as pixels are added, the *transparency mask* of the layer is modified. This transparency mask isn't visible in the way that other Photoshop masks are—it's implied. This is done in order to protect you from even thinking about the fact that there's an invisible mask inherent to each layer.

If you want to actually get access to this mask, you can load it as a selection by using either of the following two methods:

1. Command (or Control, on the PC)-clicking the layer in the Layers palette.

2. Use the Load Selection command (Select menu), and load the layer X transparency (if you've named the layer, then substitute the name for "layer x")

as a new selection; the transparency mask of the currently-active layer, provided it doesn't have a layer mask, is the default choice in the Load Selection command.

You also can save this selection into an alpha channel for later reference by choosing Select>Save Selection.

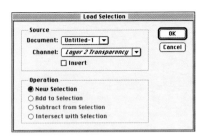

If a layer doesn't already have a layer mask, or if the current document doesn't have ancillary alpha channels, the transparency mask for the layer is automatically chosen when the Load Selection command from the Select menu is invoked.

Once the transparency mask is loaded as a selection, you can edit just the active pixels in the layer without adding new pixels. For example, you might want to paste a texture or picture into some text that already exists on a layer.

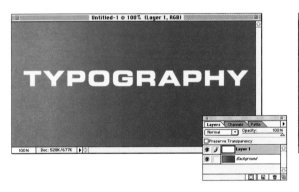

Let's say that you want to paste a texture from your clipboard into this text.

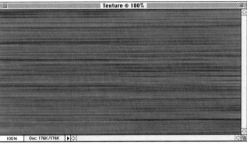

Here's the texture that we want to put "inside" the text from the previous figure. Using the Select All and Copy commands, the texture is placed onto the Clipboard.

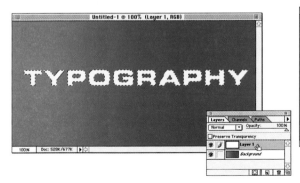

Press the Command (or Control on the PC) key and click the text layer in the layers palette. The transparency mask of the text appears as an active selection on the screen.

Select Paste Into from the Edit menu, and the texture appears masked inside of the type.

Note that the newly pasted texture doesn't become part of the text layer; instead, the pasted texture is put into a new layer, complete with a layer mask defining the shape of the selection made with the text layer transparency.

If you look carefully at the edges of the text with the newly pasted texture, you'll notice one drawback of this technique: The pasted texture is imperfectly combined with the anti-aliased pixels at the edge of the text, leaving a color fringe artifact from the anti-aliasing.

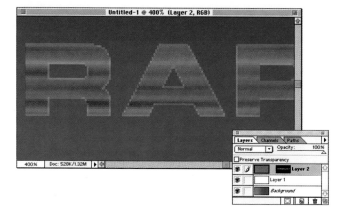

Note the white edge on the text, the results of the combination of the pasted texture with the prior anti-aliasing artifacts. A feature or a bug? You decide.

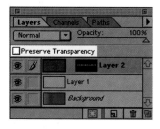

Preserve Transparency is an option available for non-background layers. It's usually turned off.

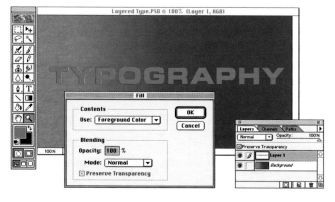

The Fill command is used to fill the text with 100% of the current foreground color. Note that the text has been changed to that color, without the anti-aliased edge artifacts of the previous exercise.

How do you get around this? The least painful answer, in the case of a text effect, is to create the text in an alpha channel (as white text on a black background) and load it as a selection for the Paste Into process. Yes, we know that this doesn't help you with situations where you are trying to work with pixels that already exist as color data on a layer. This example is yet another case where alpha channels are better than relying on comparable layer methodologies. (We'll deal with the *right* way to paste into a layer in a moment.)

But what if you wanted to change the color of the text, or use the paintbrush tool to paint color brush strokes into the text? Would you load the transparency mask as a selection and then use the Paintbrush tool? No. Instead, we would advise that you learn about the *Preserve Transparency* feature of layers. Read on.

Preserve Transparency

In the Layers palette, you'll find a checkbox labeled Preserve Transparency.

This control, when turned on, takes into account the invisible mask associated with each layer when doing any processing to the layer. If you paint on a layer with this setting enabled, the paint is only applied to places where image data already exists on the layer. This is basically the same result you'd get by activating a layer's transparency mask as a selection and then editing the layer, but without tying up any precious selections. If you turn this setting off, the paint is applied anywhere on the layer, regardless of the previous contents.

Let's say, for example, that you want to change the color of the text layer from the previous example. Select the color you want to change the type to, and make it the current foreground color. Use the Fill command to change the color of the text.

> Tip: Astute Photoshop users will probably point out that we could have used the Hue/Saturation controls to shift the hue of a layer without explicitly turning on Preserve Transparency and filling it with a certain color. True. But this method only works for operations that affect a layer globally. If, for example, you wanted to paint edge colors or highlights onto the text using the airbrush or paintbrush tools, you're going to find that Preserve Transparency is critical in order to get the results you really want.

There are two operations, however, that Preserve Transparency does not affect: using the Move tool and using transformations (commands such as Free Transform, Scale, Rotate, and so on). These tools move the contents of a layer around, keeping its discreet edges intact without clipping them to its original, implied transparency mask.

One of the most common pitfalls of using Preserve Transparency is to forget to turn it off when you don't need it. Even seasoned Photoshop users (especially when they're distracted or under a crushing deadline!) think they've encountered a bug when image editing tools (such as Paintbrush) seem to have no effect. Just uncheck the Preserve Transparency option. No bug!

Let's go back to the example of the texture pasted into the text for a moment. We mentioned that one way to get the right edge values would be to create an alpha channel of the text and use it as a selection for a Paste Into command. But, in this case, we want to use the pixel data that already exists on a layer without creating a mask.

Is there a way to take the active pixels of a layer and make them into an instant mask for other layers? Yes. The answer: *Clipping Groups*.

Clipping/Layer Groups

The name Layer Grouping is somewhat confusing (even for experienced Photoshop artisans), and isn't exactly accurate. The implication is that a Layer Group would enable you to do things to multiple layers simultaneously, which is now possible (with specific limitations) with the advent of Photoshop 4.0. In the context of the actual functionality of grouping layers together, it makes far more sense to call the entity Clipping Groups.

Why *clipping*? In the language of computer graphics (and, more specifically, in the lingo of Adobe PostScript), clipping refers to the process of blocking, or masking, image data. For example, in object-oriented graphics programs (such as Adobe Illustrator and Macromedia Freehand), using a path to contain (or mask) other paths converts the masking path to a Clipping Path.

In addition to these two levels of image transparency control, the process of creating a clipping group allows multiple layers (each with its own individual global transparency and layer masks) to be masked through an additional 8-bit mask. This mask is determined by the transparency mask of the bottom-most layer of a set of grouped layers. This bottom-most layer is called the *clipping layer.*

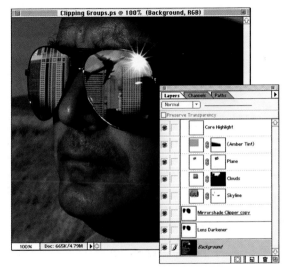

In a set of grouped layers, the bottom-most layer is the clipping layer. Note that its name is underscored, and the layers above it are indented, indicating that they're grouped with the bottom clipping layer. The transparency mask of the clipping layer becomes the overall mask for all grouped layers. Actual color image data in the clipping layer is disregarded in the *masking* process.

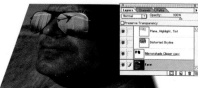

These are the layers used to create the layered-image lens effect in the previous figure. They are seen individually here, ungrouped. Notice that the top two layers already have complex, non-uniform transparencies, and the bottom-most layer is entirely solid black.

Here the three layers are grouped together, seen with the background onto which they will be composited. The top two layers interact with the clipping layer with their individual color and transparency characteristics, but are ultimately masked by the clipping layer.

The clipping group has been composited onto the background and placed over the man's original sunglasses. Because the clipping layer is all black and set to normal mode, the original lenses are entirely obscured.

Let's take a closer look at this example and examine clipping layers in more depth.

Layers can be grouped together into clipping groups in three ways:

- Open the Layers Option dialog box for the desired layer (double-click the layer in the Layers palette) and check the Group with Previous Layer checkbox. The clipping layer in the layer group appears underlined in the Layers palette.

Tip: If you look carefully, you'll notice that when you click the Group with Previous Layer button in the layer option dialog box, the change is instantly made back in the active document and the effect is shown in the image window. Make sure that your layers palette is visible (place it off to one side of the screen).

- You also can group layers by Option-clicking the divider between two adjacent layers in the Layers palette.
- The key command for Group with Previous Layer is Command + G.

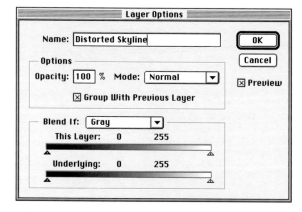

When you check the Group with Previous Layer option, the layer immediately under the currently selected layer is turned into a clipping layer, and is grouped with the selected layer.

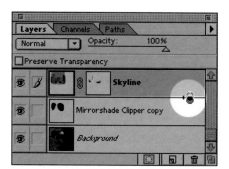

This cursor appears when you Option-click the border between two layers in the Layers palette, and groups two adjacent layers together.

Once designated as a clipping layer, the bottom-most layer in a clipping group may still be edited; any changes to its transparency, opacity, or layer mask (as you would expect) affects the transparency of any layers grouped with it.

Changing the layer's position in the Layers palette, however, can seriously alter the results of a clipping group. Moving the clipping layer above any layers grouped with it will ungroup those layers; any layers from the original group that are still above the clipping layer will remain in the layer group. If the visibility of the clipping layer is turned off, all grouped layers will be made invisible as well.

It's very important to remember, however, that a clipping layer is still a layer, with its own image data and transfer mode. While the clipping layer can be changed and edited at any time, only changes to the clipping layer's *opacity, layer mask,* or *transparency mask* affect the layers in its clipping group. Changing the pixels in the clipping layer (without actually adding or removing any pixels, which changes the layer's transparency mask) or the clipping layer's transfer mode certainly affects how the layers visibly interact—clipping layers are still image layers, after all—but does *not* affect how the clipping layer masks those layers grouped with it.

Layer Masks

Each Photoshop layer can have its own 8-bit mask. This is totally separate and different from transparency masks, layer groups, and a document's alpha channels. A layer mask determines the opacity of a single layer using the same grayscale metaphor as true alpha channels. Where the layer mask is white, the layer is visible, and where the mask is black, the layer is hidden from view. Selections can be turned into layer masks, and vice versa.

It's best to think about layer masks and layer transparency in one of two ways: *uniform* and *non-uniform* transparency. The overall *uniform* transparency of a layer is controlled with the Opacity slider in the Layers palette, affecting every pixel in that layer. The overall *non-uniform* transparency of a layer is controlled by its layer mask, enabling each pixel to have its own opacity level.

An active selection can be saved as a layer mask by using the Save Selection command; first select the layer you want to be the recipient of the new layer mask, and then select that layer's mask in the Channel pop-up menu within the Save Selection dialog box. Load Selection loads a given layer mask as a selection; again, make sure that the right layer is active in the Layers palette. The keyboard shortcut for loading a layer mask as a selection is Command-Option-\(backslash).

When editing a layer with a layer mask, you can edit either the actual layer image data or the grayscale layer mask. A thick black line around the preview of either the layer or its mask in the Layers palette indicates which of the two is editable. (If you have the Layer preview turned off, of course, this won't work.) Option-clicking the layer mask preview makes it visible in your active image window; doing the same to the layer preview makes the image pixels visible again.

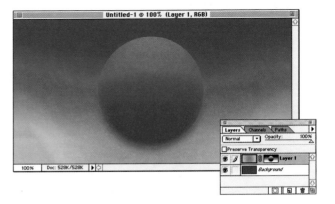

In this image, the complex relationship between the two layers is created with a layer mask. The image portion of Layer 1 is currently visible; notice the heavier black outline around the left layer preview in the Layers palette.

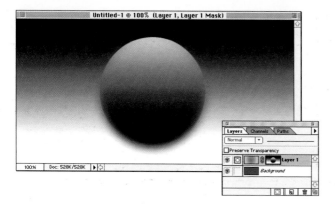

By Option-clicking Layer 1's mask preview, the mask is made visible in the image window.

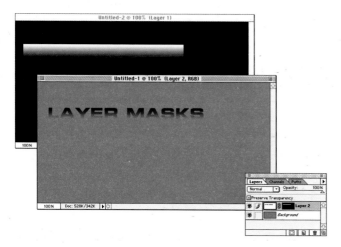

The black type layer has a gradient layer mask, a copy of which is visible behind the main image. Notice that the type layer and its layer mask are currently linked together.

The default behavior of layer masks is to be *linked* with a mask's associated image layer. This means that the layer mask moves with the image layer, as a result of using the Move tool, using the Free Transform command, and so on. By clicking the chain icon between a layer and its mask, you can move each independently. This becomes important if your layer mask is registered with, or based on, a layer beneath it, or if you merely want to re-adjust a texture or image vignette while leaving its mask in place.

The only time that an unlinked layer mask is created is as a result of the Paste Into command. Because the layer mask is based on the selection into which you wanted to Paste, it remains in place as you move its associated layer. Of course, you can link the layer and its mask together after the fact.

You also may notice that if your selected layer has a layer mask, that layer mask appears in the Channels palette. Don't confuse this with a real alpha channel; this just provides another way to access a layer mask. For example, making it visible with the combined RGB channel enables you to view the layer mask using Photoshop's overlay mode. Command-clicking the layer mask in the Channels palette loads it as a selection, just like any other alpha channel. It's there for convenience, not because it's an alpha channel for the entire document.

Layer Masks and Adjustment Layers

Because adjustment layers contain color adjustment data, the grayscale pixel content of an adjustment layer is, in fact, its layer mask. If you paint into an adjustment layer, you are affecting its layer mask directly—without explicitly creating a layer mask during the process.

Working with an adjustment layer's mask is a little different from working with a regular layer. A newly-created adjustment layer's mask is typically all white: The adjustment is global, and not constrained to any one area. This is fine for overall brightness enhancements and hue shifting, but what if you want to limit the effect? You could paint black and grays into the adjustment layer after the fact, but that's not too practical (although it's certainly useful in some situations).

One of the first things many Photoshop artists try to do is to copy the grayscale contents on a channel, alpha channel, or layer mask and paste them into an adjustment layer's layer mask. Well, because Photoshop now creates a new layer every time a Paste operation is executed, this doesn't work. A new layer containing that grayscale image data is created above the adjustment layer, leaving its layer mask unaffected. This is perhaps the most frustrating side effect of the default new-layer-on-paste "feature" in Photoshop 4.0.

The key is to define a selection *first*, based on where you want the adjustment layer to take effect, and then actually create the adjustment layer. Creating an adjustment layer while there is an active selection region automatically creates a layer mask based on the selection. For example, rather than pasting the contents of an alpha channel into an adjustment layer mask, the alpha channel is loaded as a selection, and then the adjustment layer is created. Using the Save Selection command also enables selections to be saved into the adjustment layer after the adjustment layer is created.

Let's look at an example of this method, using a common effect: selective desaturation. In order to accentuate a product in an advertisement, a full-color product is often featured within an otherwise grayscale image. Rather than tint the product itself, which often introduces unwanted colors (an important consideration if the product's colors are part of its brand recognition), one approach is to desaturate the rest of the image.

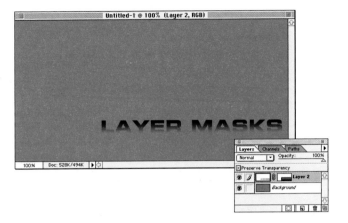

When the image portion of the layer is moved, the mask moves with it, keeping the mask identical relative to the layer's image. Look carefully at the layer mask preview in the Layers palette and you'll see the change.

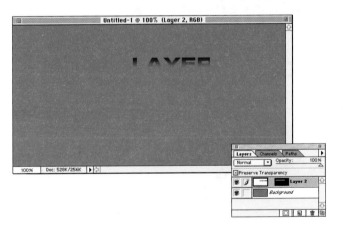

When the layer and its layer mask are unlinked, each is moved independently of the other. Moving the text, in this case, doesn't move the mask with it, hence the strange transparency effect you see here.

This image serves as a hypothetical advertisement for a clothing company; the task is to accentuate the woman's denim overalls.

In order to keep maximum flexibility, this job will be tackled with adjustment layers. We'd probably want to use a Hue/Saturation adjustment layer to desaturate a majority of the image. Assessing the mask creation process, the blue channel of this image—a natural place to start, considering that we want to base a mask on something that's almost perfectly blue—is relatively free of film grain, negative scratches, and scan artifacts. Unfortunately, we can't just copy the blue channel into the adjustment layer—that would simply create a new layer that held the contents of the clipboard. We could start to make an alpha channel, but we want to conserve as much effort (and disk space) as possible. Loading the blue channel as a selection automatically sets up the adjustment layer mask.

This product shot certainly doesn't accentuate the model's overalls; the colors are too bright, and her guitar obscures most of what we want to draw attention to.

The blue channel is loaded as a selection, the resulting selection is inversed, and a new adjustment layer is created (Layer>New>Adjustment Layer) that holds a Hue/Saturation operation.

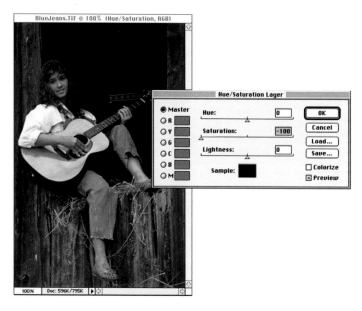

The Hue/Saturation adjustment layer is set to -100 saturation, desaturating everything encompassed by the adjustment layer's mask.

As you can see, the desaturation layer isn't perfect; we've still got too much of the background color, as well as some loss of saturation in the denim.

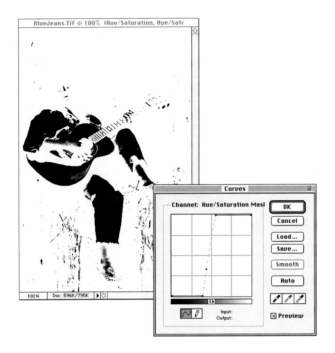

The Curves dialog box is used to massage this raw grayscale image into a more useful mask. The shadows and highlights are clamped somewhat, resulting in a significant contrast enhancement.

After some minor work painting out some problem areas, this is the final result.

Review: Layer Masking Methods

Breathe deeply, and let's re-cap the different methods of determining and manipulating a layer's transparency:

- At the most basic level, each layer has its own implicit, invisible *transparency mask*, determined by the painted, cloned, filled, or pasted pixels within that layer.

- The *Preserve Transparency* feature retains the implicit transparency mask of a layer, regardless of what you do to that layer.

- The overall, uniform transparency of a layer—such as, the same transparency throughout the layer, without variation—can be further altered by using the Opacity slider in the Layers palette.

- The transparency mask of a single layer—a *clipping layer*—can even be used to act as a mask for other layers by grouping the layers together into a layer group.

- Finally, adding a non-uniform *layer mask* to any layer further determines the layer's transparency using grayscale pixels. And all this without a single real alpha channel or path.

In summary, a single Photoshop document can hold a maximum of 99 layer masks (one per layer), 21 alpha channels (assuming it's an RGB image), and 32,000 paths. This does not include the implicit transparency masks each layer has, which can be loaded as a selection if needed. If this doesn't satisfy your masking and selection needs, you may want to re-evaluate your imaging strategy—or hold out until Photoshop 9.5.

Image Compositing Using Layer Masking

While it may not be immediately obvious, this image makes extensive use of layer masks and layer groups.

This is the original image; with the help of Photoshop's layer masking capabilities, his glasses will soon reflect an entirely new vista.

The sunglasses image is a good example of using layer masks and layer groups to composite images together. While there are no alpha channels used in this composite, many techniques for creating alpha channels were involved in deriving the layer masks in this example.

The background layer is the original image; our goal is to change the reflection in the man's glasses from a rural scene to an urban one. The first step is making a mask for the lenses in his glasses, into which other imagery will be composited. We chose to outline the lenses using Photoshop's Paths tool; the tonal and color range within the reflection are too varied to quickly mask any other way.

Next, we need to analyze how we're going to composite more images onto the glasses. Having a solid color like black or white would be helpful, but we want to keep that enormous right-hand lens flare for realism. Rather than go with a solid color or tone, the glasses should get as dark as possible without effecting the man's face or the lens flare.

In the Paths palette, dragging the Mirrorshades path onto the selection icon turns the path into a selection region.

The path called Mirrorshades is the basis for the sunglasses' lens mask.

In the Layers palette, we create a new layer and fill
the selection region with solid black. The default
(Normal) transfer mode obscures the lens flare, but
changing it to Overlay lets the flare show through
while darkening everything else.

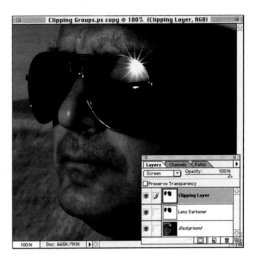

We duplicate the Lens Darkening layer, set it to
Screen mode, and re-name it Clipping Layer; this is
the basis for the layer group into which we'll composite the other imagery.

A new layer with an image of a city skyline placed in
it. The layer was bulged using the Spherize filter to
match the curvature of the lenses. The Skyline layer
is grouped with the Clipping Layer.

Why not use the Lens Darkening layer for the Clipping Layer?
Its overlay transfer mode won't let lighter images composite
well on top of it. By setting the Clipping Layer transfer mode
to Screen, we can more easily composite lighter images onto
the darker lenses. Our Clipping Layer, as the basis for a layer
group, is technically a mask: an image that determines the
opacity of other images.

Our composite is beginning to look pretty good; the lens flare
is even showing through the skyline as is should.
Mirrorshades, although reflective, don't reflect evenly across
their surface due to their curvature. By painting black into a
layer mask, we can reduce the opacity of certain regions of this
layer.

This reduces the opacity of the Skyline layer near the bottom
of the lenses, simulating the reduced reflectivity of the glasses
as they curve away from the image.

The flat blue sky in the Skyline layer, however, isn't very interesting. Because it's a large contiguous area of solid color, it
will be easy to select in and replace it with something more
dramatic.

For added realism, we add a layer mask to the Skyline layer. The transparency of the Clipping Layer was loaded as a selection, and the selection region was painted with the airbrush tool in the Skyline layer's layer mask.

We select an image of big fluffy clouds and place it in the image, giving it its own layer (called Clouds). We move it in place (over the blue sky that's visible within the glasses) and group it to the Skyline layer, adding it to the greater layer group.

Unfortunately, the lower part of the cloud layer obscures the buildings in the layer below. But, as we all know by know, layer masks are our friends...

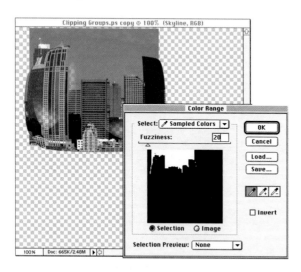

The Clouds layer is hidden for the moment, while the Color Range command (in the Select menu) is used to select the blue sky in the Skyline layer.

Selecting the Clouds layer, we use the Save Selection command to create a layer mask. Now the clouds appear only where the blue sky once was.

Why add a layer mask? Why not just use the Paste Into command once the blue sky was selected? If we pasted the clouds into the Skyline layer and the selection wasn't perfect, we'd see blue edges around the clouds; once it was pasted in, that would be it. This way we can not only re-position the clouds to taste, but we can blur, expand, or contract the layer mask until the edges look perfect.

Both Color Range and luminance masking techniques come in handy here, because the sky is primarily blue, but has some lighter clouds, while the plane is mostly darker than the background.

Not only is our man at the airport, but he wants fancier tinted Mirror shades.

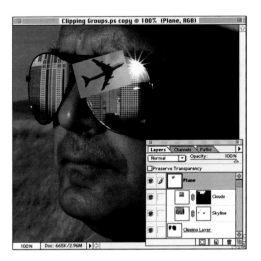

We also decide that our subject is hanging out near an urban airport; we paste an airplane into the image and add it to our rapidly growing clipping group.

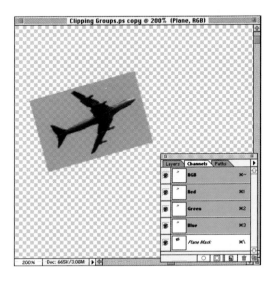

After positioning the airplane, we turn off all our other layers to get a better view and create a layer mask for the plane.

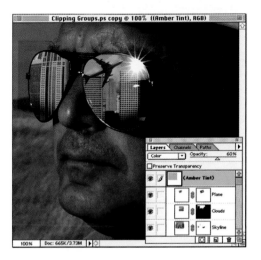

A new layer is created and a large swatch of amber color is added. This new Amber Tint layer is added to the clipping group, has its transfer mode changed to Color, and its Opacity lowered to 60%.

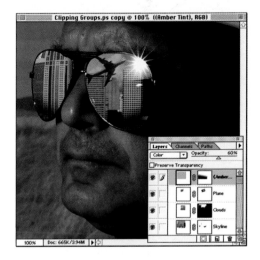

Sunglasses are often unevenly tinted, so we use the Add Layer Mask command and create a simple black-to-white vertical gradient to lessen the tint in the lower half of the lenses. The result is then added to the layer group. Practical *and* stylish.

For a final touch of realism, we enhance the apparent curvature of the lenses by adding some reflective highlights.

To reinforce the idea of having separate layers for darkening of the lenses and clipping the composited elements, watch what happens when we take some alternate approaches.

A little confused about how we used layer application modes in this example? Not to worry: There are heinous amounts of detail on that little subject later on.

Creating a new layer, some curved highlights are airbrushed along the tops of the glasses. This Core Highlight layer is set to the Screen transfer mode (for subtlety) and added to our clipping group. Our composite is complete.

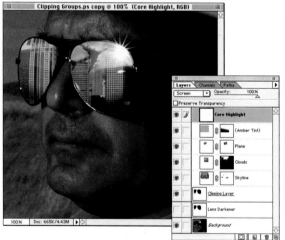

Our finished image, with the Lens Darkening layer turned off. Notice how the original tones of the lenses interfere with the new elements, specifically the horizon between the hills and the sky.

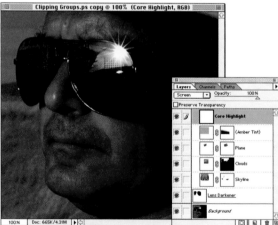

All the composited elements are now grouped with the Lens Darkening layer. It's identical to the Clipping Layer except for its transfer mode (Overlay instead of Screen), but not only does the original image now interfere with the composited elements, the layers above it are too dark.

Layer Transfer Modes

Most of the modes available in Calculations and Apply Image are available as options when working with layers. To minimize overlap, we recommend referring to Chapter 4, "Calculations," for the specific math of how these modes work. In this section, we focus on the layer-specific applications of these effects.

Along with descriptions of each layer mode, there will be up to five figures for each mode to help you visualize how each mode works. The figures are based on a number of standard image types to represent the full range of each mode's effects.

100% saturated hues, going to black, on top of an RGB image.

100% saturated hues, going to white, on top of an RGB image.

A black-to-white gradient on top of an RGB image.

An RGB image on top of a grayscale image.

A black-to-white gradient on top of a grayscale image.

These figures should give you a comprehensive understanding of how each transfer mode affects hue, saturation, and brightness.

Normal

Normal applies the layer exactly how you see it, with no special effects. The obvious choice if you're dealing with straight compositing.

Dissolve

Dissolve processes layers through a scattering effect, based on a feathered version of the new layer's transparency mask; this is one option not available in Calculations. The Dissolve effect is based on transparency; groups of pixels with low opacities are dissolved more than pixels with high transparencies. Layers whose pixels are all 100% opaque aren't affected by Dissolve.

This means that layers with anti-aliased or feathered edges will, therefore, have the Dissolve effect applied to the edges of that layer, based on how soft the layer's edge is.

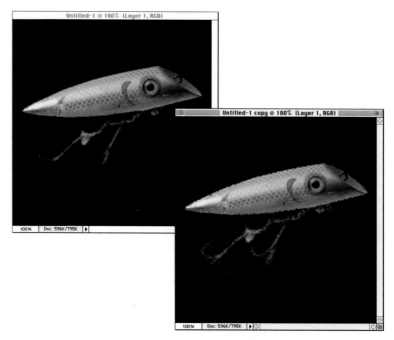

The soft edges of this layer receive more of the Dissolve effect to the foreground element
than the relatively sharp edges.

We still wish that we could control the dissolve effect itself, or at least anti-alias the effect (without blurring the layer with filters). Until then, this mode is too much of a brute force technique to be useful on a daily basis.

Multiply

A layer set to Multiply mode quite literally multiplies its pixel brightness values with those below it, significantly darkening layers beneath it. This result is then divided by the maximum range of brightness values to prevent large areas from being clipped to solid black.

Layer masks can be used to restrict where the dark tones are being applied on the underlying layers, as can the Opacity level of the layer itself. The added benefit of this technique is that you aren't making actual changes to the original image's pixel values.

Restoring color and tonal density to an overexposed (light) image is very easy using Multiply layer mode. By multiplying a grayscale or RGB layer by an exact copy of itself, it's easy to build up both tonal and color density in the areas where it's most needed. Try copying an overexposed image to a separate layer and specifying Multiply as the application mode. Layer masks can be used to restrict where the dark tones are being applied on the underlying layers, as can the Opacity level of the layer itself. The added benefit of this technique is that you aren't making actual changes to the original image's pixel values. You can stack the image more than once and try changing the opacity of the foreground layers to adjust the amount of density buildup.

Screen

Screen adds together the values of two layers, constraining the results to the maximum brightness of either layer.

As with Calculations, screening a layer by itself builds up brightness in the areas most needed, the opposite result of using Multiply to build dark densities. Try copying an underexposed image to a separate layer and specifying

Screen as the application mode. Changing the opacity of the foreground layers adjusts the amount of brightness buildup. For an increased effect, stack a screened layer more than once.

Overlay

For layers set to Overlay mode, light areas in the upper layer are screened onto the bottom layer, and dark areas in the upper layer are multiplied to dark underlying areas. As brightness values in the upper layer reach 50% gray, the screening and multiplication effects lessen. Flat 50% gray has no effect on the underlying layer.

A good way to visualize how Overlay works is to create a new layer over an image, fill that new layer with exactly 50% gray, and set its transfer mode to Overlay. It will appear as if the new layer has disappeared. Next, fill the layer with a black-to-white horizontal linear gradient. The areas under the lighter end of the gradient will look like they're being screened, the areas closer to the black area of the gradient will look like they're being multiplied, and the regions near the gray mid-tones will have very little effect applied to them.

Overlaying an image on top of itself can be used to both increase contrast and color intensity, but the effect can be pretty heavy-handed; keep your mouse over the Opacity slider to adjust the effect. This also is a good way to lay down textures onto a neutral-tone background without having the increased brightness associated with Screen.

Soft Light

Soft Light's selective lightening and darkening is great for painting exposure changes onto an image. Painting black or white (some brush transparency helps) onto an empty Soft Light layer looks like dodging and burning, with the additional control over the opacity of the effect using a layer mask or the Layer's Opacity slider. 50% gray in the upper layer has no effect on the underlying layer.

Hard Light

Hard Light, like Overlay, multiplies dark areas and screens light areas. These operations, however, are based on the color or tone in the Hard Light layer, rather than underlying layers. Unlike Soft Light, painting black or white into a Hard Light layer results in solid black or white. Whereas a Hard Light layer has values approaching black and approaching white, it overpowers the tones beneath it. Where the Hard Light layer contains primarily mid-tone grays, its effect is minimal; in fact, true 50% gray has no visible effect, like the Overlay mode.

The basic visual effect of Hard Light is easy to understand in a grayscale layered document. Where a Hard Light layer has values approaching black and approaching white, it overpowers the tones beneath it. Where the Hard Light layer contains primarily mid-tone grays, its effect is minimal; in fact, true 50% gray has no visible effect, like the Overlay mode.

Placing a duplicate layer over its original and using the Hard Light mode increases the image's contrast. The result is very similar to the Overlay mode, but the darkest and lightest tones are more overpowering.

Darken

Unlike Multiply, Darken (the Layer equivalent of Darker) can't be used to darken an overexposed image. It compares overlapping pixels and outputs the darkest tone, so identical layers applied using Darken have no visible effect. Darken can be used to reduce the contrast of an image (replacing the lightest values in the underlying layer with the darkest values in the Darken layer), but this is better handled by commands like Curves and Levels. Darken is sometimes used to composite dark text onto a midtone or light background texture.

Lighten

Lighten is the opposite of darken in both math and visual look.

Difference

The Difference mode visualizes the difference between two pixels' values. The greater the difference in hue and brightness, the brighter the Difference mode result will be; the Difference between pure white and black will be shown as white. If two pixels have the exact same value, the result is black.

One great use of Difference is when you're stitching together multiple scanned images into one large image. Imagine scanning a newspaper page (which is larger than most flatbed scanners) in multiple segments, then loading each segment into a new layer. By using the Difference command, you can establish exact registration between the overlapping layers of the scans—when two layers are in exact registration, the difference between the two is zero. The screen shows that difference as black.

Exclusion

Placing a duplicate layer over its original in Exclusion mode results in a color solarization effect. In an exclusion layer, black leaves the underlying image unaffected, while white inverts the underlying image, and grays provide an amount of blending between positive and negative based on brightness. Any color data in the Exclusion layer is inverted by the light areas of the underlying image and unaffected by the darker underlying regions.

Color Dodge

Color Dodge is similar to both Screen and Lighten in that its application tends to lighten the layers involved. Where the underlying layer is darker and less saturated than the upper layer, Color Dodge lightens and saturates those areas of the lower layer, replacing underlying hues with those of the upper layer. Absolute black in the upper layer has no effect on the tones or colors in the lower layer. The upper layer's colors tint the lower layer based on their saturation; grayscale layers have no hue or saturation effects on underlying layers. While many other modes focus on either brightness, saturation, or hue, Color Dodge has an effect on all three.

Color Burn

Color Burn is literally the opposite of Color Dodge: where the underlying layer is lighter and less saturated than the upper layer, Color Dodge darkens and saturates those areas of the bottom layer, replacing underlying hues with those of the top layer. The intensity of hue and saturation effects on the bottom layer are determined by the saturation values of the upper layer. Areas of white in the top layer have no effect on the bottom layer.

Color Burn could potentially be used to bring back contrast into washed out images (by duplicating an image layer and applying the duplicate through Color Dodge), but only if the image was extremely light and unsaturated. For example, an image that has a darkest tone of 50% gray is a great candidate for using Color Burn to bring back contrast (and Color Burn's much more effective than using Multiply in this example). But if your images are that washed out, re-shooting or re-scanning your subject matter might be better.

Combining Color Burn (in very sparing amounts) with Multiply when restoring tone and saturation to an image can yield very pleasant results.

Hue

Hue is the actual color tonality of a color value. This mode leaves the brightness and saturation alone, merely changing the color value. Hue is good mode for tinting, one that produces reasonably-saturated colors.

Saturation

Saturation is color intensity, or purity. The Saturation of an underlying layer is replaced by the Saturation of the upper layer. More saturation results in richer color, less saturation yields pastel colors, and a lack of saturation in a color image leaves only grayscale values. This is good for varying levels of saturation control, but using a Hue/Saturation adjustment layer gives you the same control (in addition to hue and brightness manipulation).

Color

Color is a combination of hue and saturation. When using this mode, the brightness values (details) of an underlying image are retained, while the hue and saturation of the overlaid element is transferred to the background. One of the preferred modes for tinting images, Color is more heavy-handed than Hue, creating super-saturated colors.

   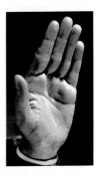

Luminosity

Luminosity changes the brightness/detail values of underlying images, with the underlying layer's the hue and saturation (or color, as in the previous entry) retained.

Using Application Modes and Layer Masking

Application modes are well-known for their capability to create special effects between two layers, but their real-world compositing uses aren't as commonly detailed. This image shows some of the more common uses of layer application modes in a photographic composite. This section uses many of the layer transparency and masking techniques that we covered earlier.

Application modes allow both subtle and obvious interactions between layers, as seen in this composite.

The image began as only two layers: the background layer, filled with a red-to-black horizontal gradient, and the model, already masked, duplicated, and placed into the new document.

The beginning of the composite: the background layer and the model. Both use the Normal application mode, because each layer ultimately needs to be totally visible.

A photograph of underbrush is added in the background for some texture. It needs to be visible, but not overpowering: It's the background, after all. Multiply and Overlay are good candidates, but Soft Light is chosen for subtlety.

Multiply suppresses the light areas of the texture, but makes the background too dark. Overlay screens the lighter areas of the texture with the background, making the texture a little too pronounced. Soft Light introduces enough variation in the background to be interesting without being distracting.

The skull composite uses three features to complete its look: reduced opacity, a clipping group, and a layer mask.

The skull is now composited on top of the model's cloak. It is grouped with the Model layer and dropped in Opacity; because this gives the desired effect, its application mode is set to Normal. For realism, a mask is made for the hands and is saved as a layer mask.

Masked and duplicated from a separate file, the wings are added next, underneath the model layer.

The light on the model seems to be coming from the front, underneath his face. A drop shadow behind the model would probably look natural and improve the edge definition of the model's cloak. The model layer is duplicated, placed between the original model layer and the wing layer, filled with black (making sure that Preserve Transparency is checked when the fill is activated), and then blurred. It is then grouped with the wings layer to make sure that the drop shadow doesn't project onto the background.

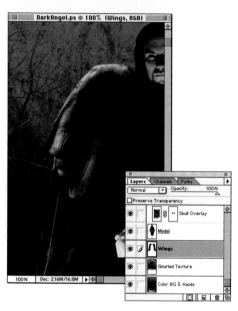

After color-correcting the wings to match the rest of this image, a few enhancements are needed to make them look better. They look a little too smooth in some areas, and the edges between the wings and the model's cloak lack contrast.

A new layer is then created to roughen the wings a little to make them match the somewhat grainy surroundings. It is filled with 50% gray, and has a small amount of Noise added to it. It's also grouped with the drop shadow and wing layers. Finally, the noise layer's mode is set to Overlay. Because 50% gray is not composited when Overlay is used, only the darker and lighter noise elements appear on the wings, simulating film grain.

For a final supernatural touch, we'll add a glow around the model, which surrounds both the figure and the wings.

The new layer is then filled with orange and blurred.

Other Layer Features

We've covered a lot of ground in our discussion of layers and their associated features. However, there are still a few options available to the layer power-user that aren't directly related to layer transparency, masking, or compositing. These additional features and techniques will help you get the most out of Photoshop's layers feature.

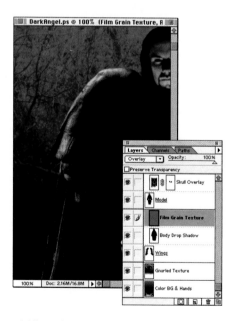

Adding a drop shadow and some artificial grain artifacts helps integrate the wings into the composite.

With the new layer selected, the Merge Visible command is invoked by holding down the Option key.

The glow is based upon the model and the wings. Only those two layers are made visible, and a new layer is created.

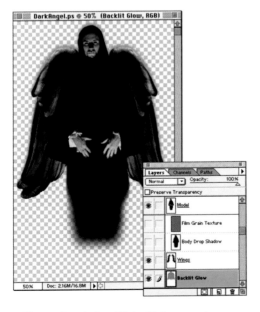

The new layer is then filled with the merged contents of the model and wing layers.

The final composite, with its component layers.

Merging Layers

You can combine multiple layers into one by merging them together. This can be crucial if you're running out of RAM, operating with limited disk space, or need to apply a Photoshop filter to multiple layers.

● When using the Merge Layers command, make sure that the eye icon is turned on for the layers to be merged. Layers that are to be kept intact should be invisible (eye icon not displayed).

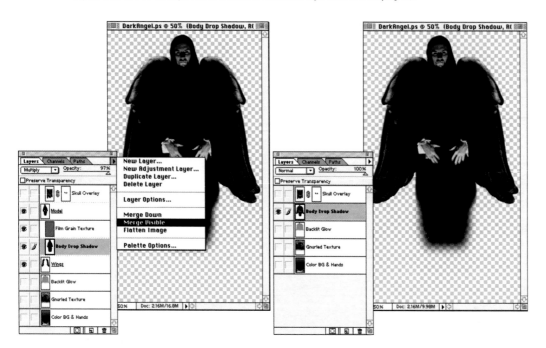

The left-hand image shows the layers palette with multiple layers—some turned on (visible), some turned off (invisible). The right-hand image, although it looks identical to the left-hand image, has had the visible layers merged into one single layer; the absence of non-visible layers is quite noticeable in the Layers palette. Only layers that are visible are factored into any Merge operation. Layers that are set to be invisible are not taken into account when merging.

● Layers with layer masks can be merged. The layer masks are processed through their respective layers before the merge is processed between the visible layers.

 Tip: In Photoshop 3.X, layers with layer masks couldn't be merged without first explicitly processing the layer mask with the respective layer. If you're still using this version of Photoshop, make sure to apply the layer masks to the layers by selecting the Remove layer mask command and choosing to apply the mask to the layer. Then proceed with the Merge.

● The Flatten Image command in the Layers pop-up merges all current layers of a document.

● The Duplicate, Calculations, and Apply Image commands (Image menu) have the ability to create merged versions of files directly, which is very useful when working with large files, among other things. There is more detail on these topics in Chapter 4.

The only current image file formats that support layers are Photoshop 3.0 and 4.0; Ray Dream Designer is slated for Photoshop Layers support as well. Fractal Design Painter (versions 4.0 and later) can also directly import Photoshop documents with layers. If you want to export Photoshop images made up of layers for use in another program (such as a page layout application or multimedia authoring program), it makes sense to duplicate a merged and flattened version of the layered document and save this version in the desired format and color space.

Sample Merged

Perhaps one of the most powerful options for specific tools, Sample Merge enables you to use certain tools in conjunction with layers capabilities to achieve a neat infinite-undo effect. We only wish that Sample Merged was available for more tools (like filters and color correction tools, among others).

The following are the tools that offer a Sample Merged option:

- Magic Wand
- Smudge
- Focus Tools (Blur and Sharpen)
- Aligned and non-aligned Clone and Clone Pattern

Sample Merged is activated by checking the option in the tool Options palette for any tool that offers it as an option.

If you choose the Sample Merged option from the preceding list of tools and make a layer—other than the background layer—active, your effect samples data from the *background* layer and is rendered into the *active* layer. If you turn off the eye icon on the background layer, you should notice that only the pixels that were modified or painted appear in the layer. The background layer remains unchanged.

> **Tip:** Like other commands that refer to and utilize merged data from more than a single layer at a time, the Sample Merged option uses only the currently displayed layers in the current document. Any layers that aren't visible aren't factored into the merge operation. There's something to keep in mind when using a defined pattern made up of a Photoshop document with multiple layers: all of the visible layers of the source-defined pattern are used when using the rubber stamp tool set to Pattern, which is why the Sample Merged checkbox is always on.

One of the more useful applications of Sample Merged is using the Rubber Stamp tool for cloning/retouching multiple layers onto a new layer. This is crucial in implementing a non-destructive approach to image restoration tasks. By placing retouched pixels on their own layer, the result is as follows:

- You can always retain the ability to revert back to the base image without using an Undo buffer.
- You can observe the amount of modification between the base image and your work by changing the transparency setting of the clone target layer.
- It's easy to show a client the results of extensive image restoration or retouching by turning the clone layer on and off, for an instant before-and-after effect. This is very effective in helping you explain why it took so long to get the job done right (and why you charged them so much money!).

Matting—Defringe

As discussed in Chapter 2, one of the most common pitfalls in compositing is the presence of matte lines, remnants of the background color found on the edges of the composited element. While good selection habits and efficient mask-making techniques often yield good edge results, matte lines sometimes go unnoticed until the selected foreground element is actually placed on top of its new background.

The Layer menu's Matting submenu is intended to fix the problems associated with edge fringes from different source backgrounds. Just as the Modify submenu alters the edges of selections, and as the Minimum and Maximum filters alter the edges of a mask, the Matting submenu holds tools for enhancing the edges of layers that have already been composited. Unlike the other methods of edge enhancement, however, the Matting commands actually alter the color content of your actual image data, and they should be used with caution.

The Defringe command (Layer>Matting>Defringe), an option that once resided in the Select menu, is a special layer function that helps deal with unruly matte lines. Defringing works by replacing a layer's edge color with colors sampled farther inside that layer, effectively pulling color from inside the layer towards its outer edges. The hue that's used to replace the discolored fringe is sampled from pixels inside the layer itself, a uniform distance from the layer's edges. This distance is entered in the Width text box in the Defringe dialog box.

Defringe replaces edge colors with colors from pixels inside the layers; how far inside the layer that replacement colors are chosen is determined by the Width parameter.

When compositing, the Defringe command is especially helpful when the overall hue or tone of a new background is significantly different from that against which a foreground element was shot. The flower example shows how defringing can help, even with a mask that's relatively accurate.

An orange flower from the overhead shot needs to be composited into the planter in the other image.

This orange flower has already been masked, primarily using Color Range; its mask is loaded as a selection, and the flower is copied.

While the fringe has been eliminated, a new problem has been introduced: a lack of anti-aliasing, because the layer's interior color has now been spread to the edge of the layer. It's especially noticeable in the lower-left and upper-right areas of the previous figure.

The edge of this layer needs to be anti-aliased against its new background. Blurring the edges of the layer is the best way to accomplish this, but we need a way to blur the edges without affecting the inner details of the layer. It's time to invoke the Border command.

The orange flower is pasted into the planter image. At a first glance, it doesn't look too bad...

...until we zoom in and see that the mask we made picked up some dark artifacts. These are a result of picking up the flower's anti-aliased edge against a dark background. The good news, however, is that this dark fringe is only about one pixel in width.

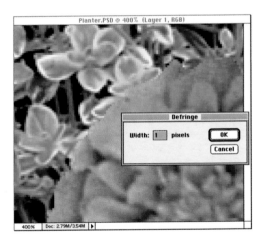

Using Defringe, the colors 1 pixel from the edge of the layer are pulled out to replace the dark fringe.

The transparency mask of the flower layer is loaded as a selection; the Border command is set to a value of 2.

A Gaussian Blur of 0.5 pixels does just the trick, creating an anti-aliased edge.

With some shadows and minimal brightness matching, our composite is in much better shape.

As with most edge-enhancement techniques, Defringing only takes you so far. If you find that you're Defringing at widths higher than 9 pixels, re-creating your mask might be in order. High Defringe settings result in strange color banding, and simply don't look right. It's quicker and easier to get a well-made mask in the creation phase than to do major surgery to the edges of a poorly-made mask.

 Tip: Always keep in mind the source resolution of your image—a high-res, 300-DPI image displays less of an effect when a Defringe of 10 pixels is applied to it, as compared to the same 10 pixel setting on a 72-DPI image. The basic rule of thumb: If you find yourself entering Defringe values greater than 9 pixels at any time (regardless of source image resolution), you'll probably be better off recreating your selection/mask with a tighter edge on the object you're trying to mask.

Matting—Remove Black/White Matte

A common requirement of many Photoshop tasks is to create a mask to isolate a foreground element that was shot against black or white, a common procedure in catalog-oriented photography. The Matting submenu has two additional one-shot commands to simplify matte line problems against solid white or black backgrounds: Remove Black Matte and Remove White Matte.

As their names imply, the Remove Matte commands remove slight matte lines that are predominately white or black, as a result of a foreground image being shot on a white or black background. Like Defringing, the Remove Matte commands are best used on images with one-pixel matte lines; matte lines wider than this simply are not fixed by Remove Black Matte or Remove White Matte.

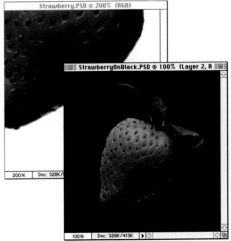

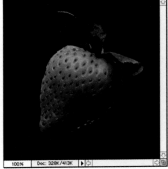

This strawberry, copied from a flat white background, has a slight halo of white around it.

With Remove White Matte, the white highlight is gone. However, much like Defringe, the edges of the object have been aliased by the edge enhancement.

Using the Border command to constrain a slight Gaussian Blur, as in the previous Defringe example, to re-introduce some anti-aliasing on its edges.

In real-world applications, we've found that these two Defringe options are often of little practical value. Try simply using the normal Defringe command if you find that the Remove While and Black Matte commands don't yield acceptable results.

Cool Layer Tricks

There are a multitude of hidden and/or subtle tricks we've run across using Layers. Here are some tips that will probably make your layer-management tasks less painful:

- With the Move tool selected, you can nudge a layer in any direction, one pixel at a time, by using the cursor keys on your keyboard. Hold down the Shift key while pressing the cursor keys, and you'll nudge the selection 10 pixels at a time.

- Pressing Option while clicking on a layer's eye icon makes that layer the only visible one (all other layers turn invisible)—sort of a quick solo option for the selected layer, or a mute option for all other layers. Doing so again makes all the other layers visible again.

- Pressing Option while clicking on a layer mask icon (in the Layers palette) makes the layer mask visible on screen, enabling you to directly paint into the layer mask.

- Pressing Option while positioning the cursor directly over the lines that separate layers changes the cursor and enables you to turn grouping on and off without opening each individual layer options dialog box or using the Layer>Group with Previous command.

- Pressing Option while clicking the new layer icon (at the bottom of the Layers palette) invokes the New Layer dialog box. Note that this is the opposite of how Option often defeats the invocation of dialog boxes for other commands, like Duplicate.

- Holding down the Option key while choosing the Merge Layers command (in the Layers menu) produces a new merged layer while leaving the original visible layers intact. The merged contents of this operation are put into the currently-active layer (as long as it's visible), so it's best to create a new, empty layer before trying this trick. (Photoshop used to *automatically* create a new layer in version 3.0; we'll hope that Adobe reintroduces this feature in the next version of Photoshop.)

- Pressing Shift while clicking a layer mask icon turns the layer mask off (while retaining it for later use; the mask *is not* deleted).

- Double-clicking a floating selection turns that selection into a new layer; Option-double-clicking creates a new layer without invoking the New Layer dialog box.

- Any time you have an active selection defined anywhere in a document, you can save it directly into a layer mask. Choose Save Selection and look at the top option in the Destination Channel pop-up. The currently selected layer appears as an option, and a new layer mask is created if there isn't one already defined for the layer.

- Layers can be copied between documents using Photoshop's new drag-and-drop technology. Simply draw an active layer from one document onto the active area (not the Layers palette) of another document, and drop. This technique keeps the clipboard clear, which is very handy if you already have something in the clipboard and don't want to lose it when copying layers between documents. Holding down the Shift key while dragging-and-dropping automatically centers the layer in its destination document.

Layered Typography—
A Little Bit of Everything

Getting the most from layers takes some practice and slight rethinking of how you work. In the following example, we've created a fairly complex text effect using the flexibility of layers with Photoshop filters. This is an example you can follow and recreate on your own computer—grab your favorite typeface and hold on!

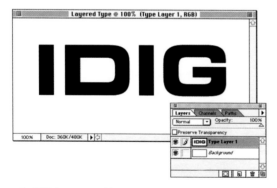

An RGB document with a white background is created, and a layer of type is created. Choose a typeface that has thick letter forms so you can better see the in-line effects to come.

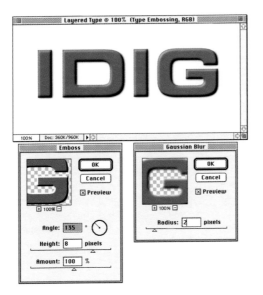

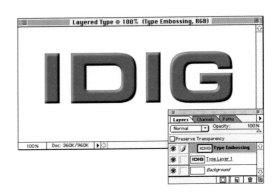

Our two type layers are grouped together; the Type Embossing layer covers Type Layer 1, but the blur applied to it is constrained by Type Layer 1.

The type layer is duplicated; the Emboss filter is applied with a light angle of 135°, a height of 8 pixels, and an amount of 100%. It is then blurred using a Gaussian Blur filter with a radius of 2 pixels.

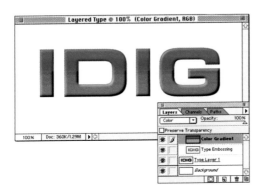

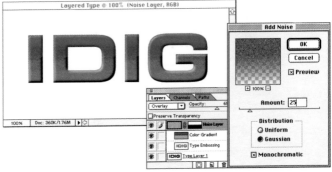

A new layer is created and grouped with the two type layers. A horizontal color gradient is applied and the layer's mode is set to Color.

Another new layer is added to the existing layer, filled with 50% gray and monochromatic Noise (Amount set to 25), and set to Overlay mode. A layer mask is added and filled with a simple horizontal white-to-black gradient so that the noise fades away at the bottom of the type. This layer is added to the layer group.

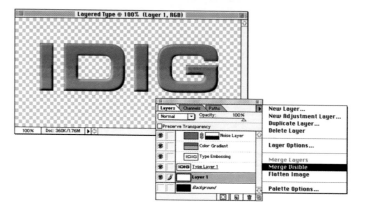

The background layer is inverted, making it black. A final layer is created and positioned just above the background layer. The new layer is selected, the background layer is made invisible, and the Merge Visible command is invoked by holding down the Option key.

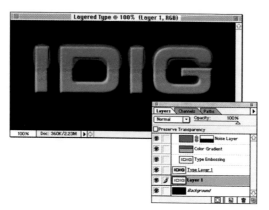

The visible layers are all merged into the new layer, which is then blurred to create a glow effect. Making the background layer visible again, our type effect is complete.

The Power & Performance Division of Newer Technology, Inc.

A little bit of layer savvy goes a long way; this logo is built almost entirely on layer effects.

More Layer-Based Type Effects

Producing type effects is a common task for anyone involved in graphic design, especially for multimedia and the World Wide Web. Sometimes a client will want a fully rendered 3D flying logo, but more often adding dimension and character to a 2D logo is all that's required. While many artists spend quality time and money searching out one-stop third-party filters to do their type effects, results that are just as stunning (and ultimately more controllable) can be created just by using layers.

This logo treatment was done by our company, IDIG, for a World Wide Web page. Unlike the previous example, only one filter—Gaussian Blur—was used in the creation of this image. All the visual effects seen here are a result of layers.

The first two layers that were created were the logo itself (named Type) and the corporate tag line beneath it (named Tag Line). The Type layer was then duplicated, filled with black, and had a 3-pixel Gaussian blur applied to it for a drop shadow. A blank layer also was created, the Type layer was activated as a selection, and a black stroke was applied.

The next step is to add an embossing effect to the Type layer. A very common approach to this is a short filter recipe. Duplicate the Type layer, change its application mode to Overlay so that the 50% gray areas will be transparent while the highlights and drop shadows will show, apply the Emboss filter, and then perhaps add some blurring to the Emboss layer.

There are some limitations to this approach. The Emboss filter approach does not, for example, allow the highlights and shadows to be moved independently of one another. Also, the highlights and shadows cannot have their opacities affected independently. These types of custom embossing effects are possible; however, if the embossing effect is simulated using independent layers (instead of just using the Emboss filter by itself on a single layer of data).

A new layer is created and grouped with the Type layer. The Type layer is activated as a selection, feathered by 3 pixels, then inverted. This selection is then filled with black. Dropping the selection, the Move tool is selected and the keyboard arrow keys are used to nudge the new layer (named Emboss, Shadow) up and to the left.

The Emboss, Shadow layer is duplicated and inverted using the Image>Adjust>Invert command. It is then nudged down and to the right, creating the highlighted edge of our emboss effect. It is named Emboss, Highlight. These two embossing layers can now have their opacity, position, or even amount of blurring independently controlled.

For some added visual spice, we'll add some layers to give the type a metallic appearance without obscuring the basic color scheme (often important to clients with specific corporate colors).

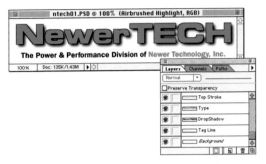

The basic elements of the type treatment; very flat, but we've only just begun...

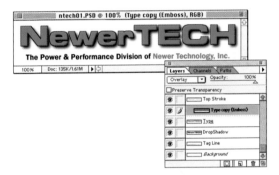

This is the result of using the Emboss and Gaussian Blur filters to add dimension to this text. As you'll see later, this approach isn't very flexible.

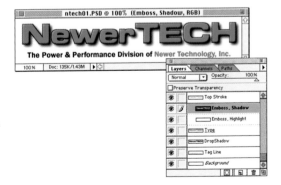

This highlight portion completes the effect. This approach enables independent control over the light and dark areas of the embossing effect.

The Chrome Gradient layer, to add some reflective highlights to the logo.

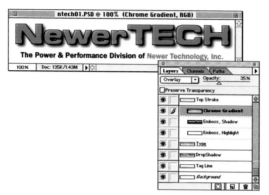

With the addition of both shadow and reflective lighting, this logo is starting to look much more dynamic.

A basic chrome lighting pattern is easy to do. A new layer is created and added to the Type layer group. The oval selection marquee tool is used to define a selection, starting in the upper-left corner and going about halfway down the image. This selection is then inverted and filled with a black-to-white horizontal gradient.

The Chrome Gradient layer's opacity is reduced to 35% and its application mode is set to Overlay, so the layer only accentuates tonality without replacing hue or reducing saturation.

We'll also include an inner ridge effect to further reduce the flatness of the letters. The result looks like the letters in the Type layer have a raised outer lip. We want the ridges inside the letter to appear near the edges of the embossing layers. In order to define that area, we'll use the embossing layers as the basis for a selection.

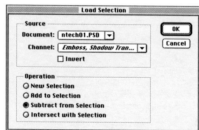

The Emboss, Shadow layer's transparency is subtracted from the existing selection.

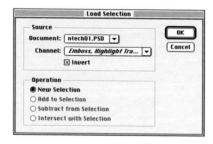

The Emboss, Highlight layer is activated as a selection and then inverted.

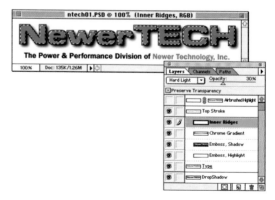

The resulting selection is now perfectly (and literally) defined by the edges of the embossing layers.

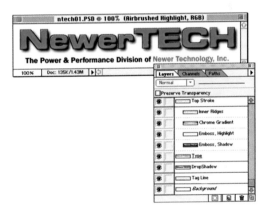

Now that we have a selection, let's define a highlight. The selection area is stroked with white, with a thickness of one pixel. This layer is re-named Inner Ridges.

While this produces a highlight inside the letters, it isn't realistic. If the letters have a lip around their edges, and the light is coming from the upper-left corner (as the embossing and drop shadow would indicate), the upper-left edges of the lip should be casting a shadow while the lower-right edges of the lip will be highlighted.

This highlight isn't perfect, but using layer transparencies as a selection has helped get in just the right place.

The Emboss, Highlight layer's transparency is once again loaded as a selection. Making sure a selection tool is selected, the keyboard arrow keys are used to nudge the selection over the top and left portions of the Inner Ridges layer. The Inner Ridges layer is then inverted, changing the white highlights to black shadows.

The Inner Ridge layer is now dropped to 35% Opacity (for subtlety) and has its application mode changed to Hard Light. Now only the darkest and lightest tones punch through.

Once again, layer transparencies come to the rescue. The result: our much-improved inner ridge effect.

For a final touch, some subtle highlights on the upper-left corners of the letters might add a little more dramatic flair. Painting this effect by hand will be quick and easy—but we want the effect to be seen only where the embossing highlights are located. Creating a new layer for our final highlight effect (naming it Airbrushed Highlight), we activate the Emboss, Highlight layer as a selection and save it as the Airbrushed Highlight layer's mask.

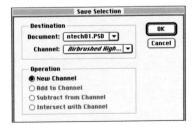

Making a layer mask for this layer enables quick and loose painting without worrying about obscuring underlying edges.

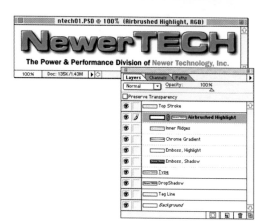

It's not a one-stop, filter-based solution to embossing, but this multi-layer approach is more versatile and affords greater creative control.

The preliminary tree texture, created by filling and filtering a rasterized Illustrator outline file.

After a little airbrushing with solid white, our image is complete. If the client wishes any changes to any aspect of this type treatment, every element can be edited separately from any other element.

Layer-Based Foliage

Making realistic tree foliage is an interesting challenge; while many people fudge it, abstracting foliage and simulating its patterns, sometimes more attention to detail is required. This example illustrates how to use layers to produce both detail and depth.

The first step is to create a sketch of the scene. The outline of the shapes in the scene were made using Adobe Illustrator. Once the shapes were finished, they were copied into the clipboard and pasted into a layer within Adobe Photoshop. A new layer was created and filled in with color; a combination of the Add Noise and Mosaic Tiles filters achieved the desired texture of tree bark. Using the Airbrush tool, various sizes of shadows were added to the tree and lines were cut into the back, adding realism to the texture.

Now comes the challenge of creating the leaves. In a new file, a series of shapes are created to form leaf clusters.

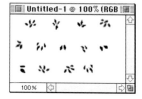

These leaf clusters, made in a separate file, are going to be used as brush templates.

Each of these various shapes is selected with the Rectangle selection tool, and the Define Brush command is chosen from the Brushes palette to turn them into brush shapes.

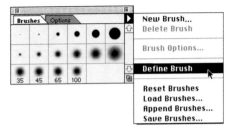

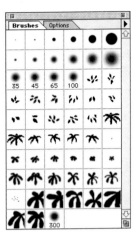

These brush strokes are used to define different custom brushes for the foliage...

...that then appears in the Brushes palette.

With the Paintbrush tool and the various leaf cluster shapes, the leaves were added to the trees.

Using various shades of orange and different Opacity settings, additional leaves were created to be the leaves in front that seem to be illuminated by the (hidden) street-level light source below. The same techniques were then used to create the bushes and all the other trees visible throughout the image.

The primary light source in the image is a street light, visible behind the foliage on the left. In the Background layer the gradient of blue is applied with the Gradient tool. The light source is created by using the Airbrush with different sizes and various shades of orange and white.

First, using black, a layer of leaves is created to serve as the overall shape. As more detail is added, this layer will also represent the leaves in shadow.

Depth is built up in the foliage by using custom brushes and painting with increasing opacity and brighter colors.

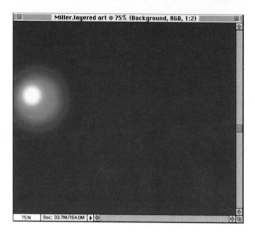

The light source is created using a radial gradient placed in the background layer (seen here with the leaves layer turned off).

The layer with the tree in front of the light source (just leaves, filled with black) is made visible by clicking the eye icon in the Layer's palette.

The tree foliage layer, in front of the light source, is duplicated and placed behind the original layer.

A layer mask is applied to this duplicate layer so that the light reflected on the leaves fades away the further the leaves are from the light source.

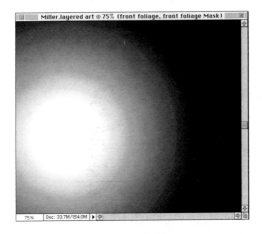

This radial gradient is used as a layer mask to simulate reflective falloff in the tree's foliage.

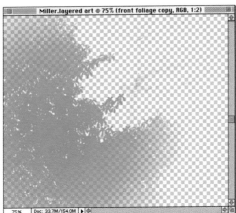

The duplicate layer is filled with orange.

This layer is then offset slightly so that it's visible just at the edges of the topmost black foliage layer.

This offset layer gives the impression of reflections of the light on the edges of the leaves.

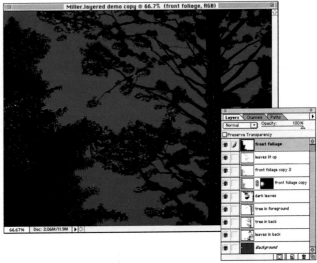

This is the finished image, with full lighting effects.

Our psychedelic eye, destined for a multimedia-oriented application.

Layers, Masks and Multimedia

This sample image was created as a background screen for the *Haight-Ashbury in the Sixties* CD-ROM. Our goal was to create a close-up of an eyeball, the surrounding skin of which had a psychedelic pattern. A QuickTime animation then plays within the iris of the eyeball. It's not only a great example of using layers to composite elements together, but also of using masks *outside* of Photoshop. Because we've already covered alpha channels making masks and layers, this is a great time to illustrate how they can all work together.

First, let's look at the layers in this image.

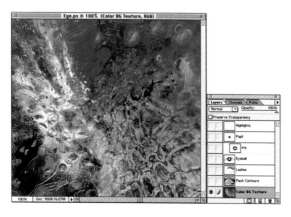

This color image is a composite of a number of different textures created with the advanced texture editor in MetaTools' KPT Bryce. It's going to act as the texture of the face surrounding the eye.

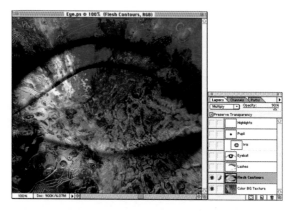

This layer is going to define the contours of the eye socket. It was hand-painted in grayscale and applied with the Multiply transfer mode; this simulates an eye socket illuminated from above, darkening the regions that would be in shadow.

Understanding how layer application modes work is essential to planning this kind of effect. If Overlay was used, it would screen the highlights of the Flesh Contours layer; unfortunately, instead of gently adding highlights where they were needed, a large portion of the lighter Color BG Texture layer would look overexposed, and the shadows would be less dramatic.

While the edges of the Iris layer are close to being perfect (not overlapping the skin outside the Eyeball layer), the edges were grouped with the eyeball layer to make sure that the iris is fully contained within the naturally visible area of the eyeball itself.

When time came to place the animation in the eyeball's iris, an immediate problem came to mind: QuickTime movies are inherently rectangular. A mask would have to be placed over the QuickTime animation, showing the movie through a white circle. The eye was first duplicated, flattened, and cropped down to the area just outside the iris. It was then imported as a layer into Adobe After Effects, as was the equally-psychedelic QuickTime animation.

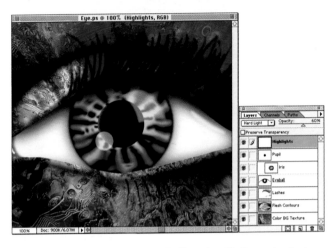

These hand-painted layers all use the Normal application mode, simply because we want them to be fully opaque. The Iris layer is grouped with the Eyeball. The Highlights layer adds white core highlights to the eyeball.

After Effects has the ability to use Bézier paths as masks; you can even interpolate the Bézier points over time and feather the Bézier mask itself. A circular path was created around the animated layer for a mask and placed over the still layer of the eye. Once the animation's mask was feathered to taste, the After Effects project was saved as a QuickTime movie: the psychedelic movie plays inside of the circular mask, surrounded by the eye background.

Now for the last step. Importing the new QuickTime movie and a flattened, uncropped version of the original eye into Macromedia Director (the main authoring tool used in the *Haight-Ashbury* project), the two were carefully aligned on Director's stage. Because the eye background of the QuickTime movie was a cropped version of the original eye, the edges match up perfectly. Beyond some slight compression artifacts, the result was just what was needed: the illusion of a round QuickTime movie, playing within the iris of the full-screen eye.

What's wrong with layers in Photoshop 4.0?

As great as Layers are, they're not perfect; there are a number of problems with Photoshop's implementation of the Layers paradigm. Some are minor, while others are serious problems in production environments.

- **No way to apply filters to multiple layers simultaneously.** Before the advent of adjustment layers, this used to be true of color correction as well.

- **No Add or Subtract application modes for layers.** What happened?

- **Not enough functions and tools have Sample Merged capability.**

- **Layer grouping options need to be more powerful.** Hierarchical or nested layer groups would be wonderful.

- **The fact that using the Paste command** *always* **creates a new layer is often just what you** *don't* **want to happen.** A classic example is copying the contents of a layer into an adjustment layer to create an adjustment layer mask. You can't paste directly into an adjustment layer, and regular layers cannot have their contents merged into adjustment layers.

CHAPTER 4

Calculations

Ever since the very first version of Photoshop, most digital artists go about their work in more or less the same way, using the many tools in the main tool palette and steering clear of the dreaded Calculations commands (which have more or less remained the same in all permutations and revisions of the program).

Calculations are considered the dark art of Photoshop, a deep, shadowy chunk of its functionality that few people *really* understand. Some artists we know (who consider themselves right-brained thinkers—more creative, less analytical) seem intimidated by the simple fact that Calculations, as its name implies, actually performs mathematical comparisons and calculations between two chunks of image data. Well, be intimidated no more. Calculations represents some of the most potent image processing methods that digital imaging can afford. Once you understand the basic methodology of Calculations, the math is relatively painless.

Comparison with Layer Functionality

In Photoshop 4.0, the addition of layers has expanded the opportunities to use interchannel image processing operations, or *CHOPS* (our acronym for **channel operations**), but the separate Calculation (Image>Calculations) and Apply Image (Image>Apply Image) submenus are still important for a variety of tasks not directly related to the use of layers. Much of what can be accomplished with Apply Image and Calculations can in fact be exactly duplicated with layers and the use of application modes (most of which are identical to the Calculations modes).

The drawback of this strategy is that adding a handful of layers to a large image slows down Photoshop rather significantly. Photoshop needs to internally re-composite every layer together every time a change is made to the image, and that costs RAM overhead (to composite the layers), disk space (to store the proper temporary files for display, Undo, and Revert), and time. Apply Image and Calculations, on the other hand, work via a direct internal data pipeline, which speeds up processing and keeps memory overhead lower, especially with print–resolution images. Previewing the results of an Apply Image or Calculations operation doesn't take up a significant amount of RAM. Seeing the results of layer interactions with application modes not only needs to be calculated and held in RAM, but any change in a layer's state also needs to be written to a temporary file on the local scratch disk. Experimenting with Apply Image and Calculations is the way to go, especially with larger image files.

The Channel Operations Commands

The commands relating to calculations activities are grouped together in the Image menu. You'll notice that these commands are separated from the rest of the contents of the Image menu (like everything else in Photoshop menus, related commands are segregated together). The commands are as follows:

- Duplicate
- Apply Image
- Calculations

These are the commands that unleash Photoshop's real power: the channel operations commands.

Duplicate

Duplicate is the fastest way to make a copy of an active document and all of its channels and layers (Duplicate is certainly faster than saving the file to disk with another name, then opening the newly saved file). Previous versions of Photoshop also used the Duplicate command to move selections and alpha channels around; this functionality is now basically handled by the Apply Image command (covered in more detail later in this chapter).

If a document has active layers, you can choose to duplicate a merged version of the layers (instead of the separate layer elements retained as such). Notice that the Duplicate dialog box contains a checkbox labeled Merged Layers Only. When checked, this option automatically merges *all visible layers* in the source document into a single-layer, flattened target image.

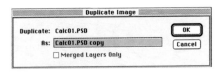

The Duplicate Image dialog box enables you to designate a new name for the results of the duplication operation. You can give the duplicate file any name you want by typing it directly into the text entry field.

Duplicate tip: Hold down the Option (ALT on the PC) key while selecting the Duplicate command to make the duplicate of the document and all of its active layers without invoking the Duplicate dialog box. The new document automatically has the word *copy* appended to the file name. The Merged Layers Only option cannot be invoked when using this shortcut. In order to create single-layer target documents from multiple layers, you need to explicitly invoke the Duplicate dialog box.

Apply Image and Calculations

These two menu items contain the bulk of the raw image processing prowess of Photoshop, and are different in very subtle and, frankly, confusing ways. The main function of these interchannel tools is to compare the pixels of two documents, layers, or channels, and create new pixels from the operation. These calculation modes are primarily based on the brightness levels found in an 8-bits-per-channel world.

Remember:

0 = black

128 = medium gray

255 = white

There was a time when the functionality of Calculations and Apply Image was integrated into a single Calculations command. This Apply Image/Calculations schism resulted in overlapping functionality and arbitrary limitations in the new Apply Image and Calculations commands. There is really no win, in terms of functionality or ease of use, to separating the original Calculations command, especially in light of the limitations that have been introduced into each of the resulting "features." If the relationship between these two commands has ever seemed a little strange, it is. Getting the most out of these powerful imaging tools just requires understanding both their similarities and differences.

There are some essential rules that are important in understanding how both Calculations and Apply Image work:

- These commands both require a minimum of two source images/channels/layers in order to work. In the case of Apply Image, the currently active document is automatically considered one of the sources.

- All potential source files must currently be opened into Photoshop. You cannot specify a file that's on a local hard drive but not already open in Photoshop.

- With either of these commands, both source images must be the same historical size and pixel resolution. When the Apply Image command is used, the Source pop-up menu only shows the currently open image documents that are the same size as the currently active document. Calculations behaves in the same fashion, even though you can choose two documents as sources that *are not* the currently active document (but are the same size as the currently active document).

For example, if you're working with a document that's 4×3 inches at 72 DPI, the *only* other image files you'll see available as sources are open documents that historical are exactly 4×3 inches at 72 DPI.

> The historical reason for the image size requirement of all calculations is related to the fact that Photoshop had its first production exposure at Industrial Light and Magic, where one of the two brothers who wrote the original version of the program, John Knoll, is a Visual Effects Supervisor. Originally, Photoshop was used to process multiple scanned film frames that were already perfectly registered (most of the time). This pre-registration of the plates needed to be maintained during subsequent image processing using Calculations (remember, this is in the days before Photoshop had any type of layer functionality). For this reason, Calculations wants images of the exact same physical dimensions.

- If the source documents have multiple layers, you can choose to process either specific layers (a single layer at a time) or a merged version of all of the visible layers of the source documents.

> As in all other instances of the Merged option, only currently visible layers are factored in the merge operation.

- Apply Image and Calculations can be used to process documents that are in different color spaces. For example, you can process the individual channels of an RGB document with specific channels of a CMYK file, as long as file sizes and resolutions match up.

 Tip: Bitmapped and Indexed Color modes are the two exceptions to the preceding feature. When images are in these two color modes, they cannot be used, in any way, with Calculations.

There is one other specific limitation of calculations between images with different color modes. The Apply Image command, as you'll see shortly, enables you to process the combined channels of an image (the combined RGB channels of an image in that mode, or the CMYK composite image of a pre-press file).

- Both Apply Image and Calculations can be used to move active selections between documents. If you have a selection defined, and open either of these commands, you'll find that Selection is an available option for the Channel of either source.

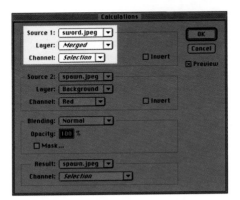

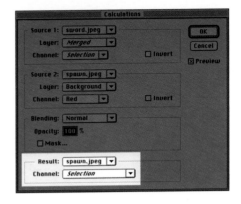

If you have an active selection, and choose the Calculations command, you'll find that a new option in the Channels pop-up menu is Selection, enabling you to move the active selection to another document.

If you want to move this selection to another document as a selection, choose Selection as the channel for the Result.

Try playing with the Opacity settings when using these commands. This enables you to try out percentages of an effect without further post-processing.

Apply Image

The Apply Image command is specifically used to process the currently active document/channels/layers as a source (which is designated as the *Target* in the Apply Image dialog box) with another document, and enables you to process multi-channel data (RGB as the primary example) with other discrete channels or multi-channel data in other source documents.

> ### Authors' Note
>
> For some strange reason known only to Adobe, the Apply Image command is also largely different from the Calculations commands in that it enables you to process the full RGB composite of an image; as we'll see later in this chapter, Calculations *does not* allow you to process RGB simultaneously, a seemingly arbitrary (and completely frustrating) limitation.

When you open the Apply Image command (Image>Apply Image), you are presented with a single dialog box.

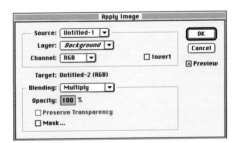

The Apply Image dialog box enables you to specify a document to process with the currently active document and the desired calculation and masking modes.

Let's examine each parameter:

- **Source:** This is the document to be processed with the document that was active when the Apply Image command was invoked. As expected, it must have the same resolution and size as the active document (also called the Target elsewhere in the Apply Image dialog box).

- **Layer:** This enables you to specify which layers of the Source document are to be used. The Merged option uses a merged combination of all of the currently visible layers of the Source document.

- **Channel:** This is where you choose whether to process the overall composite of the channels (with RGB files, for instance, you can select the overall RGB data), individual color channels, and transparency masks (when individual layers are selected as the Target, you get the additional option of choosing the transparency mask for that layer).

- **Target:** This is the name of the currently active document, as well as the currently active channel or layer. If you invoke the Apply Image command with a specific channel or layer selected, you'll see the specifics in this field. This is the data that the Source will be processed with.

- **Blending:** The calculation/application/transfer/effect mode (yes, we've seen all of these terms used to describe these commands) used for the processing between the two sources.

- **Opacity:** This is the percentage of the Source document that's taken into account on the calculation process. By lowering this percentage, more of the original target document is mixed with the overall resulting effect.

- **Preserve Transparency:** If your selected Target layer has transparent pixels (such as type created on a layer within Photoshop), you have the ability to preserve the layer transparency in the overall resulting calculation.

- **Mask:** The overall results of the calculation can be masked through a grayscale channel to limit the operation to occur only within a specific region of the image. As expected, the channel can come from any open document with the same size and resolution. If you select a layer as the mask, you have the further option of choosing a single color channel of the layer, the overall luminosity (expressed as the gray channel in the channel pop-up), or the transparency mask of the selected layer.

- **Invert:** This option, available for the Source and the Mask, is equivalent to applying the Invert command (Image>Adjust>Invert) to the channel/image/layer before invoking the Apply Image command. This is especially useful when using alpha channels as sources, enabling you to flip the polarity of the mask without leaving the Apply Image dialog box.

- **Preview:** When this option is checked, the results of the currently specified calculation are displayed in the currently active document area (which, in effect, acts as a preview proxy).

Tip: The actual data in the document is not overwritten during a preview; but be careful about clicking the OK button, because if you do, the results will *definitely* overwrite the original information in the document.

The Apply Image mode is different from Calculations in several ways, but perhaps the most important is that Apply Image supports composite image mode operations, whereas Calculations can only process a single pair of component channels at a time. With Apply Image, if you are currently working with an RGB or other multi-channel document and the composite view of the image is active, you'll have the option of processing all three channels simultaneously. (In the case of RGB, the composite view would be all three channels of red, green, and blue that are currently active, displaying the full color image.) This is especially useful for operations that involve processing an entire image with itself (see the "Building Density Using Calculations" example using the Multiply mode later in this chapter).

In its default state, the results of the Apply Image are always sent to the currently selected layer (or channel) of the source document.

The most Important Apply Image Tip in the known universe: Holding down the Option key while opening the Apply Image command provides a new option at the bottom of the dialog box, a pop-up menu labeled Result. This enables you to direct the results of the Apply Image to a new channel, document, selection, and more.

Now for the bad news: This hidden command also has an accompanying hidden bug. If you have an active selection region in your document, holding down the Option key won't give you the Result and Destination options. If there's an active selection in the document before you invoke the Apply Image command, you simply can't designate a destination other than the currently selected channel/layer. This is, in the authors' opinions, the worst bug currently in Photoshop. And, to add insult to injury, this bug also existed in Photoshop 3.0.

This becomes especially problematic if you want to use Apply Image to move selections between images. In this case, you'll have to make sure that the currently active target document is the one you want to receive the selection before you invoke the Apply Image command.

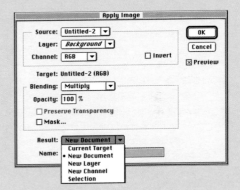

The alternate Apply Image command, invoked by holding down the Option key, enables results to be saved into different destinations.

Calculations

The Calculations command is specifically designed to process multiple *single* channels of any open documents, saving with the results saved in either the current document or a new document. Calculations enables you to control almost every aspect of your interchannel operation, and can even utilize active selection regions as if they were stored as alpha channels (figuring that unselected pixels are black, that selected pixels are white, and using grays to represent varying levels of feathering).

One of the main drawbacks of Calculations is that you can't specify the color composite channels as a source, which is easily manageable with Apply image. This restricts the use of Calculations to processing pairs of single channel data.

The relationship between the options within the Calculations dialog box are similar to the parameters found in Apply Image. We'll go step-by-step and follow the path of data through the Calculations process, starting with the dialog box's individual parameters.

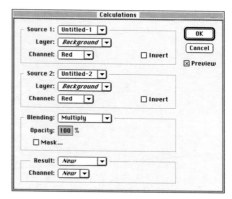

The Calculations dialog box has four basic elements: two source files, a mask through which the calculation will be applied, and a target for the result.

- **Source 1 and Source 2.** Calculations can process two channels at a time. These channels can be in the same document or different documents, and either can be a component color channel or an alpha channel. In a multi-layered document, the color channel or transparency of a specific layer (or the merged image) can be used as a source. If you have an active selection, it can be used as a Source as well: Calculations treats it as an alpha channel, as if the selected pixels were white and the unselected pixels were black. Source 1 is essentially applied *on top* of Source 2.

- **Blending.** Blending has three parameters: application mode, Opacity, and Mask. The *application modes* are discussed in detail in the following pages. *Opacity* indicates the opacity of the Source 1 channel. *Mask* uses a channel (color or alpha) as a mask for the Source 1 channel, *not* for masking the Calculations result onto a pre-existing Result channel. In this way, it behaves like a layer mask, masking part of Source 1 so that portions of Source 2 remain unaffected.

- **Result and Channel.** This is the single-channel (color or alpha) destination of the Calculations results; both the Result document and channel may be specified. In a multi-layer document, the result can be placed into a layer mask.

A Calculations operation, then, starts with Source 1 being processed with Source 2. This is modified by the application mode used and the opacity of the Source 1 channel. Source 1 is then applied through the mask (if any) onto Source 2, and the result is output to the Result destination.

A particularly strange Calculations feature/bug: If you hold down the Option key while invoking Calculations, you'll notice that the font used to display the dialog box is significantly smaller than the font normally used to display the dialog box—making the dialog box noticeably smaller on screen. This feature/bug isn't present in the Windows NT 4.0 version of Photoshop we use at IDIG. The ironic part of this is that the smaller display font is actually preferable all the time, and should be the default. Anyone from Adobe reading this?

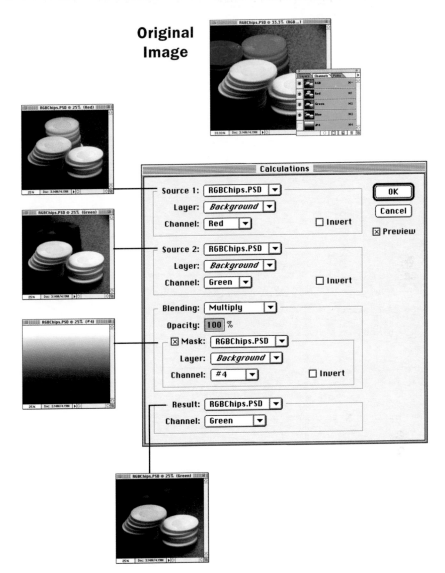

A representation of how the Calculations dialog box corresponds to an image's channels. In this example, the Red and Green channels are multiplied together through a mask, replacing the original Green channel with the Calculations result. The top part of the Green channel is now significantly darker.

Let's look at the previous Calculations example, but use Apply Image to get the same effect. The Target is fixed, based on your currently-active channel: to affect the green channel, for example, the green channel must be selected in the Channels palette (or by using the Command-2 key command). You must invoke Apply Image while holding down the Option key, of course, to get the option to specify a Result document and Channel destination. Otherwise, the Result overwrites your Target channel. The rest of the procedure is identical to that in the Calculations dialog box.

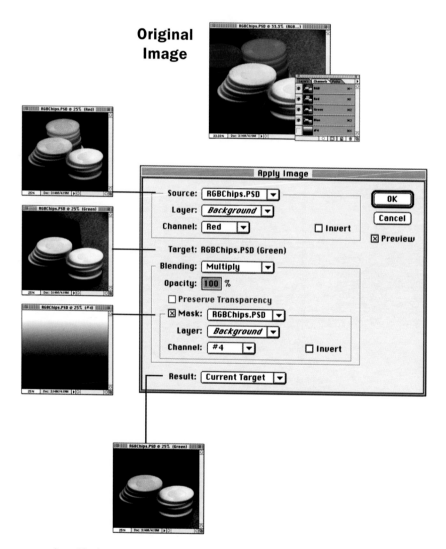

The Apply Image command, used in the same process of multiplying the Red channel onto the Green through an alpha channel mask. With a few quirky differences, Apply Image is very similar to Calculations.

Understanding the Math

Getting practical use out of the Calculations commands requires some background and understanding of the math behind the modes available in both layers and calculations. While some of the commands are obviously more useful than others, it's good to have an idea about how each one works.

Normal

Normal applies the image or channel exactly as you see it, with no special functionality. It simply replaces all the pixels in the target channel(s) with that of the source channel(s). The only parameter that changes the appearance of the composite is the source's opacity.

This mode was most useful in previous versions of Photoshop as a mechanism to move channels between documents. Photoshop 4.0's Duplicate Channel and Duplicate Layer commands, found in the Channels and Layers palette pop-up menus respectively, are arguably more convenient ways to move channels and layers between documents.

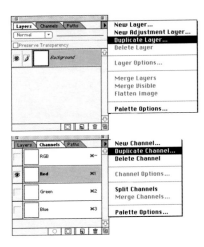

While the Normal mode can be used to transport channels directly from one document to another using Calculations, the Duplicate Channel and Duplicate Layers commands are simpler to use for such a basic operation.

Multiply

Multiply is one of the more useful interchannel application modes, and can be put to use in processing alpha channels together, as well as many other things.

The way to understand the basic functionality of the Multiply command is to try it out as its direct function: the same basic multiplication you learned in grade school. 2×2=4, right? Well, it gets a bit more involved as we dive deeper into Photoshop, but the basic idea is intact. Math is math!

So let's use the concept of simple multiplication using pixels as the bait. Most of the time, this multiplication involves grayscale images or alpha channels—but we'll start with something even more basic, a simple binary situation consisting of two values: pure black and white. First, visualize a one-bit image: white is designated as one, black is designated as zero. If two channels (or layers) with black and white pixels are multiplied together, it's pretty easy to predict the output values:

Black = 0

White = 1

Anything multiplied by White (1) = Anything

Anything multiplied by *Black* (0) = Black

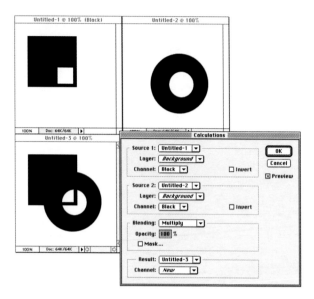

The top two shapes are being multiplied together and the result appears in the lower document. Notice that the shapes cut out of each image only appear where they are both white; any pixel overlapping a black pixel is multiplied by zero, making the resulting pixel black as well.

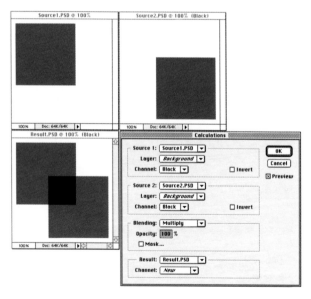

When composited using Multiply, these swatches of 50% gray are darkened to 75% gray where they overlap. The area where the swatches do not overlap is multiplied by white, so they're not darkened at all.

This gets more complex when you deal with grayscale images. Any grayscale pixel has a brightness value ranging from 0 to 255 (darker pixels, of course, have lower values). The Multiply mode compares the pixels of each source; if the pixels of the underlying source (Source 2) are equal to or lighter than the pixels in the upper source (Source 1), the lighter pixels in Source 2 are darkened as a result.

The straight math: The two pixels' brightness values are multiplied together, then divided by the maximum range of brightness values:

(*Pixel* Value A * Pixel Value B) / 256 = New Pixel Value

For example, two swatches of 50% gray (brightness value 128) multiplied together yield a swatch of 75% gray (brightness value 64):

$(128*128)/256=64.$

Because the initial multiplier is divided by the maximum brightness range, the mixture of dark gray values is gradual, making Multiply incredibly useful for combining masks with masking effects, such as laying a gradient down into a blurred-edge mask.

Another useful application of the Multiple mode is to automatically restore dark density to overexposed images.

Building Density Using Calculations

Unlike crystal-clear, perfectly balanced photographs, overexposed photos are *easy* to make, making them all too common in our daily imaging routine. Photoshop and other image editing programs are built specifically for fixing such overexposed images, but, like many other things in life, there's more than one way to do things.

Photoshop tools such as Levels, Curves, and Variations can certainly restore density and darken an image, but they affect an image globally. If you use masks and selections to limit your color corrections, that eats up time and inflates your file size, which also occurs if you start to use layers or adjustment layers.

As an alternative method of rebuilding poor tone and color density on an image quickly and interactively, we offer you the "Calculation method." We'll literally be multiplying an image by itself, increasing the image's density without using a single color correction command, selection region, adjustment layer, or clipboard procedure (in other words, no cutting, copying or pasting). You'll only need one overexposed image, one alpha channel, and just a little time.

Note that we'll need to use the Apply Image command, because Photoshop's Calculations can't process composite RGB channels.

In the original image, the darker regions of the image actually look fine; the colors are moderately saturated and the detail is all there. It's the bright areas that have very little detail and contrast, especially on the right side of the image. ("What verandah? What view? I want my money back!")

Because this is the case, even Calculations needs to have its effects limited to only the areas that need it. The next step is to derive a mask from the image, through which the calculation will be processed. This is where critical viewing and problem-solving skills are essential—analyzing images for potential masks.

The original, overexposed image.

The individual channels of the overexposed image.

Looking at the individual color channels, this image's high-contrast data actually lies in both the Red and Blue channels. The Red channel has the most pronounced contrast, but the Blue channel (quite free of dust, grain, and junk this time around) has robust tones over the areas we want to mask. We need to combine the two channels and get the best of both worlds.

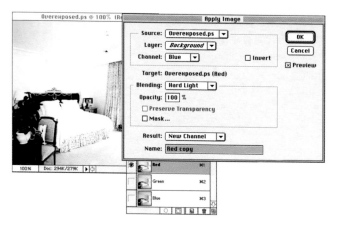

The Red channel is selected in the Channels palette. The Image>Apply Image command is invoked, holding down the Option key. With the Blue channel as the source and the Red channel as the target, the Hard Light blending mode is selected at 100% Opacity. The result goes into a new channel called Red copy.

The resulting channel is just what we need: Those dark areas are masked while the bright areas will be affected.

The Apply Image command, this time with the combined RGB channel selected in the Channels palette. The target and the source are the same (RGB), and are multiplied together at 100% opacity.

While the image's density is back, the darker areas are starting to get muddy. Notice the lack of color and detail in the headboard, the table, and the potted plant.

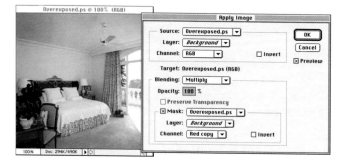

The Apply Image command, this time with the Mask box, is checked and the Red copy channel is selected as the mask.

Both detail and color have returned to the overexposed areas, but the darker regions of the image are masked from the effect, yielding a great overall balance of color and tone densities. Having control over the Opacity of the Apply Image command lets us adjust how much density is restored; in this particular image, however, 100% looks fantastic.

For complete control over color density with unlimited Undo capability, layers can be used in the same way. Background layers can be duplicated and multiplied on top of themselves, with layer masks determining the mask for the effect. This previous example, however, is a lot more RAM-friendly than doing the same thing with layers: your image size (on hard disk and in RAM) doubles every time you duplicate a Background layer, and grows even larger if you add layer masks to each duplicated layer!

The final image.

Screen

Screen is an incredibly useful command for combining color images and masks. Related to the Add command, Screen is much more intelligent (and, ultimately, more useful) for most applications.

Screen combines the values of two images/values, but constrains the results to not exceed the maximum brightness of either of the images/values. To understand this, let's get into Photoshop's 255 mindset (black is 0, white is the maximum value at 255) and visualize two grayscale images with black (0), white (255), and a 50% gray (127).

$$255-[((255-Source\ 1)(255-Source\ 2))/255] = New\ Value$$

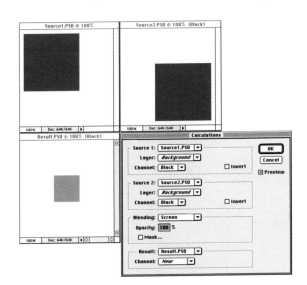

If you have a pair of overlapping soft edge masks, the best way to combine them is to use Screen; because Screen's equation can't exceed 255, the areas of combined light grays may burn out and have unwanted harsh edges where they overlap.

Our previous example, involving two image with overlapping 50% gray swatches, looks much different in Screen mode; the result is 75% gray where the two swatches overlap. The white areas still remain white.

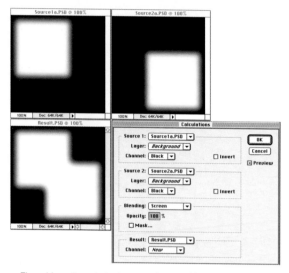

These blurred masks look great when combined using Screen, but their edges are still uniformly soft. And for comparison...

...this is the same result using the Lighter command. Notice, because only the lighter pixels of the two are composited, that the edge where the masks overlap becomes problematic.

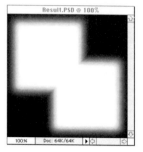

The other mode that's related to Screen, Add, produces different problems. Because Add doesn't constrain the result to the brightest of the two sources, the blurred edges are burned out by adding up to 255 (white) in the areas where middle grays overlap.

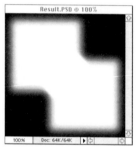

Another great application of Screen is the process of restoring reasonable brightness to an underexposed (dark) image. This, though, is often easier to control when used between the same image duplicated into a pair of layers, with the top layer set to Screen.

Overlay

An interesting combination of Multiply and Screen, the dark areas of Source 1 are multiplied onto Source 2, while the light areas of Source 1 are screened onto Source 2. Mid-tones have little effect—in fact, a channel filled with flat 50% gray appears to have no effect when applied with Overlay. The color of the background is mixed with the foreground image, based on the saturation of colors in Source 1.

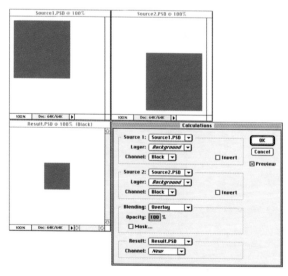

The two gray swatches appear as 50% gray where they overlap—having no appreciable effect on either original—but the white areas of each dominate where the swatches don't overlap.

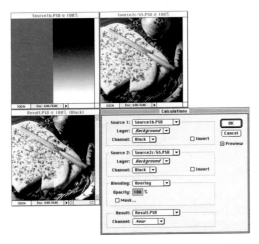

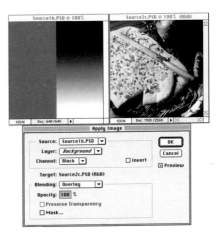

In this figure, the gray swatch in Source 1 has no effect on Source 2. The effect of the gradient, located on the right side of Source 1, is easily seen. The dark tones result in a Multiply effect and the light tones have a Screen effect.

Overlay's various effects behave almost exactly the same with color images as they do with grayscale images. Color shadows exhibit super-saturated colors, much like the Multiply mode.

Soft Light

Soft Light is similar to Overlay, except that its effects look closer to Lighter and Darker than Screen and Multiply. Generally speaking, if the foreground color or image is lighter, the results are also lighter. If the foreground is on the darker side, the results go towards dark, while neither situation ever results in pure black or white.

Soft Light can simulate dodging and burning by dynamically using layers or channels.

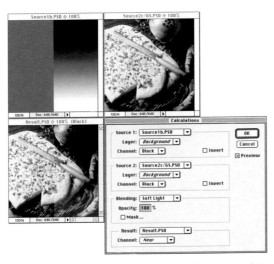

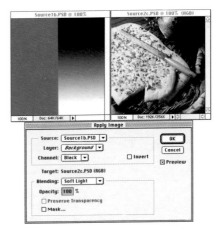

The extremes of highlight and shadows in Source 1 are darkening and lightening Source 2, respectively. This effect is more subtle as Hard Light and Overlay. 50% gray in Source 1 does not effect Source 2.

Unlike Overlay, Soft Light doesn't saturate color shadows; notice how only the brightness is primarily affected in this color example. Areas of highlight in Source 1, however, overexpose Source 2.

Hard Light

Hard Light is a harsher version of the effect achieved with Overlay; what Overlay is to Multiply and Screen, Hard Light is to Darken and Lighten. Unlike Overlay, however, dark foreground tones totally suppress lighter tones beneath, using the Darker mode, and light foreground tones override dark areas below, using Lighter. Similar to Overlay, however, mid-tone grays have no effect. Saturation also seems to have an effect on transparency of the composite; heavy saturation in the color values of the top layer seems to increase opacity of the layer.

For example, take an image (Image A) and apply an image (using Apply Image) that contains top-to-bottom, black-to-white gradient, using Hard Light mode (Image B). This results in totally black tones at the top of the image (Image B's shadows), totally white tones at the bottom (Image B's highlights), and very little change in the middle (Image A showing through), where the Hard Light image contains neutral tones.

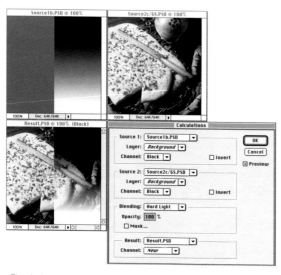

The darkest and lightest parts of the gradient in Source 1 total-ly overwhelms the tones of Source 2. As with many of the other modes, 50% gray in Source 1 has no effect.

The overwhelming effect of Hard Light is easily seen in color as well; here you can see how black and white are simply composited over Source 2, its Opacity dwindling as both shad-ows and highlights get closer to 50% gray.

This color image will serve as our Target image as we explore Color Dodge and Color Burn.

Color Dodge

Color Dodge has a superficial resemblance to both Screen and Lighten, but its operation is more complex. Where the underlying image (Source 2) is darker and less saturated than the upper image (Source 1), Color Dodge lightens and saturates those areas of Source 2, replacing underlying hues with those of Source 1. Absolute black in Source 1 has no effect on the tones or colors in Source 2. While many other modes focus on either brightness, saturation, or hue, Color Dodge operates on all three.

There's an interesting correlation between the Color Dodge mode and the Dodge tool in Photoshop's toolbox. The result of a flat 50% gray image and a color RGB image, applied with Color Mode at 100% Opacity (using either Apply Image or layers) is *identical*, as if you had used the Dodge tool set to Highlights, at 100% Opacity, over the entire image. It appears that Color Dodge and the Dodge tool use similar mathematics when re-assigning pixel values, hence the mode's name.

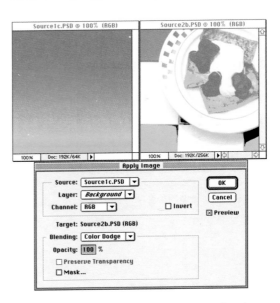

Using a black-to-white gradient for Source 1, Color Dodge's effect is easily seen on the color Target image. The upper potion of the Target image looks normal, but its contrast is significantly increased the brighter Source 1 gets.

Changing Source 1 to a color gradient imparts its color onto the Target image.

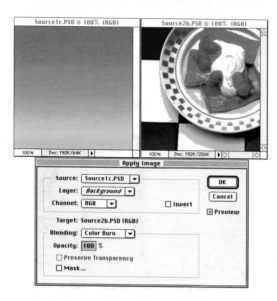

The red-to-yellow color gradient is drastically saturating and darkening the Target color image, replacing the hues of the Target with that of the Source.

Color Burn

Color Burn is literally the opposite of Color Dodge. Where the underlying image (Source 2) is lighter and less saturated than the upper image (Source 1), Color Dodge darkens and saturates those areas of Source 2, replacing underlying hues with those of Source 1. Areas of white in Source 1 have no effect on Source 2.

Color Burn has its own relationship to Photoshop's Burn tool. The result of a flat 50% gray image and a color RGB image, applied with Color Mode at 100% Opacity is the same as using the Burn tool set to Shadows at 100% Opacity over the entire image.

Darker

The Darker mode compares overlapping pixels and sets the darker of the two as output. It's not exactly the most finessed of the composite modes.

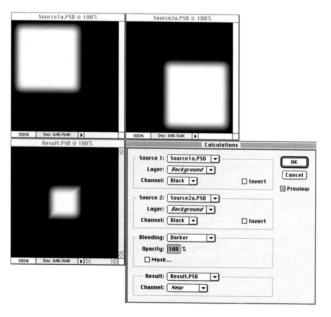

Simply showing the darkest pixels of the two combined Sources, you can see that Darker isn't very good at combining soft-edged masks.

Lighter

The Lighter mode compares overlapping pixels and sets the lighter one of the two as output.

When Lighter is applied to color images using Apply Image, background pixels (the Target) that are darker than foreground pixels (the Source) are both lightened and tinted to the foreground color values.

> Darker and Lighter are both essential for bluescreen and greenscreen work. Please refer to Chapter 5, "Bluescreen and Greenscreen Compositing," for more info!

Add

Add combines channels and adds up the results, always going towards white/brightness. If you were to add together a 50% gray (Brightness level 128) and a 25% gray (Brightness level 192), the results would peak out at white:

$$50\% \text{ Gray} = 128$$
$$25\% \text{ gray} = 192$$
$$128 + 192 = 320$$

Because there's no 320 white, the results are clipped at 255 (white). That's why you'll often seen blown-out, overexposed areas of white.

The Scale and Offset settings don't refer to size and pixels, as they do in other contexts. In Calculations, they are further variables in the Add equation. Scale is the number by which the added pixel values are divided, and can range from 1.0 to 2.0. A Scale of 1, for example, doesn't affect the result at all; any number divided by one remains unchanged. A Scale of 2 results in the average of the two compared pixel values (adding the values and dividing by 2). The Offset parameter is a number added after the

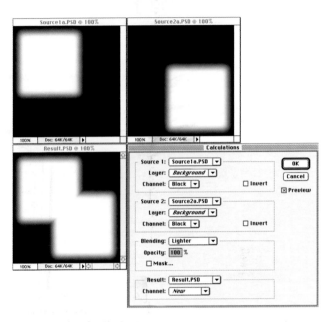

The Lighter mode's simplicity is what creates strange clipping shapes when used with soft-edged masks.

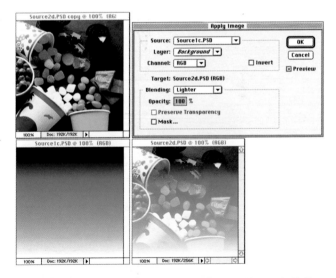

The top of this gradient has very little effect (because it's very dark). The lightest of the middle jellybeans still retain some color (because they're lighter than the gradient in those areas) while the dark table gets heavily tinted and brightened, and the pure white at the bottom overwhelms the Target image entirely.

pixel values are added and divided by the Scale; this results in a uniform change in pixel values, from –255 to 255.

The extended Add equation is as follows:

[(Source 1 + Source 2)/Scale] + Offset = New Pixel Value

Add can be used for some rather unorthodox image processing techniques; one of the most interesting examples of how Add works is to embed a custom watermark into one channel of an RGB image.

Of course, a watermark isn't useful if you can't extract it out of the image. The Difference command, in brief, calculates the exact difference in pixel values between two images, channels, or layers. Even if the difference between two channels is one brightness level, Difference reveals it. (For more information, see the extended definition of the Difference mode, discussed in the next few pages.)

Here we see an RGB image ready to be watermarked and a grayscale image that will serve as the watermark shape itself. The grayscale image contains a logo that is only 1 level of brightness higher than black; the text has been selected for visibility.

The first step is to Add the watermark to the color image. You probably won't even see the finished watermark.

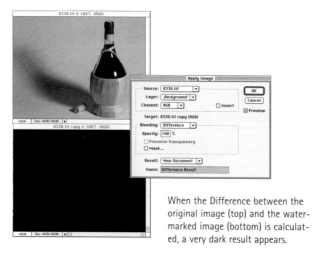

When the Difference between the original image (top) and the watermarked image (bottom) is calculated, a very dark result appears.

The Difference is output to a new document. The Levels command can be used to increase the contrast of the result, revealing the watermark.

This graphic text needs some dimension; we'll be adding an inline shadow to simulate rounded letters. This would be very easy if the text was still in its own layer, but the image has been flattened. Luckily, we still have an alpha channel for the text.

Subtract

Subtract literally subtracts pixel values in one channel from another channel; this almost always results in darker tones.

Another way to look at this is to think in terms of pure black and white, where black =0 and white =1.

White (1) – Black (0) = White (1)

White (1) – White (1) = Black (0)

Black (0) – White (1) = Black (0)

Remember that there are no negative numbers in the world of Photoshop brightness values. Everything ends at 0, or black, so if the result is less than zero, it is represented as black. The mathematics of Subtract are almost identical to those of Add, but the Source 1 and Source 2 values are subtracted, rather than added.

[(Source 1 – Source 2)/Scale] + Offset = New Pixel Value

To begin working on our inline text shadow, a duplicate of the original alpha channel is made.

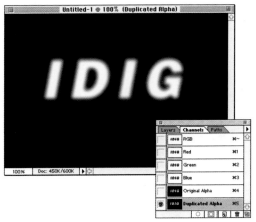

The duplicated alpha channel is offset by four pixels up and to the left, and a 4-pixel Gaussian blur is applied to it.

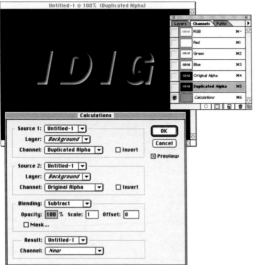

The blurred duplicate (designated as Source 1) is now subtracted from the original (Source 2). The black areas of the duplicate are subtracted from the white areas of the original letters; the result is put into a new channel.

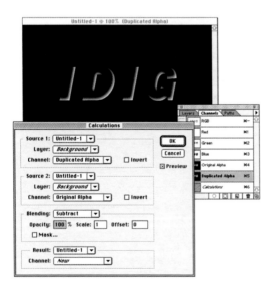

If the order of channels is changed in the previous Calculations example, observe what happens: The white areas of the original alpha channel are subtracted from the white areas of the blurred alpha channel, resulting in black. Because the black areas of the original are literally subtracting 0 (zero) from the blurred duplicate, the softened and offset edges are still visible.

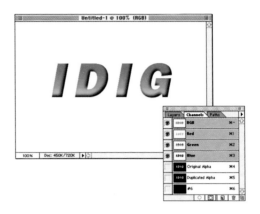

This new channel is loaded as a selection and filled with black.

The results of Subtract vary significantly, based on the order in which the two channels are processed. For example, if pixel value 128 is subtracted from pixel value 64, the result is lower than zero (64–128=–64), and therefore results in black. If value 64 is subtracted from 128, however, the result is 25% gray (128–64=64).

Here's another practical example of adding depth to an image by using the Subtract command to process alpha channels for a specific set of special effects. For this example, this image of the earth needs to be heavily altered; we want to add some drama, and plan to have the sun peeking out from behind the earth's left side, casting the majority of the globe (from the viewer's point of view) in a night-time shadow.

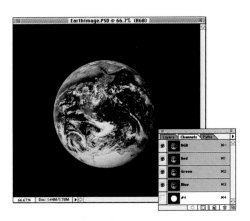

By the time we're done, this image of Earth will be a lot more dramatic. Notice that we already have an alpha channel for the planet.

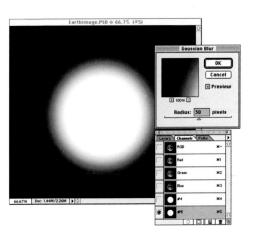

This alpha channel is copied, and the copy is given a hefty Gaussian blur.

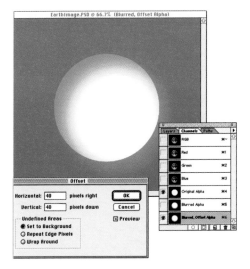

The blurred channel is duplicated and offset down and to the right, to mask the darkening of the planet's night side. The sharp, original channel is kept visible to aid in the proper placement of the blurred copy.

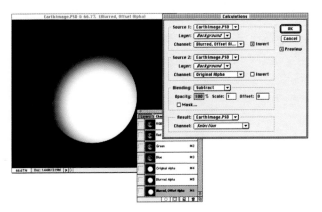

In the Calculations dialog box, the original planet mask (inverted in the Calculations dialog box) and the blurred, offset alpha channel are subtracted from each other. The result is a selection, which is used to darken the night side of the planet.

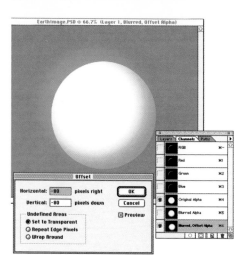

This new selection is filled with black.

The image won't be complete without the sun rising behind the planet's left edge. The blurred and offset alpha channel is offset again, this time up and to the left. The original mask is made visible for reference.

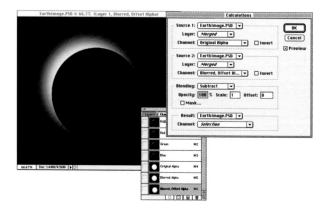

The original mask and the offset mask are once again subtracted from each other, resulting in a new selection.

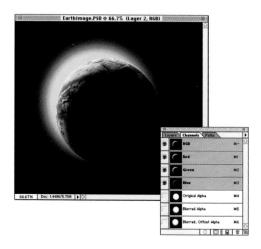

This new selection is filled with a white-to-yellow radial gradient, to simulate the sun coming out from behind the planet.

Difference

Difference takes into consideration the spread between overlapping pixels, and gives you the absolute number between the two values as a result.

If you use difference on two images that are exactly the same, the resulting image is purely black, representing no difference between the two. The greater the difference between two pixels, the brighter the result.

Let's look at an example in order to understand how difference is different from subtract, a question we're frequently asked.

This RGB image consists of a simple white circle on a black background.

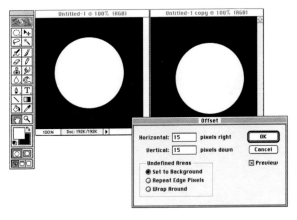

The subtraction is the remainder of the offset sphere with the original sphere removed.

The difference is the total, or absolute amount of movement of the offset sphere in relation to the original; the difference between the two images lies on both the upper-left and lower-right edges of the sphere.

Duplicate the file and move the sphere 15 pixels down and to the right (using the Move tool, the keyboard arrow keys, or the Offset filter). Set the background color to black so that no white edges appear when the image is offset.

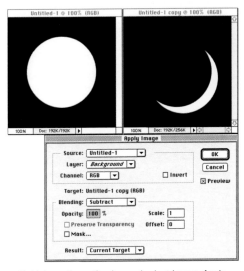

Hold down the option key and select Image>Apply Image. Set the original file as the Source (the Offset duplicate is the Target), and select the Subtract Blending mode and 100% Opacity.

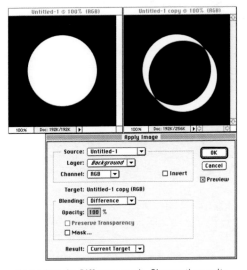

Now select the Difference mode. Observe the results.

Difference Tip: in the previous example, try changing the opacity setting when differencing to see the relative position of the overall shapes with respect to the difference mask.

This mode leads to a whole method of mask creation: difference masking.

The difference between a fixed background and the same background with an object in it is, essentially, the object—and any visual interactions between the object and the surroundings, such as shadows.

Let's look at another example of how Difference can be used in a practical production context. Many artists find themselves scanning artwork too large for a typical desktop scanner platen. Such artwork is typically scanned in pieces and stitched back together in Photoshop. Difference winds up being a very useful layer mode with which to register and align pictures scanned in pieces. This example may seem more at home in a discussion of layers, but this is a great way to further understand the math behind the difference mode.

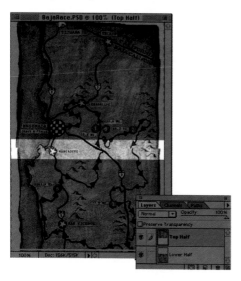

This drawing was too large to fit on an 8" x 14" flatbed scanner, so it was scanned in two separate pieces. They are brought into the same document as different layers. The misaligned seam is highlighted for visibility.

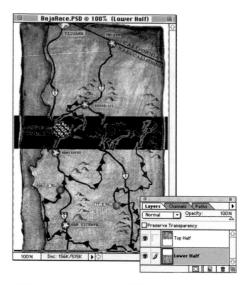

With the topmost layer in Difference mode, it's easy to see where the two pieces aren't registered.

The top layer is set to Difference mode. Where the scanned image is white in both layers, the overlap is darker. Where the overlap is lighter, there is a significant difference in pixels values; this indicates that the two layers aren't properly aligned.

When the two layers are properly aligned, the overlapping area should turn very dark; with little to no difference in pixels, the top and bottom pieces are guaranteed to be in alignment.

The further complication in this example is the fact that this image was scanned from a magazine; because the scans weren't made at the exact same angle, the moiré patterns that appear in each half of the scan won't line up perfectly. In this case, Difference will never result in an entirely black overlap. The areas to watch are the high-frequency edges of the drawing, not the larger grayscale areas; as long as those go as dark as they can, the drawing will be acceptably aligned.

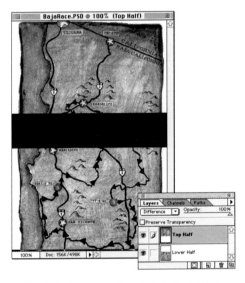

The dark stripe across the middle indicates that there is little difference between the pixels in the upper and lower layers; the image is pretty closely registered.

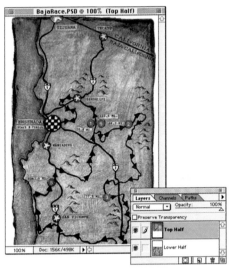

This image is the same as in the previous figure, but the upper layer has been set back to Normal mode. Notice how close the alignment is.

Exclusion

One of the more esoteric of the new application modes in Photoshop 4.0 is Exclusion. Let's look at an example between a grayscale source and a color target. Where the source is black, the target won't change; where the source is white, the target will be inverted. The brightness of any grays in the source produce a percentage blend between the original and the inverted result. A 50% gray tone in the source produces a flat 50% gray: a half-and-half of a positive and a negative results in gray.

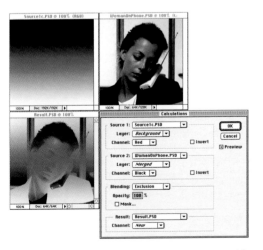

In this example, you can see that the darkest areas of Source 1 have no effect on Source 2, and that the lightest areas of Source 1 have inverted Source 2. The band of 50% gray across the middle of Source 1 results in 50% gray, a half-and-half blend of negative and positive.

Between two color sources, things get a little more complicated. Areas of high saturation in the source show through in the darkest areas of the target. This is similar to lighten, but with a more rapid fall-off in effect between the darks (heaviest effect) and mid-tones (least effect) in the target image.

If two identical images are calculated together using Exclusion, a solarization effect occurs. In fact, the effect is similar to the Solarize filter, but Exclusion tends to increase contrast while muting the tones and colors in the mid-range. (We'll venture a guess that this filter might have been created to offer a more flexible and interactive option to the Solarize filter, which has no user-definable parameters.)

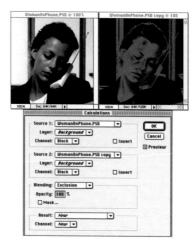

This grayscale image has been Excluded with a copy of itself; it looks like a common solarized photograph.

When used with color images, Exclude changes both the Target's brightness and hue based on the Source's brightness.

Using Exclusion to composite a color image onto itself yields a color solarization effect. Unlike the standard Solarize filter, Exclude offers an Opacity setting and a masking parameter for better control.

Calculations in a Better World

Prior to Photoshop 3.X, the Calculations commands weren't separated into the two current splinter math commands, Apply Image and Calculations; the authors of this book feel strongly that this interface addition is detrimental to the understanding and use of Calculations, and should be corrected in future versions of Photoshop.

Authors' note

And while we're at it, many of you might not know that Adobe acquired a product a few years ago, Ulead PhotoStyler, that had an intuitive visual interface for that program's Calculations functionality (this acquisition happened when Adobe purchased Aldus, which had been publishing PhotoStyler at the time of the buyout). Instead of digging up an old copy of PhotoStyler and showing you what its Calculations dialog box looked like, we've decided to show you a mock up our own version of an *idealized* Calculations dialog box.

To further make our point—and further illustrate how Calculations works—we've created a hypothetical Calculations dialog box that, in our opinion, both streamlines and better illustrates the Calculations process.

Perhaps the most important aspect of our hypothetical Calculations dialog box is that the user is better able to visually follow how Calculations works. The dialog box's new left-to-right layout mimics the order in which Calculations' image processing occurs: Source 1 is applied—using a particular blending mode and opacity level—to Source 2 and, processed through a mask, is applied to the Result/Output. The arrows between each preview literally indicate the Calculations processing pipeline.

The next improvement is the addition of live, real-time preview windows for Source 1, Source 2, the Mask, and the Output. Calculations would interactively display how each changed parameter affects each source and the ultimate result. The user

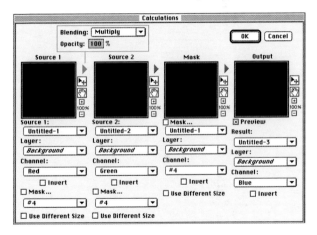

This is our idealized Calculations dialog box: easier to use, easier to understand.

could zoom in and out of each preview, pan the image within the window at high magnification levels, and even move the image itself to introduce manual offsets between each source image. Want to move the Source 1's green channel five pixels to the left before applying it to Source 2, but leave your original image unaffected? Choose the Move tool and nudge it over in the preview window! Each window has its own independent magnification level. To optimize speed, the Output window gives you the option to turn its Preview off.

The subsequent pop-up menus underneath each preview define what part of which image are used in the calculation. Most of these parameters are found in the current Calculations dialog box (such as the ability to specify source documents, layers, and channels), but some are entirely new. For example, Source 1 and Source 2 each have their own mask, chosen from the available alpha channels and layer masks in the currently-selected document. More importantly, though, each Source can be of a different size, something that's impossible to do with the current implementation of Calculations. With the Use Different Size option checked, the Output's size is the largest of the two Sources; the smaller Source can then be shifted using the Move tool for proper alignment with the larger Source. The same option is available for the Mask.

One of the most important improvements that *isn't* immediately obvious is the ability to process composite color channels (RGB, LAB, or CMYK), individual color channels, alpha channels, individual or merged layers, layer masks and/or layer transparency masks *in the same dialog box*. This would effectively eliminate the usefulness of the Apply Image command, rolling its functionality back into the Calculations environment. All this, in one convenient, easy-to-use package.

Authors' note

If there is anyone from Microsoft reading this chapter, we encourage you to contact us about using our metaphor in whatever imaging software you end up designing to go head-to-head with Adobe's Photoshop. The nice folks at Adobe seem less than interested in our ideas about how to handle Calculations. And you folks have more money.

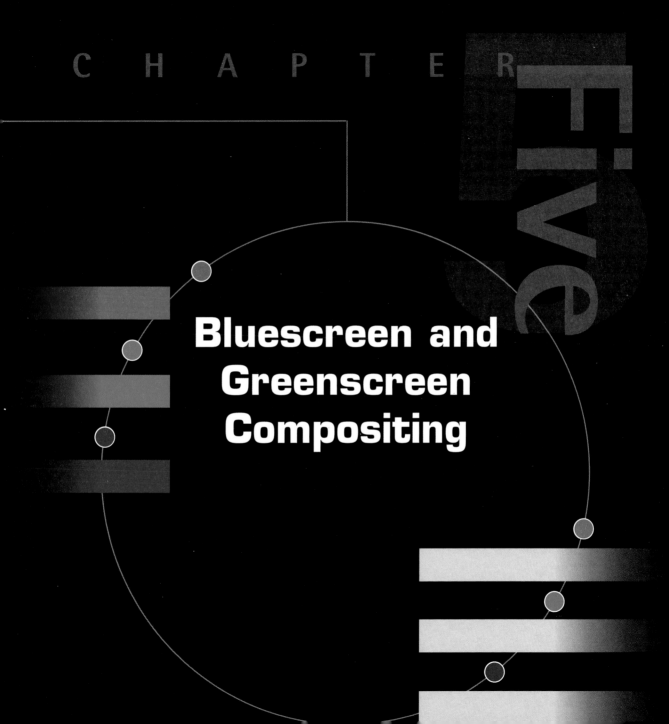

Five

Bluescreen and Greenscreen Compositing

The concept of creating masks for objects shot against solid colors isn't new. The optical photographic world has long used various techniques for masking and compositing images. The concept is based upon the behavior of colors in RGB space and the way that exposed film behaves in a laboratory, and allows for extremely precise masks that would be difficult to create with manual selection tools. One of the techniques used with the greatest success has been the process known as bluescreening.

No doubt you've noticed that this chapter not only covers bluescreen masking and compositing, but also puts the technique in context of "greenscreen." Using a green screen can be more beneficial than a blue one in some cases. A number of movies and television series make use of these alternate colors based on foreground/background color considerations. While it all sounds quite different, the only thing that's changed is the screen color; when done properly, the math and interchannel operations involved are the same as bluescreening. This chapter focuses on the more traditional bluescreen method, but as you'll see, this technique is used to derive masks for greenscreen subjects with the same level of precision.

The circle of people who *truly* understand the theory behind bluescreening and its variant techniques (greenscreen, spill suppression, and other related subjects) is quite small, and the amount of hard information on the subject is relatively sparse. With this chapter, we hope to break down some of the walls of the bluescreen ivory tower, and to help demystify this high-end professional compositing process. The reality is that you can do this type of compositing, using Photoshop, on any microcomputer.

Even though we're only covering Photoshop-specific information in this book, some of you might also be videographers and/or animators and versed in the intricacies of Adobe After Effects, one of the leading 2D animation tools for microcomputers. The expensive version of After Effects (called the Production Bundle) includes a series of additional plug-ins for creating pro-quality compositing between multiple layers of video and still images. The plug-in called Color Difference Key is a direct implementation of many of the ideas expressed in this chapter, and is the best way to handle bluescreen and greenscreen for animation and video.

The Color Difference Key filter in the Production Bundle version of Adobe After Effects contains much of the power of bluescreen and greenscreen compositing that we will cover in this chapter.

Bluescreen vs. Chroma-Keying

Bluescreen compositing is a commonly misunderstood process, and is often compared to (or mistaken for) a process called *chroma-keying*. In fact, there are only a few details about each process that are even similar.

Anyone who's seen a television weatherman in front of an animated weather map has seen chroma-keying at work. It is a process wherein one single color is chosen and made transparent so that a different background image can show through. Perhaps the biggest reason that bluescreen has been equated with chroma-keying is that the color used in many chroma-key studios is blue. The fact is, though, that any color can be used for chroma-keying: orange, green, purple—you choose it. Using blue as the key color for chroma-keying does *not*, therefore, make it bluescreen. It simply means that blue is designated to be the drop-out color.

Another difference between bluescreen and chroma-keying is that the latter is a process that can happen in real time at a relatively low cost, hence its popularity for live video broadcasts. Bluescreen isn't a real-time process, practically speaking. The bluescreen process involves some very intensive manipulation of RGB channel information, as well as direct interchannel mathematics (the basics of which are covered in this chapter). Chroma-keying is much less mathematically sophisticated, and is more related in functionality to the Magic Wand tool in Photoshop. While there are in fact high-end turnkey hardware/software systems for accomplishing comprehensive bluescreen compositing in real time, these systems are quite costly and not likely to be in the arsenal of the average imaging artist or garage videographer. If you want to do real-time bluescreen, you have few options outside of an ultra-expensive Silicon Graphic Onyx computer with large numbers of parallel processors (we'd rather buy a yacht, or at least a truckload of microcomputers and software, with that kind of money).

The sad fact of life is that the quality of chroma-key compositing is noticeably inferior to bluescreen methodologies, in terms of the quality of the edge of the foreground object or subject (the element shot against the bluescreen). There's only so much that can be done to smooth out the edges of a chroma-keyed foreground element. And if your weatherman is wearing clothing that's the same color as the chroma-key background, those portions of his clothing become transparent and literally blow a hole in your on-air personality. Chroma-keying is relatively easy to do with all sorts of software, including most 2D imaging applications, such as Premiere and After Effects (the standard retail version).

Bluescreen and chroma-keying do share a few common traits, from a production standpoint. Both require a good deal of pre-planning and preparation to do properly. They need even lighting on the color background to ensure a clean mask or composite. In the end, they even serve the same basic compositing need. But when you compare the final results, bluescreen comes out on top in the realm of quality, and that's why you'll find bluescreen one of the hallmark compositing techniques in the motion picture industry.

The Bluescreen Process

As with many other kinds of digital effects, there are three essential stages to bluescreening: *planning, production.* and *post-production/processing.*

Planning

The more work you do in the preparation stage of a bluescreen (or greenscreen) shoot will save precious time and money in front of the computer once the processing stage begins. There are some very important issues to deal with when doing a real bluescreen shoot.

Bluescreen or Greenscreen?

First, the colors in the actual foreground subject/object need to be evaluated to determine the best background key color, which is probably going to be either blue or green.

The basic rule of thumb goes like this:

- If there is any significant amount of red coloration in the subject, blue is the right color for the background, so use bluescreen.

- If there is any significant amount of yellow in the foreground subject/object (such as blond hair), use a greenscreen.

Red is the complement to green, and yellow is the complement to blue. In the actual mask derivation process, this relationship can cause problems in getting the cleanest possible mask.

Objects to be shot on bluescreen present problems if they have any shade of blue in the makeup of the actual object; yellow shading might also present problems (because it's the complementary color to blue).

Screen Preparation

Once you decide to go with either blue or green, the next step is procurement of the materials or paint that will be used to create the blue or green background. Going down to the local hardware store and buying some bright blue paint right off the shelf won't work for compositing. You'll need to get paint specifically designed for bluescreening.

Even better than paint, though, is a particular type of cloth material that's often used for bluescreen. Besides the fact that a cloth backdrop is easy to transport and set up (and can accommodate situations where you don't have the option of painting the scene), the cloth is less likely to have specular highlights (points of bright light that would be seen on a shiny, reflective surface). This is due to the surface characteristics of soft cloth, which have little reflectivity and surface shininess (hey, we're talking cloth, not silk!).

When lit, the color should be consistent throughout the background and the material should have no visible creases. Dirt and scratches on the material can also complicate a bluescreen shoot. These problems necessitate at least some digital retouching as a post-production process before any mask creation begins.

Tip: So where can you get the right paint or material? In the U.S., you might try these two outfits:

Rose Brand East, 512 West 35th St., New York, NY 10001. 1-800-223-1624

Wildfire, 11250 Playa Court, Culver City, CA 90230-6150. 1-800-937-8065

Also, any professional photo supply store is likely to have appropriate materials. Look in your local phone directory, or even better, on the Internet!

Production

As with any creative endeavor, it helps to think out specific issues of your particular bluescreen problem before even getting near a copy of Photoshop, much less a computer. Some simple production preparation will help appreciably in doing the actual bluescreen composite in Photoshop.

Proper Lighting

Perhaps the most important aspect of preparing to shoot bluescreen foreground elements is the issue of lighting, both of the background blue screen and of the actual subject being shot in front of the screen. Good lighting can sometimes compensate a little for poor bluescreen material.

Even lighting is the primary factor, besides the material itself, in getting consistent background color. Lighting can be used to eliminate shadows from creases and seams in the bluescreen material. You're going to need more than a single light source, and professional lighting is the way to go (no spotlights picked up at a garage sale!). Approach the process assuming that two sets of lights are required:

1. The lights for the actual bluescreen.
2. The lights for the subject to be shot.

Try a combination of diffuse lights both in back of and in front of the actual screen; use the lights to create a consistent brightness value across the entire area of bluescreen background. Yes, it's also time to acquire a professional light meter, the hardware version of Photoshop's Info/densitometer control. A light meter enables you to objectively and accurately measure the lighting at any point in the background screen; as expected, the values should be as consistent as possible (and, being the real world, assume that different readings along the entire area of the blue background will display some degree of brightness differentiation–this is normal and acceptable).

Proper backlighting and edge lighting is also important to visually separate the foreground subject from the bluescreen. The edges of the foreground subject should have a definable lightness value, which will help separate the object from the bluescreen background. Try using diffuse orange lighting on the edges of the foreground subject, which will help create a discernible light edge around the foreground subject, making it easier to pull the final mask from the blue background.

Color Spill and Component Control

When you place something in front of a brightly lit bluescreen, it's inevitable that some of the blue coloration will leak around the edges of the foreground subject and spill onto the internal detail of the subject. Shiny, reflective portions of the foreground subject (such as metal props that are part of a costume) might also display traces of the lit background blue or green screen. This color spill problem often isn't dealt with properly at composite time, and the results are a color halo on the inside edges of the foreground subject.

Specific techniques can assist in the elimination of color spill at shoot time, including moving the subject as far away from the background bluescreen material as possible, and using color gels on the lights used to create edge lighting on the subject (for example, yellow gels often help reduce the effects of blue spill along the edges of a subject). Proper (as in *sufficient*) key lighting on the main subject also brings out the color details of the subject. An object shot against a bluescreen without enough foreground lighting on the subject itself naturally allows the bright blue background to dominate the overall scene, and in fact possibly adds a strong blue color cast to the entire frame (whether shot on film or video).

Spill suppression can also be accomplished with some color normalization techniques described later in this chapter.

On-Set Color Component Monitoring

The ideal bluescreen shoot would include a computer on the set to capture video data and sample the RGB values of the bluescreen background in real time. This is as simple as having a copy of Photoshop running with the Info window open and in use; digital still frames can be brought into the computer using any of a number of digitization schemes, and the eyedropper tool can be used to sample and evaluate the RGB values of the scene.

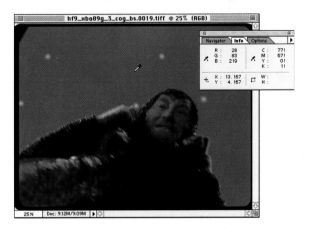

It's often a good idea to use a computer on set to sample color values of bluescreen plate photography, in order to ensure that you're getting the right red/green/blue channel mix.

Tip: While you might be tempted to use a cheaper digital camera to shoot instant stills on set for the purposes of color component analysis, be warned that the CCD arrays in most of the cheaper digital cameras simply aren't sensitive enough to give an accurate and useful RGB read. Trial and error is the only way to determine whether your digital camera can be of any assistance.

This process can help guide lighting and filming efforts to get the perfect bluescreen color: all blue, some green, and little to no red (in the best case scenario).

In summary, a large part of having a successful bluescreen shoot is minimizing any problems before the digital post-processing stage. Digital enhancement can certainly salvage a less-than-perfect bluescreen shot, but nothing can correct a bad one. One of the keys to efficient film or video production has always been getting shots right the first time, not fixing shoddy work in post-production. It's an important goal to keep in mind.

Post-Production/Processing

Once you have your digital foreground bluescreen element and your desired target background, it's time to get into Photoshop and accomplish the following generalized steps:

1. Make a duplicate of the bluescreen plate (using the Duplicate command).
2. Clean up the blue screen plate (wire removal, blue value enhancement, garbage matting).
3. Derive the mask for the object.
4. Process another duplicate of the original plate into the desired color normalization scheme, rendering the blue background into one of three main density/brightness ranges: light, dark, or median.
5. Do any final edge choking/enhancements on the derived mask.
6. Do any final color/brightness/density matching between the foreground object and the target background.
7. Do the composite.
8. Go boating.

The specifics of this process are dealt with in the detailed example described later in this chapter.

Mask Creation vs. Mask Usage

Generally speaking, the process of *deriving the mask* for the foreground object (by applying interchannel mathematics) is separate from *compositing the object* onto a new background. Don't worry if you mess up the foreground object's original coloring while creating a mask. You can always use an original, unprocessed version of the foreground object image when doing the actual compositing step.

The Background Is Just as Important as the Foreground

The new background for the masked bluescreen object may possess any variety of lighting and brightness conditions (a dark night scene, bright sunny day, cloudy and overcast sky, and so forth), but the nature of the background will influence the process used to remove blue spill from the foreground image. The three main brightness parameters are somewhat obvious:

- Dark
- Medium
- Light

In a photographic background meant to be composited with a bluescreen derived element, all three situations might be present.

Color Matching

In order to look convincing, the brightness, contrast, and lighting conditions of the bluescreen object must closely match those conditions in the background image. It's often crucial to run a series of preliminary composites of the foreground/background, with the foreground object processed through a series of varying color corrections in order to determine the optimum color correction values.

In the case of this image, all three brightness ranges are represented.

As you can see, much of the believability of a composite is accomplished by matching the color and brightness values of the foreground and background elements. In these examples, the bright and off color foreground Spawns are obviously out of place in the scene, regardless of the quality of the derived mask and composite.

Proper Screen Preparation

Having exact blue as the background was very important for the optical bluescreen process. In digital bluescreen, however, a bit of green component in the blue (resulting in a brighter, slightly paler shade of blue) can be very useful in helping with color spill removal.

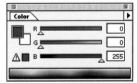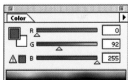

Using the standard Color slider palette in Photoshop, set to RGB mode, we can see a pure blue (255 blue) that is normally thought to be the best tone for bluescreen backgrounds. In reality, adding some green component to the blue (resulting in a lighter blue) results in more color background control when creating the composite later on (as we'll see later in the chapter, the presence of green in the bluescreen background will allow us to convert the blue background to a cool, medium gray, very useful for minimizing blue spill). In order to achieve this blue tone for the background, sample the bluescreen values on the shooting set and brighten the backlighting to produce a lighter tone in the bluescreen.

Bluescreen Compositing Using Photoshop CHOPS

OK, it's time to take a look at a typical bluescreen composite. It's important to note that it would be less than practical for us to try and cover every single problem and issue that you're likely to come across in doing a blue or greenscreen *comp* (short for composite, and a term you should get accustomed to if you ever plan on doing professional motion picture blue or green screen work!). For the purposes of this edition of our book, we're going to look at an example taken from the motion picture *Spawn*.

Authors' Note

Disclaimer: even though we're using plates from *Spawn*, our company (IDIG) didn't do the actual comps for the movie (we did a bunch of other special effects for the film, which is the reason that you're not reading this book in the summer of 1997—this book ran late because of our involvement in the movie). A southern California firm, Santa Barbara Studios, did the actual comp work for the movie using high-end, UNIX-based hardware and software solutions for bluescreen compositing. The kind folks at New Line Cinema gave us permission to use these plates for our book, thanks to the cooperation of the producer of the film, our pal Clint Goldman. Thanks, Clint!

For this example we're going to use a plate of the Spawn character riding the back of the evil Violator monster. The background plate is from another part of the movie, and is set in Hell.

Here you can see that the bluescreen plate has some elements that need to be dealt with before the comp happens—the string coming out of Spawn's back, the white marks on the bluescreen, and the overall blue values of the bluescreen. The background is a completely computer-generated Hell scene.

In this particular example, we have the benefit of intelligent shooting on the set. The color and density values of the bluescreen element closely match the overall tones of our destination background (note the predominance of dark red, golden, and brown colors in both the Spawn/Violator element and the Hell background). We've also taken the liberty of *garbage matting* the bluescreen element. There were extraneous elements in the edges of the frame (light booms and some other hardware that was on the bluescreen set). The process of blocking out, or eliminating, the undesired elements on the edges of the frame is called *garbage matting*.

In real film production, given that the elements are often pre-registered in position, a matte is created to hide the edge elements (leaving the original file size unchanged), instead of just cropping the images we've done for this example.

Another important note: For convenience and brevity, we'll often refer to the bluescreen element as the *FG* (ForeGround plate) and the target background as the *BG* (BackGround).

The very first thing that must happen with the FG plate is that the undesirable elements in the bluescreen background must be painted out—namely the string coming out of Spawn's back, as well as the three white registration points seen above and below Violator's head and behind Spawn.

Using the Paintbrush tool in Photoshop and the foreground color set to pure blue (no red or green), the undesired elements in the FG plate are manually painted out. Absolute accuracy in painting out artifacts is overkill; just cover-ups suffice (with the exception of the string, where we want a clean blue edge where the string meets Spawn).

Now it's time to get deep. Really deep.

Let's take a look at the three channels (RGB) of the FG plate, and examine the characteristics of the individual components. It's important to keep in mind that we're looking for significant brightness differences in the bluescreen background in each of the individual channels of the FG image.

The trick to doing bluescreen mask extraction is to take advantage of the differences in the red, green, and blue channels of the FG plate.

Given that the predominant color component of the background is blue, we would expect that the blue channel would display near white values in the background.

Select the blue channel of the image (Command—3).

Select the red channel of the image (Command—1).

Using the eyedropper tool and the Info palette, the actual brightness value of the blue channel is displayed—in this example, it varies between 135-185.

While there's a large amount of blue component in the bluescreen, it's not pure blue—it's 255 of the blue component. Part of the art of bluescreen is to get this value as high as you can.

On to the red channel.

In an optimum blue background, there's very little red component. In this example, the red channel is a dark gray in the background area; optimally, this should be black—or 0 red component.

The first crucial part of bluescreen matte extraction is based on the differences between the blue and red channels of the FG plate. This has nothing to do with the difference application mode found in calculations; we're simply talking about relationship between the extremities of dark (in the red channel) and light (in the blue channel) in the areas of the image that contain bluescreen background. This behavior of the red and blue channels can be processed with a calculation in order to begin to derive a mask for the foreground object.

Before taking this next step, the blue and red values of the FG plate should be pushed out to their maximum levels: 255 for blue, 0 for red. The Curves control is used to punch up these channels.

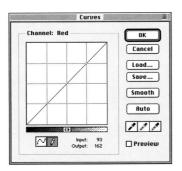

The Curves control with the red channel activated.
The goal is to make the red background component go
to a minimum value of 0.

Use the Duplicate command to make a copy of the FG plate;
the mask derivation process will alter the color values of the
foreground subject. This is alright, because we're working on a
duplicate FG plate. Make the Red channel active. Open Curves.

 Tip: If Curves is opened while viewing the composite RGB
view of the FG plate, the desired channel must be selected from within the Curves dialog box.

In order to pump down the red values of the background, the
bluescreen background area is sampled by clicking on it in the
active document with the Curves dialog box open. The area
from the left of the interactive ball indicator in Curves should
be clamped down to 0.

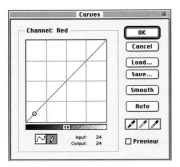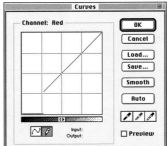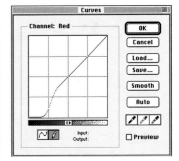

Using the pencil mode in Curves, draw a straight line from just to the right of the "ball" indicator to the left corner. Then
click on the Smooth button to soften the transition from hard black to dark grays.

This makes the background of the red channel of
the FG plate go to pure black.

It's time to address the blue channel and bring the background values to pure white. Select the blue channel and open the Curves control. As we sample the bluescreen background area, we find that it's far from pure white. Using Curves, we'll push all of the grays in the bluescreen area to white.

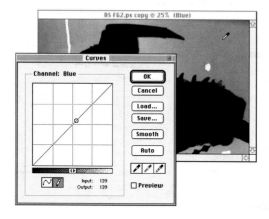

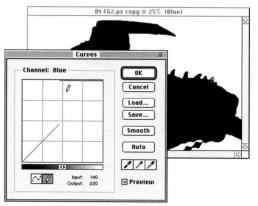

Using the Curves control with the blue channel selected, the blue background is sampled (with the eyedropper tool) along the darker areas of the background. Take note of the interactive ball readout along the curve.

Using the Pencil tool in the Curves dialog box, draw a straight line from the top, left-most part of the transfer curve to just beyond where the interactive ball indicator was from the previous figure. This makes all the light gray values go white.

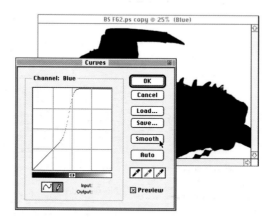

Pressing the Smooth button is the last part of the clamping of the blue channel; now the entire bluescreen background area should be white. Use the Eyedroppper tool and Info window to verify this.

We now have a version of the FG plate that will enables us to pull a good bluescreen-derived mask. If you look at the image in full color, you'll notice that some of the color values of the foreground subject might have changed. This doesn't matter; this version of the FG plate is used exclusively to create the mask. The actual foreground subject for the composite will come from a modified version of the original FG plate.

Time for Calculations between the red and blue channels. The basic theory is as follows:

● The red channel is inverted

● The inverted red channel is multiplied with the blue channel

The goal is to combine the dark densities of the inverted red and the blue to derive the first generation of our mask. Going back to the image resulting from the previous red-blue enhancements steps, we invoke the Calculate command.

The next step is to apply a global Invert command to the entire channel. Use the Invert command (Image>Adjust>Invert).

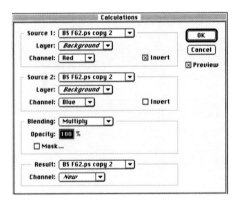

If an inverted version of the red channel (left) and the blue channel (right) of the image are compared side-by-side, you'll notice that wherever the red channel displays dark values on the foreground subject, the blue channel tends to be lighter. We've brightened up the blue channel a bit so that this relationship is more visually obvious.

In Calculations, the red channel (with the Invert check button set to on, inverting the red channel within Calculations) is multiplied with the blue channel. The results are sent to a new channel/alpha channel in the document.

The results of the inverted red multiplied with the blue channel. This is the very beginning of our mask.

The inverted results of the previous figure. The mask is beginning to emerge.

The Curves control is now used to punch out, or *clamp*, any of the light gray values inside of the mask area to white.

Very often, multiple passes of the Curves control must be done to isolate all of the gray values inside of the white portion of the mask. If you can't get all of the gray values to go to white on the first try, then apply Curves more than once to the same image. Inversely, you might also find it necessary to use Curves to clamp the dark pixels in the background back down to a true 0 black.

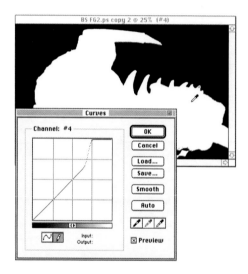

The Curves control is used to sample and clamp all values inside of the mask to white. The Smooth button is also used to soften the edges of the mask.

Now that we have a mask, we'll try using it to composite the original FG plate file with the background. There are many ways to do this (such as moving the mask back into the original file as a channel, loading it as a selection onto the FG plate, copying and pasting into the target background), but in a real-world production environment, use of Calculations is recommended. For this example, we'll use the Apply Image calculation command (which allows us to process the full RGB set of channels, unlike Calculations).

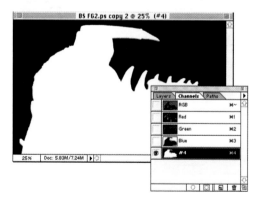

The Curves-processed mask.

With the target background file (the Hell image) active, the Apply Image command is invoked.

 Tip: Remember that you can zoom into the image while the Apply Image dialog box is open by pressing Command-spacebar to zoom in, Command-Option-spacebar to zoom out.

The process for removing blue spill from the inside details of the foreground subject involves some interchannel processing, which will result in the bluescreen background being driven to one of three overall brightness values: dark, medium, or light. You might be wondering how the background blue can be converted to another color without explicitly selecting it. Calculations is the answer.

In order to get a better grip in our next step, let's take a look at individual RGB channels of the FG plate with the foreground subjects masked out.

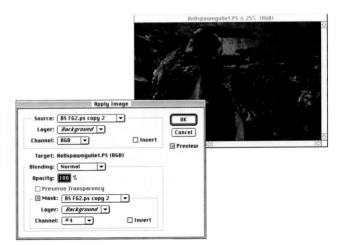

After making the Hell background image active, the *Apply Image* command is opened. The Source is the original FG plate file, the target is the background image, and the mask option is activated to load the derived bluescreen mask from its base file. With the preview button activated, we can see that the composite looks pretty good, with the exception of the blue spill on the Violator's neck (the right side of the FG subject), as well as a little blue spill on Spawn's head.

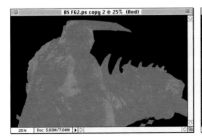  

Looking carefully at the individual channels of the processed FG plate, we see that, in the bluescreen background area, the red channel is black, the green channel is gray, and the blue channel is white.

By creative use of the Light and Darker commands in Calculations, we can force the overall bluescreen background of the FG plate to go to one of three brightness values—light, medium, or dark—without actual chromatic, or color, values.

> Remember that if the brightness value of a pixel is exactly the same in all three red, green, and blue channels, the overall RGB value of the pixel will be a shade of gray, with no color (given that the value of the pixel in any of the individual color components is exactly the same).

Let's start by processing the green and blue channels together, with the final goal being the darkening of the blue channel background from white to a more neutral, gray density.

If we now process the red and green channels with a Lighter command, we'll force the lighter background pixels of the green channel into the dark background of the red channel.

Looking at the overall RGB composite of the FG plate after these operations, it's clear that the gray values of all three channels are the same in the previous bluescreen background. Instead of being blue, the background is now an overall gray. Look at the areas of blue spill on the Violator from the previous composite example; instead of blue, the spill values are now simply displayed as being brighter areas, with no chromacity. The blue spill is effectively eliminated.

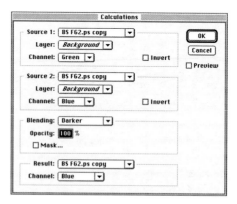

In Calculations we'll compare the pixels of the green and blue channels and put the darker pixels of the two into the blue channel. This forces the gray background of the green channel into the white background of the blue channel.

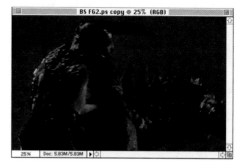

Using Calculations, we'll do a Lighter between green and red, and replace the red channel with the results.

The color-normalized results of the previous two calculations passes.

So what happens if the color values of the foreground subject shift noticeably after this process? No problem—just use your favorite color correction commands to bring the colors back to their original values. Because the background now contains no significant chromacity/color value, the relatively slight color correction shifts needed to restore the original colors have little to no effect on the background. If you're still concerned, remember that there's a derived mask for the foreground object that could be loaded as a selection before color correction occurs. This will protect the neutralized background from shifting color to *any* degree.

So what does this new, spill-suppressed FG plate look like in the target background?

The new foreground subject composited into the background, with no color spill. Looks like a final!

A close-up view of the composite. There are almost no edge artifacts between the Spawn/Violator subjects and the background.

In the previous example, we wanted to put the FG plate subject against a relatively neutral background (The Hell image). The brightness values of the target background might not have been as dark as they are in our example, though. In these cases, you'll want to process the bluescreen background into one of the other two extremes—black or white. This can be done by altering the color spill suppression calculations slightly to take the darker, black background values of the blue channel, or the lighter, white background values of the red channel as the goal for all channels. The math is as follows:

The FG plate processed with the preceding parameters, in order to make the background go light/white. This image is now ready to be composited into a predominantly light background.

- Lighter (this sequence should occur in the exact order described)

    1. Lighter of Green & Blue into Green

    2. Lighter of Red & Green into Red

- Darker (this sequence should occur in the exact order described)

    1. Darker of Green & Red into Green

    2. Darker of Blue & Green into Blue

These two versions of the FG plate are now ready to be composited into predominantly light or dark backgrounds, with minimal edge halation. In fact, by using alpha channels you can mix and match the portions of the FG plate needed for a background with varying brightness values.

Tip: If anything weird happens to the color or details of your foreground element, fear not: You can always choke the derived mask down a bit, use it to copy the internal portion of the original FG element on blue, and paste it down onto the *precomp*. (The precomp is the result of pasting the spill-removed FG onto the background, which takes care of the edges).

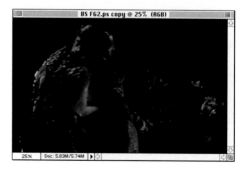

The FG plate processed with the preceding parameters, in order to make the background go dark/black. This image is now ready to be composited into a predominantly dark background.

What About Greenscreen?

Greenscreen employs the same basic process and calculations as bluescreen, except that the inverted red channel is multiplied by the *green* channel (instead of the *blue* channel) with the same color enhancement pass to facilitate making the mask (clamping procedures done in order to make the greenscreen go pure green).

In this example, the original greenscreen plate of Clown (our favorite character from the movie *Spawn*) is processed in order to maximize the green and red values of the greens background, and the inverted red is multiplied by green channel and inverted/clamped in order to make the mask for the Clown character.

What about the color spill suppression? Here's the answer: Once you understand the spill suppression pass for bluescreen, the greenscreen formula will jump out at you like a hungry snake. Look at the channels of a greenscreen FG image, and look at the Calculations recipes from the figures immediately preceding the green screen plates, and it will hit you. We're not trying to tease you, but it's important that you grok the bluescreen spill suppression process, because once you do, applying it to greenscreen will become effortless.

So there you have it. You now have the basic skills to approach bluescreen and greenscreen mask derivation and compositing. Don't be frustrated if it takes some effort to fully understand. You're looking at one of the toughest Calculations processes found in Photoshop.

Take time, drink it in, and when you grok it, you'll wonder how you ever lived without Photoshop Channel Chops.

six

Paths

Finding the Path to Happiness

Most of this book deals specifically with bitmapped graphics, given that Photoshop is essentially a bitmap editing program. But the fact remains that vector graphics–the kind normally associated with illustration and drawing software–have a significant role to play in Photoshop, both internally and when exporting Photoshop images to other programs (such as page layout software, and even Illustrator).

The Path tool is the expression of Photoshop's vector-based drawing and masking capabilities. Using the Path tool found in Photoshop, you can do the following:

- Have up to 32,000 paths associated with a single document, which can be turned into selections or alpha channels at any point. (Though, we have to admit, the thought of actually trying to scroll through 32,000 path names is rather frightening.)

- Save silhouette-style alpha channels as paths, which take up very little memory compared to alpha channels (vector entities are inherently more compact than any bitmap equivalent). Note that the inherent detail of the original channel, using true pixel data, dictates the viability of saving the channel as a path, which uses mathematical representations of curves to form the path's outline. The more fine-edge detail found in the original bitmap channel makes it more difficult to represent the mask as a path. Special effects masks such as gradients aren't well-suited for conversion to paths.

- Create cool custom brush effects by stroking paths with a variety of Photoshop painting and retouching tools.

- Imbed a path into an EPS or TIFF file for high-quality, resolution-independent masking of bitmapped images when placed into page layout programs or drawing software. This is perhaps the most typical use of Photoshop paths for most users.

> In this book, we primarily deal with Adobe Illustrator as the reference example of vector-based graphics. Why? Mostly due to the fact that Bert, our resident vector genius, is a longtime Illustrator aficionado, and simply has never found a reason to use MacroMedia Freehand. But fear not–the general techniques described in this chapter are useful no matter what drawing program you're attached to. The overall concepts inherent in using a path-based drawing tool are similar in just about all vector drawing software, regardless of computer platform.

Paths are an important masking tool for Photoshop. While the focus of this chapter isn't necessarily the complete, total understanding of every intricacy related to using the Path tool, we feel that many Photoshop-specific books gloss over some of the finer points on using (and understanding) the successful creation of paths. Here are some thoughts on the proper feeding and care of Photoshop paths.

Paths: The Basics

The Path tool is one of the most flexible and powerful selection tools found in Photoshop; however, it's also one of its most underutilized and misunderstood procedures for selecting elements of an image. The main reason for the neglect of this rather powerful tool is its less-than-perfect interface, as well as the fact that it presents a working methodology that's distinctly different from any other selection tool in Photoshop.

The tool appeared in the very first version of Adobe Illustrator back around 1986. Upon its debut, it was generally put down by the artistic community because it didn't conform to the way people were used to working with graphics tools on a computer. Of course, it's also fair and accurate to note that the concept of drawing smooth, curved lines with any meaningful level of control was still largely unknown to the small band of digital artists actively working at the time.

Typically, in most graphics software, clicking and dragging with any tool produces a visual and, usually, printable result. Clicking and dragging with the Path tool produced an anchor point with a handle. The mechanics of the path-based drawing tools have often eluded even seasoned digital illustrators: How long should the handles be, and at what angle? In what direction should they be dragged? Where are the points placed to make a certain shape?

In this chapter, we will, once and for all, make it clear how to use this tool. Once you have mastered it, you'll wonder how you ever got along without it.

Let's start by comparing it to traditional tools of the trade. The Path tool is the equivalent of using any tool such as a brush, technical pen, pencil, or even art knife in conjunction with a set of French curves. The use and limitations of French curves are the perfect analogy to get your brain around in order to make the most of Photoshop's paths. (If you're not familiar with the French curve, it's simply a plastic shape used as guides for any tool to create a flowing, curved line. The main challenge in using these analog devices is selecting the specific curve that will give you the longest and most accurate sweep.

A French curve.

It's often necessary to switch shapes or change the position of the French curve to follow a particular sweep. With the Path tool, a similar approach is vital. You must try to create the longest distance between two points as possible, to keep paths as simple (with as few control handles) as possible. The more points you have in a path, the longer it will take Photoshop to process it. This is especially true in the case of a clipping path (discussed in greater detail later in this chapter).

When to Use the Path Tool

The Path tool provides the user with a variety of functions. The created paths can be used to make difficult and precise selections. There are many times when isolating a part of an image is difficult or far too labor intensive for the other selecting methods and tools. There are times when many of the techniques we discuss in other parts of this book simply don't work for creating masks, such as images that don't have significant dynamic range or hue differentiation between foreground and background elements.

If you wanted to separate the head of the sphinx from the background in the following figure, it would be impossible using the Magic Wand tool. The alpha channel techniques discussed elsewhere in this book wouldn't work here either; the color and brightness ranges in the image and its channels are too similar. The other selection tools wouldn't be very accurate and would require an unreasonable amount of intensive labor. The Path tool gives you the ability to isolate the areas you need accurately and quickly—and the masks produced with it are *editable*. You can fine-tune the path to suit your needs, at any time, as they are maintained as vector-based, discrete entities.

Of course, paths are jacks of many trades. They can be used as a drawing tool, or filled with color, or stroked using any of the tools in the tool palette. Even the eraser tool can follow a path.

Using the Path Tool

Let's start by defining a path.

A *path* is any shape or line that either outlines a form in an image or creates a new shape. It is made up of *anchor points* that determine the starting and ending of each line segment. These anchor points can have *handles*, which produce curved lines. An anchor point without handles makes corner (or sharp) points, which produce straight lines. These paths are saved with the document and can be modified any time they are called up.

There are simple rules to remember when using the Path tool. The most important is to click and drag in the direction that your line (path) will be traveling.

The next figure demonstrates this procedure. The click-and-drag action produces a handle. This handle is *not* the line itself, but simply a tool to manipulate the line that's to be created. The actual line of the Path is created when the second anchor point is placed: the result is a line between the two anchor points. The handle should follow the tangent of the curve being created. Note that in the illustration, the handle seems to be resting or balanced on the proposed line.

All the elements in this image have a similar hue and luminosity value.

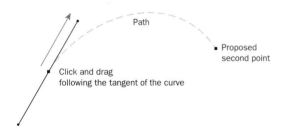

Producing handles with the Path tool.

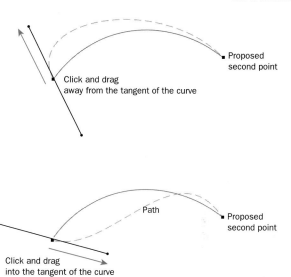

Path
Line to be matched

Proposed
second point

Click and drag
away from the tangent of the curve

Proposed
second point

Path

Click and drag
into the tangent of the curve

Lines can be changed based on the angle of a point's handle to the proposed line.

You can have a handle that goes towards or away from the path you want to draw, but handles have a definite effect on the resulting path. The figure to the right of this paragraph shows the effect on paths when the handles don't follow the tangent of the curve.

The length of the handle determines the height or depth (also called the *inflection*) of the curve.

To create an even, smooth curve, the length of the handle should be approximately a third of the distance to the next point. The following figure shows the effects on lines when the handles are exaggerated.

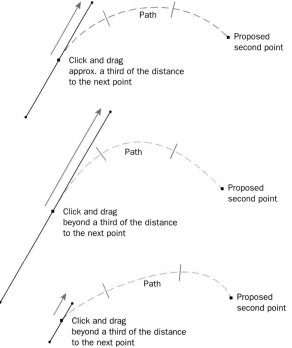

Path

Click and drag
approx. a third of the distance
to the next point

Proposed
second point

Path

Click and drag
beyond a third of the distance
to the next point

Proposed
second point

Path

Click and drag
beyond a third of the distance
to the next point

Proposed
second point

The length of the handle determines the height or depth of the curve.

Exaggerated handles and their effects on the lines they create.

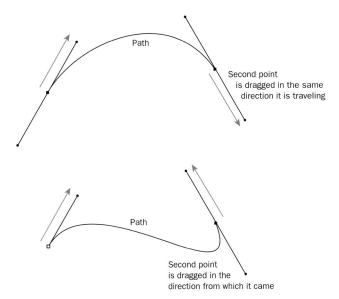

Path

Second point
is dragged in the same
direction it is traveling

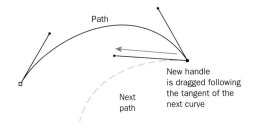

Path

Second point
is dragged in the
direction from which it came

Dragging handles in opposing directions.

Path

New handle
is dragged following
the tangent of the
next curve

Next
path

Holding down the Option key lets you drag one handle independently of
the other.

The nautilus on the left has been outlined with the Path tool, and has 18
points on its path. The one on the right has been outlined using only four
points.

The second point also is clicked and dragged in the direction in which your line is traveling. If you drag in the opposite direction, the result will be an S curve, as shown in the figure to the left.

The same procedure is done for each successive point. There are times, however, when the next point must follow a different curve. In this case, it's necessary to create a new handle from the last anchor point to follow this new curve. Pressing the Option key while clicking and dragging on the anchor point produces a new handle that can be set to an entirely new angle, as shown in the next figure to the left of this paragraph. It's important to note that you click and drag from the *anchor point* and not the handle of the point. If you click on the handle it produces a new anchor point in that position.

As mentioned before, having the fewest possible points on a path is better, speeding processing and improving smoothness. The shell figure shows a comparison of a good path to a path with too many points.

The shell image on the left has a path that was made using 18 anchor points. This is the result many artists get when they're unsure about where to place the anchor points. The shell image on the right has a path of only four anchor points. Note the strategic placement of each point to maximize the effectiveness of the curve with the least amount of points. Note that the points are placed only where the curvature of the shell significantly changes in inflection. It takes some time to "see" the curves of an image in relationship to the Path tool, but some experimentation and hands-on use of paths will get you right into the groove.

An encouraging thing to remember is that the Path tool is very forgiving: If you don't get it right the first time, you can always adjust it later. After a path is created, you can click on any line segment and drag it to a new shape, or click on the anchor points of that segment and the handles will appear.

Dragging the handles adjusts the line to the desired shape. During the adjustment period, if you find it impossible to get the proper line with the existing points, you can add more.

Paths to Enlightenment

Now that you've seen the basics of the Photoshop Path tool (and hopefully experimented with it a bit), you're ready to enter into a deep look at Paths and their inner workings.

The Path Tool: An In-Depth Look

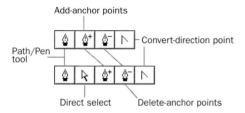

Top- Illustrator tool palette
Bottom- Photoshop tool palette

Add-anchor points

Path/Pen tool — Convert-direction point

Direct select   Delete-anchor points

The Path tool palette in Illustrator and Photoshop.

The Add Point tool adds a point to a line segment wherever you click. The new point assumes the attributes of the original points at either end of the line to which you have added the point. For example, if you add a point to a curved line, the new point will be a smooth point with handles. If you add a point to a straight line, the new point will be a corner point without handles. Any extraneous anchor points can be deleted with the Delete Anchor Points tool.

The attributes of the anchor points can be changed at any time. The Convert-direction point tool found in both Adobe Illustrator and Adobe Photoshop gives you this flexibility. The same concept for handles in the creation process applies to this tool. If you click on a point, you get a corner point without handles. If you click and drag on an existing point, you get handles.

A path saved in Photoshop can be composed of various line segments or individual shapes. If there is more than one shape to a path, it's considered a single path and all actions attributed to it affect all elements uniformly. The following figure shows three shapes that have been filled with black. If any of the shapes intersect each other, the area in which they intersect will act as a compound path, creating a hole in the shape. (Note that you get similar effects if you overlap outlines drawn with the Lasso tool.) The next figure shows the same three shapes, with the same fill, but an overlap of the shapes creates a compound path.

Three shapes within a path have been filled with black.

Three intersecting shapes within a path have been filled with black.

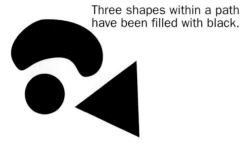

Non-overlapping shapes drawn with the Path tool.

Overlapping shapes create compound shapes, shown here as negative areas.

Special Features—Making Selections from Paths

Now that we've created paths, what can we do with them? In Illustrator, they are the shapes that make up the image itself. In Photoshop, they can add a variety of effects. The first and most common use of the Path tool, as discussed at the beginning of this chapter, is to make a selection.

As with the other selection tools in Photoshop, a feather radius can be assigned to the selection beforehand. This makes the selected area into a soft-edged shape with the vignette effect's fade dependent on the radius set in the dialog box.

Making the path a selection can be accomplished in a number of ways. Make Selection can be selected from the path palette submenu. This brings up a dialog box where attributes, such as the feather amount, can be specified. The path also can be dragged over the Make Selection icon in the path palette. If this method is used, the resulting selection takes on any attributes previously assigned in the Make Selection dialog box, for example, a feather radius. Once a selection is made, the selected area can be color-corrected, duplicated, filtered, or any of the other functions within Photoshop can be applied to it, leaving the rest of the image unmodified.

If an area of the image is currently selected, making a path a selection gives you the capability to have the path interact with the current selected area. The path can override the current selection and make a new selection based on its shape and attributes. It can use its shape and attributes to add to, subtract from, or intersect with the current selected area. In the last of these functions, if a path intersects an area currently selected, the result will be the area where the two intersect.

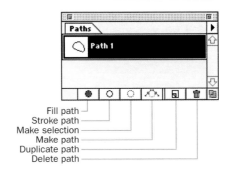

Fill path
Stroke path
Make selection
Make path
Duplicate path
Delete path

The Make Selection icon.

Paths and Alpha Channels

Paths complement alpha channels and masking due to their capability to interact with pre-existing selections. It's important to realize, however, that while paths and alpha channels can both be used to make selections, each has its own strengths and peculiarities.

As versatile as paths are, however, they aren't a replacement for alpha channels; for example, while a path can be feathered on all of its edges, it cannot be feathered more in one area than another. With an alpha channel, you can get increased feathering by selecting an area of the alpha channel itself and applying any blur filter. Unlike alpha channels, however, paths take up practically no additional storage space. They're just mathematical representations of curves, not pixels. As powerful as alpha channels are, you still can fit only so many into a given image file (between 1 and 21, depending on image file format). As we mentioned earlier, you can have up to 32,000 paths in a single Photoshop document.

The following example is a good illustration of how a specific effect can be created using both alpha channels and paths. The illustration is of a dark room with a window visible on the left, casting outside light into the room.

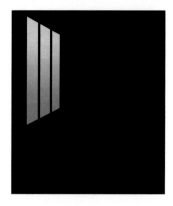

Original room with window.

Using the Path tool, three polygons were created to resemble the reflection of the light cast onto the floor.

Paths created for light reflections.

The light was to fade away as it gets farther from the window. An alpha channel was created that would expose the area of the floor where the light would fall.

Figure alpha channel to determine light fall-off.

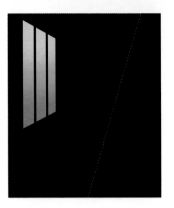

Alpha channel is made active.

The alpha channel was used to make a selection on the image.

Paths are activated.

The path of the reflection was activated by selecting it in the path's palette.

The new path-based selection intersects a the selection made with the alpha channel.

Make Selection was then chosen from the path palette submenu.

In the dialog box that pops up, Feather Radius is chosen to soften the edges. Because there was a selection currently active, the Operations section of the dialog box is totally active. Intersect made the area of the alpha channels selection active only within the confines of the path. The area was then filled with a color, and the result is shown in the figure to the right.

The color-filled image result.

Filling Paths

Filling a path can be accomplished in a variety of ways. The path can be dragged over the Fill Path icon in the path's palette. It also can be made into a selection and then filled using any of the fill functions within Photoshop.

There are shortcuts for these fill functions: Pressing Option-Delete fills the area with 100% of the foreground color, and pressing Shift-Delete will pop up the Fill options dialog box.

Special Features—Stroking Paths

Stroking the path gives an outline to the shape or lines that make up the path. The path can be dragged over the Stroke Path icon in the path's palette. This defaults to the pencil tool and the currently selected foreground color to stroke the path.

You can choose the paintbrush, airbrush, dodge, burn, sponge, smudge, blur, sharpen, pencil, rubber stamp (Cloning tool), or the eraser to stroke a path. If you choose the Stroke option from the Path palette submenu, a dialog box enables you to choose the tool you want to use. The current foreground color will always be the color used for the stroke, as will the tool's current settings in the Brushes and Options palettes. If a particular tool is selected in the Tool palette, dragging the path over the Stroke Path icon in the palette uses the selected tool to stroke the path.

Making Paths from Selections

Any active selected region within an image (which, by definition, means the contents of any alpha channel that's loaded as a selection), regardless of the selection method, can be converted into a path. To accomplish this, once the desired area is selected, Make Work Path is chosen from the path's palette submenu.

The Make Work Path command, in the path's palette pop-up menu.

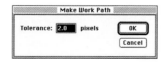

The Make Work Path dialog box.

A dialog box that allows you to set up a Tolerance for the path being generated is displayed (see the following figure). The values can range from 0.5 to 10 pixels and determine the sensitivity of the path to slight changes in the selection being converted. The higher the value, the fewer anchor points will be created in the resulting path.

The Make Path Icon

The Make Work Path dialog box.

It's crucial to remember that if the path isn't perfect, it can be modified by hand, and that anchor points can be added or deleted later. The shortcut is to click on the Make Path icon in the Path palette. This turns the previous selected area into a path that can be manipulated like any other path.

Clipping Paths

Turning selected areas into paths becomes especially handy when you're creating clipping paths. Let's say you have an image that was shot against a stark background for easy contrast, as shown in the figure of the parking meter. You want this image to serve as a silhouette in your page layout program. In other words, it will allow any other text or images to be seen behind it; this is commonly used to clip product shots in catalogs or for images in magazines. To achieve this affect it's necessary to create a clipping path.

In the case of the following image, it's quite simple. With the magic wand, the area of the background is selected. The Select>Inverse command is used to select the object. Finally, Make Work Path is chosen from the Path palette submenu.

To turn the path into a clipping path, choose Clipping Path from the Path palette submenu.

This brings up the Clipping Path dialog box.

The Clipping Path command, in the path's palette pop-up menu.

This parking meter is an easy target for the Make Path command.

The Clipping Path dialog box.

Here you can choose which path will be used to clip the image. The Flatness of the path, measured in device pixels, represents how smooth the resulting curves will be—as well as how much processing power is going to be needed to render the final path/mask on the target output device.

To better understand how this enigmatic parameter works, let's take a brief look at how output devices resolve PostScript curves.

A PostScript device actually prints curved lines by creating a series of straight line segments, thus simulating, rather than printing, real curves. The flatness setting for the clipping path determines the length of each line in device pixels. (Remember that *pixel* just means picture element; a 600-DPI laser writer has 600 device pixels per inch.) A value of 2, then, creates one line segment the length of two device pixels (that is, 300 line segments per inch on our 600-dpi laser writer). Lower values thus create more line segments and a smoother curve, while higher values make each line segment longer and result in a rougher curve.

Flatness values can range from 0.2 to 100. A flatness setting from 4 to 6 is recommended for high-resolution printing (1200 to 2400 dpi), simply because lower Flatness values might produce so much PostScript data that it would be possible to choke the output device as it tries to render a complex path with small device pixels. A setting from 2 to 4 is better for low-resolution printing (300 to 600 DPI). If the setting is left blank, the image is printed using the default settings of the printer.

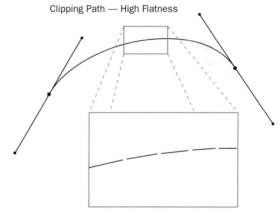

Clipping Path — High Flatness

Magnification: Individual Line Segments

> The flatness setting for the clipping path determines the length of each line in device pixels.

A diagram of Clipping Path Flatness; line segments making up a PostScript curve. If we look closely at a clipping path with a high Flatness setting, we find that each line segment is longer, resulting in a rougher path. The lower setting creates shorter line segments, making the path look much smoother.

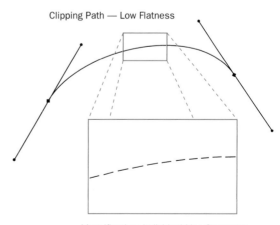

Clipping Path — Low Flatness

Magnification: Individual Line Segments

To further illustrate the need for a clipping path, let's actually see the effects of the clipping path when used in a page layout program. The next figure shows an image of a coffee cup shot against a black background. The cup is to appear as a silhouette on the lower right of a page with a large colored box (where the text will go) placed behind it.

Using the path tool, a path is created to fully encompass the cup. By applying the techniques outlined earlier in this chapter, the edges of the cup and saucer are carefully outlined using the least amount of points possible.

Note that the opening of the cup handle also is outlined. Because this path is inside the outer path of the cup, it acts as a compound path, creating a hole for that area. Compound paths, as mentioned earlier in this chapter, are created when multiple paths that overlap each other are created. The area where they overlap, or intersect, becomes transparent.

It seems logical that if you want the background of an image to disappear, you simply select it and press delete. The following figure shows the background deleted. This was accomplished by making the path a selection and pressing the Delete key.

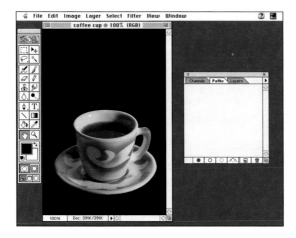

A screen shot of a Photoshop file of a coffee cup—this is the original image of the coffee cup shot against a black background in Photoshop.

The coffee cup with path applied. With the Path tool, the path to outline the cup is created along the edges of the cup.

The background deleted to white. The path was made a selection and the background was deleted.

Unfortunately, this doesn't eliminate the background; it simply makes it white. When imported to a page layout program, the white appears. The figure to the right shows the cup in a QuarkXPress document.

Notice that the white of the background shows through. Choosing Background None from within the Modify dialog box in XPress eliminates the background color for the picture box, but not the background color of the picture itself.

This is where the clipping path comes into play. Within the Photoshop file the path is designated as a clipping path. When imported into the page layout program with the clipping path, the cup becomes a true silhouette.

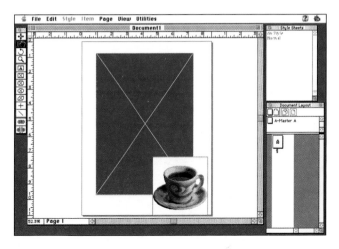

The cup image in QuarkXPress. The image of the cup, when imported into a page layout program, retains the white of the background.

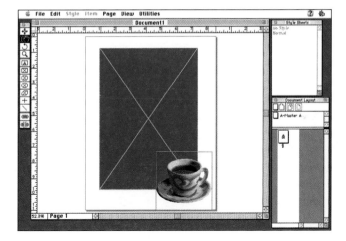

The cup clipped in XPress. With the clipping path, the cup takes on the silhouette effect that the exercise called for.

Follow the Path

Paths should never be overlooked as tools for special effects, selection handling, and masking; the Path tool is as versatile a tool as you'll find anywhere. Take advantage of its accuracy and low memory usage. Use it as an alternative method of saving tight selections. Utilize clipping paths to clean up and tighten the edges of your photo illustrations in page layouts.

Be aware of the weaknesses of paths, though, such as the inability to accurately represent gradient or variably feathered masks. The Path tool takes some getting used to (as does everything in a program as complex and deep as Photoshop), but spending some quality time learning how to use it will pay off in the end.

M

Q

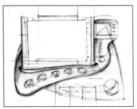

CH 1—PLANNING

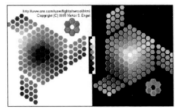

CH 2—PALETTES & WEB

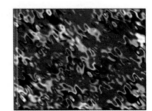

CH 3—TEXTURES

Interface Design
with Photoshop

offers direct, step-by-step creation of Web and multimedia interface elements in Photoshop. Each chapter focuses on an important aspect of interface design, including textures, beveling, embossing, and more. With each chapter providing full coverage of one element, you receive all the textual and visual information you need to plan and design interfaces unrivaled by your competition. From the planning stages to creating unique variations, this book will show you how to use Photoshop's power and utilities to your best advantage.

REAL WORLD

CH 13—SLIDERS

CH 12—STOCK IMAGERY

CH 4—BEVELING

CH 5—EMBOSSING

CH 6—GLOWS & SHADOWS

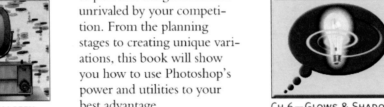

CH 11—3D IMAGERY

CH 7—CHROME, GLASS, PLASTIC

CH 10—DISTORTIONS

CH 9—VARIATIONS

CH 8—BORDERS

Chapter 1: The Big Picture: Sending Graphics Over the Web

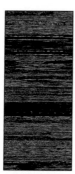

Chapter 2: The Big Squeeze: Compression

Chapter 3: Bit Depth and Palettes Once and For All

Chapter 4: Molding Images for the Web

Chapter 5: Backgrounds and Texture

Chapter 6: Transparency

About
Photoshop
Web Techniques

Photoshop Web Techniques shows you how to harness the power of Photoshop as a web graphics tool. Author Scott Hamlin comprehensively covers several Photoshop techniques through hands-on tutorials and real-world examples, as well as provides several "Beyond Photoshop" sections to show you how to incorporate your graphics into such popular web-based technologies as JavaScript and Shockwave. In 11 full-color chapters, you'll learn everything you need to know about creating web graphics with Photoshop and using those graphics to create web pages that will leave your visitors always wanting more.

$50.00 USA/$70.95 CAN/£46.99 Net UK (inc of VAT)
ISBN: 1-56205-733-2

Chapter 7: Working with Text

Chapter 8: Bullets and Buttons

Chapter 9: Imagemaps: The Old and the New

Chapter 10: Creating Images for Shockwave Files

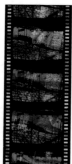

Chapter 11: Web Animations with Photoshop

Publishing for Professionals

Inside Adobe Photoshop 4
Gary David Bouton

You can master the power of the world's most popular computer graphics program with *Inside Adobe Photoshop 4!*
Covers the latest version for Windows and Macintosh
1-56205-681-6 ▲ $44.99 USA/$63.95 CDN
864 pp., 7 3/8 x 9 1/8, Accomplished - Expert
Available Now

Designing Web Graphics.2
Lynda Weinman

The updated and expanded second edition of this best-selling, full-color, step-by-step guide will teach you the most sucessful methods for designing and preparing graphics for the web.
1-56205-715-4 ▲ $55.00 USA/$77.95 CDN
482 pp., 8 x 10, Full Color, Accomplished - Expert
Available Now

Essentials of Digital Photography
Akira Kasai and Russel Sparkman

This complete workbook and tutorial bridges the knowledge and experience of traditional photographers and the power of digital tools.
1-56205-762-6 ▲ $60.00 USA/$84.95 CDN
360 pp., 8 x 10, Full Color, All User Levels
Available Now

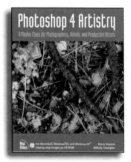

Photoshop 4 Artistry
Barry Haynes and Wendy Crumpler

This book is a masterful, in-depth course for photographers, artists, and production artists who want to create the best photographic images.
1-56205-759-6 ▲ $55.00 USA/$77.95 CDN
320 pp., 8 x 10, Full Color, Intermediate - Expert
Available Now